T0114151

Also by Stanley Aronowitz

From the Ashes of the Old: American Labor and America's Future

The Jobless Future: Sci-Tech and the Dogma of Work (with William DiFazio)

Post-Work: The Wages of Cybernation (with Jonathan Cutler)

The Death and Rebirth of American Radicalism

Dead Artists, Live Theories, and Other Cultural Problems

False Promises: The Shaping of American Working Class Consciousness

Roll Over Beethoven: The Return of Cultural Strife

The Politics of Identity: Class, Culture, Social Movements

Postmodern Education: Politics, Culture, and Social Criticism (with Henry Girou

Science as Power: Discourse and Ideology in Modern Society

The Crisis in Historical Materialism: Class, Politics, and Culture in Marxist Theo

Working Class Hero: A New Strategy for Labor

THE KNOWLEDGE FACTORY

THE
KNOWLEDGE
FACTORY

**DISMANTLING THE
CORPORATE UNIVERSITY
AND CREATING TRUE
HIGHER LEARNING**

Stanley Aronowitz

Beacon Press   Boston

Beacon Press
25 Beacon Street
Boston, Massachusetts 02108-2892
www.beacon.org

Beacon Press books
are published under the auspices of
the Unitarian Universalist Association of Congregations.

05 04   8 7 6 5 4 3 2

This book is printed on acid-free paper that meets the uncoated paper
ANSI/NISO specifications for permanence as revised in 1992.

Text design by Preston Thomas
Composition by Wilsted & Taylor Publishing Services

Library of Congress Cataloging-in-Publication Data

Aronowitz, Stanley.
    The knowledge factory : dismantling the corporate university and
creating true higher learning / Stanley Aronowitz.
        p.   cm.
    Includes bibliographical references (p.   ) and index.
    ISBN 0-8070-3122-4 (cloth)
    ISBN 0-8070-3123-2 (pbk.)
    1. Education, Higher—Aims and objectives—United States.
    2. Education, Higher—Social aspects—United States.   I. Title.
LA227.4.A76   2000
378.73—dc21   99-34355

TO MY MOTHER, Frances Aronowitz-Helfand, who, after attending the Borough of Manhattan Community College and the Center for Worker Education, received at the age of seventy-four her bachelor of arts, magna cum laude, at City College of the City University of New York, 1987.

Contents

Preface

Although I have been accused of being chronically gregarious, I have always loved learning new things, an activity that periodically takes me away from the social world and into books, articles, and libraries. Nothing gives me more pleasure than to discover some idea that knocks me on my rear end. But in the course of a fairly long life, I am occasionally at pains to remind myself to be cautious about rejecting the "new," particularly when it challenges what I have taken for granted. The more violent my response, the more certain I am that eventually I will embrace the strange and often despised idea(s), at least for a time. For this reason I have tended to be suspicious of received wisdom. Perhaps this is the reason I have never trusted institutionalized knowledge.

I come to write this book out of personal engagement, not alone as a result of the intellectual curiosity that sometimes inspires in me dispassionate inquiry. I teach sociology and cultural studies, but I have also found time to try various types of educational innovation, both within the system of public secondary and higher education and outside of it. From 1970 to 1972, I was a planner and director of the first experimental New York City public high school in the post–World War Two era. By May 1999, I had completed more than twenty-six years as a teacher in four American institutions of postsecondary education—a community college, a leading public research university, an Ivy League school, and finally the graduate school of the largest urban university in the country. But, I must confess that although I am *in* the academy, I am not *of* the academy. Like many who have completed various stages of their education, I was never sure why I was there. My unorthodox professorial career began in 1972 when I was appointed assistant professor in the experimental school of Staten Island Community College. I was thirty-nine years old and possessed only a bachelor's degree from the New School, a credential I obtained in circumstances virtually unimaginable today.

Until I graduated high school, the most memorable experience of my schooling was in the sixth grade under the tutelage of Dr. Helen Harris, whose degree was in languages. Later, my mother told me PS 57 in the Bronx had been designated a "progressive" experiment by the Board of Education. The experiment consisted in a transdisciplinary curriculum in which, excepting math, all of our subjects were integrated. We learned something of the geography, culture, and history of Italy, Mexico, and

Russia. We sang their respective national anthems in the original languages and read stories by native authors. I know I learned something in Dr. Harris's class because I can still sing these anthems, although I've forgotten some of the words, and I have never lost my affection for the culture of the three countries.

From Dr. Harris's perspective, I was a bright but disruptive child who used my skills of persuasion to lead many less talented students away from the beaten path. Consequently, my friends and I spent large chunks of time in the principal's office for disruptive behavior, and my mother was hauled into school on more than one occasion to answer for my indiscretions. Yet in Dr. Harris's class, I discovered for the first time since kindergarten that school knowledge could be pleasurable and intellectually stimulating. Sixth grade became the benchmark against which I measured my subsequent schooling and, invariably, found it wanting. Seventh grade was not a complete washout because it was there that I learned to type, without which, given my atrocious handwriting, I am sure that this and my other books would never have been written, let alone read by prospective editors.

I was in the "rapid advance" program, which enabled me to complete two years of junior high school in one, and sometime early in the eighth or ninth grade I learned of the exam for New York's Music and Art High School, which survives today as part of the much larger La Guardia High School. Although I was never a good enough violinist to contemplate a career as a professional musician, I passed the M and A test for music because it was based on identifying tonal intervals and rhythms, which required no particular training. I took the test because my neighborhood high school was, even in the late 1940s, one of the classic "at risk" public high schools in New York. What I didn't realize was that, music and art subjects aside, M and A was an academically "challenged" school. As a group, its teaching staff was of indifferent quality; some even bordered on incompetent. No English teacher inspired me, the math was rote, and the science actually off-putting. Only one social science teacher managed to engage my attention. Like many in the department, unless he was cheating on the dues, Mr. August Gold was probably a card-carrying Socialist Party member and an official in the then vibrant consumer cooperative movement. He was a follower of Charles Beard, whose economic interpretation of the Constitution and other aspects of American history was considered quite avant-garde in

an era when the prevailing textbook interpretations proclaimed the doctrine of Manifest Destiny, and of the centrality of Great Men. The historians of what Richard Hofstadter has called the "progressive" school
were regarded as dissenters from received wisdom, and sometimes condemned incorrectly as Marxists.

Like many other good enough high schools, what saved M and A
were the students. They divided into two groups: the professionally oriented, most of whom, in music, aspired to performance and in art were
equally divided between the commercial and "fine" art camps; and an
equally large group of those, like myself, who had some artistic incli-
nation, but were there primarily to escape the parochial environments
of our neighborhoods. Many were sons and daughters of New Dealers,
some of thirties radicals, mostly of the communist variety, a distinction
often blurred by the virtual end of intellectual radicalism by the war's
outbreak. Some were members of the labor Zionist movement and had
broad left-wing sympathies, but since they were destined to emigrate to
the newly formed state of Israel, kept their distance from involvement in
American politics. Those young radicals who were not Zionists tended to
hang out together, and in the immediate postwar period, a substantial
minority joined the prevailing CP-led "progressive" youth groups. In a
school of some 1,800 students, our chapter of the Young Progressives had
250 members and, in the 1948 presidential election, carried our school's
straw poll for third party candidate, former vice-president Henry A.
Wallace. We met in the local club of the American Labor Party and had
about a hundred students in monthly attendance. Most of us performed
well enough in school but reserved our real education for the drama and
study groups we formed among ourselves.

Some of us attended the CP-controlled Jefferson School of Social
Science, where we learned everything from drama to Marxist orthodoxy.
Jefferson School turned out to be my real university. At age sixteen, I enrolled in the Marxist Institute, which, among other subjects, exposed me
to philosophy. We read Thales, Anaximander, and Heraclitus from the
pre-Socratics, Plato's *Republic* (but only in order to refute it), and Aristotle's *Metaphysics* as a precursor to Hegel and Marx. We studied Descartes
and the English empiricists, especially Locke, Berkeley, and Hume, a
demonstration in the futility of bourgeois idealism. We learned how
Marx turned Hegel on his head by preserving the dialectic and throwing out the idealism. The interpretation was, to say the least, incomplete,

but I got to read large portions of the *Phenomenology of Mind* in the turgid translation of the English Hegelian, John Baillie. Finally, I studied Marx's *German Ideology, Capital,* and the historical writings. A hefty menu of Lenin and Stalin brought us to the apex of human knowledge. Some of my teachers were stimulating: in particular, Marx Wartofsky, later of Boston University and Baruch College, and Harry K. Wells, a rather orthodox Marxist who wrote his dissertation at Columbia on Alfred North Whitehead and later published an unrelenting attack on pragmatism and a more modulated materialist critique of Freud.

As I look back, my group was quite separate, not only from the future Jascha Heifetzes and Vladimir Horowitzes or the prospective abstract expressionists who had no place in the art curriculum, but from the apoliticals in our midst—although we probably had some ideological influence on them. I made a few enduring friendships, but the curriculum had little impact on me. I was completely uninterested in science and mathematics, and my high grades in social studies and English were accomplished through my reading of alternative texts. Indeed, by the time I reached college age, I was truly unclear as to what I might do there. But the aspirations of my parents prevailed over my strong impulse to postpone further formal education.

In fact, I barely qualified for entrance into Brooklyn College. Founded in 1931, Brooklyn was one of only four senior public colleges in New York and had slightly lower admission requirements than the famed City College. Like the other New York municipal colleges at the time, Brooklyn was tuition-free. Otherwise I would not have been able to go to college, since my family was unwilling—and probably unable—to pay the tuition fees. As it turned out I did not stay very long, for when I arrived at Brooklyn, McCarthyism was in full swing.

New York State's legislature had enacted the Feinberg law, which prohibited communists from teaching in public schools and colleges. Brooklyn's president, Harry Gideonse was, in fact, if not formally, a practitioner of Sidney Hook's idea of academic freedom: faculty would enjoy freedom of expression, provided they were not communists or followers of their line. Students would have the right to question authority, but within the rules of "civility," that is, no student had the right to transgress campus facilities to demonstrate against the administration and its policies. In my freshman year, the administration banned the student newspaper for an editorial opposing its refusal to grant official club status to the Labor Youth League, a procommunist student organization. As a member of the Young Progressives (which did have official status) and president of the Philosophy Club, I joined seven other student leaders in sponsorship of a demonstration at the dean of students' office. Four hundred students sat in, and the eight leaders, including myself, were suspended for "conduct unbecoming a student." We were offered a reprieve if we apologized for our unruly behavior. Some seniors recanted in order to be eligible for graduation and to prevent a report of their activities on their transcript. I was one of three who refused to apologize. Suspended, I happily retired from college, for the next fifteen years.

In rapid succession I became a factory worker, got married, had a child, moved to Newark to be near my job, had another child, and became active in union and community affairs. For me, the 1950s were not dismal; they were exciting. If the 1950s were years of very local concerns, in the 1960s I found myself in the swirl of the new social movements, in the first place civil rights, and then the student and peace movements. By this time I had moved back to New York, leaving my estranged wife and my children behind in New Jersey. I saw them on weekends and provided for their financial support, but I had relinquished everyday parenthood.

In reality, my academic career began in 1964. It was then that I was invited to join the editorial board of *Studies on the Left,* started only four years previously by a group of William Appleman Williams's graduate students in the history department of the University of Wisconsin and probably the most influential intellectual journal of the growing new American radicalism. At the time, I'd just left the Amalgamated Clothing Workers, where I'd been running the union boycott and some of its national organizing campaigns, to take a job as an organizer for the Oil, Chemical, and Atomic Workers in the northeast region. I think the invitation to join *Studies* was mainly related to my trade union experience and also to the fact that I was associated with the Students for a Democratic Society. I served as an advisor to the SDS Economic Research and Action Project, a community organizing program to send college students into black and white poor communities in major northern cities. I had arranged for an SDS group to go to the Clinton Hill section of Newark, where an active community organization, of which I had been vice-chairman, was fighting city hall on a host of neighborhood issues. At seminars and workshops and innumerable meetings to plan the community organizing activities and in informal conversations with prospective

organizers, I taught the fundamentals of organizing, some political economy, and the history of the labor movement.

As a result of these experiences and because I had witnessed firsthand the devolution of the once promising industrial union movement
into a series of bureaucracies that functioned more as insurance companies than as social movements, I began to think about writing a book on
the American working class and its movements. Since the United States
had few, if any, Borgias to support someone who aspired to write such a
tract, at the back of my mind I was considering whether it would be a
good idea to get a B.A. as a preliminary step toward an eventual teaching career. The opportunity arose when I learned of a Ford Foundation
program at Brooklyn College that enabled what we now call "adult
learners" (I was thirty-one) to obtain a baccalaureate degree. I didn't
know whether I could make time for this three-night-a-week regimen,
but I applied and took the requisite Graduate Record Examinations in
verbal, quantitative skills, and the humanities. My math scores were mediocre, but I scored high on the other two tests and was admitted.

I attended classes for one week and dropped out, I told myself, because the organizing duties presented insuperable scheduling conflicts. I
guess that was part of it, but the main reason for my departure was that
I found the classes boring. I don't remember whether it was the relatively
"basic" content or the pedagogy or both. But it was clear that the same
underlying impulse that drove me out of Brooklyn College fourteen
years earlier was still at work: I simply lacked the motives to tolerate
boredom for the four years of the program, which didn't acknowledge
"life experience" as a legitimate curriculum component.

Nevertheless, I started to write longer pieces than leaflets for organizing campaigns. In the winter of 1964, I published a review essay
of three books on labor for *Studies,* and subsequently wrote occasional
pieces for the *Village Voice,* the *Nation,* and *Liberation.* But it was not until I
took leave of union organizing in spring 1967 that I tried again to reenter
academia. Through the generous offices of Norman Birnbaum, then a
sociology professor on the faculty of the New School, I presented my
GRE scores, some of my published writing, and my resume to the dean
of the graduate faculty, Joseph Greenbaum. My proposal was to waive
the B.A. requirement and enter the graduate program in sociology. He
demurred, insisting that I spend at least a year "in residence" in the general studies program as a B.A. student. I was to be assigned a mentor and

was required to write a "major research paper," although I was spared the obligation to attend classes. Since meanwhile Birnbaum had accepted a position to teach at Amherst, Trent Schroyer, an assistant professor of sociology and a recent graduate of the Ph.D. program, was assigned to work with me. I wrote a seventy-five-page paper titled "The Fate of Historical Materialism in Advanced Capitalism," a critique of Marxism along the lines of the Critical Theory of the Frankfurt school and, after receiving my degree in 1968, entered the graduate school in sociology.

This time I went to classes filled with high hopes. The New School enjoyed an international reputation as the intellectual and political refuge for outstanding European scholars. At the time, its faculty included the political philosopher Hannah Arendt, the great phenomenologist Aron Gurwitch, the economist Adolph Lowe, whose classes I sometimes audited while writing my senior paper, the historical sociologist Hans Speier, and ethicist Hans Jonas. When I arrived, visitors from a more recent generation of mostly German academic intellectuals also graced the faculty: Iring Fetscher, the eminent Marxologist, and Albrecht Wellmer, one of the bright lights of the second-generation Frankfurt school, whose best-known member was, of course, Jürgen Habermas, another regular New School visitor. I was especially drawn to a less well known figure, Hans Peter Dreitzel, a sociologist from the Free University of Berlin, whose work had a much more empirical bent. He brought his students into his home and sponsored miniature salons on a wide variety of topics. On balance, my first semester in graduate school did much to allay my fears that my history in institutions of higher learning might repeat itself.

Meanwhile, I participated in several experiments in radical education, notably the Free University of New York—founded in 1965 as a non–degree granting, noncredit school situated in a loft on West 14th Street—and its successors, the Free U and the Alternate U (the "U" being a concession to the New York State Education Department, which forbid the schools to use the designation "university"). I taught courses in politics, labor, and culture. My colleagues included James Weinstein, editor of *Studies;* another *Studies* editor, Staughton Lynd, then in the throes of a tenure battle at Yale; the social ecologist Murray Bookchin; the well-known economist and follower of Frederick Von Hayek, Murray Rothbard; his friend, libertarian political theorist Leonard Liggio; Rosalyn

Baxandall, who taught women's social history; and Susan Sherman, among several writers who taught poetry. Grace Paley taught short-story writing. Tuli Kupferberg of the Fugs, a performer and song writer, was a student in one of my classes, as were Ellen Willis and Robert Christgau, both of whom were among a small group who were just beginning to invent rock criticism. There were writing and painting courses, children's programs on Saturdays, and music and theater workshops. It reminded me of Jefferson School, but without the Stalinist or any other dogma.

What impressed me about these schools was that students of all ages came to learn new things as well as to meet people and socialize without the expectation of a credential that would prepare them for a job or a career. Most of them were young radicals, many burning to change the world. So the Free Universities were not institutions of "useless" knowledge, except from the perspective of the economic and political system. But unlike American colleges and universities, private as well as public, they were not founded to serve the state or to transmit what had been thought and said by icons of national culture. Instead, in the minds of the founders, we were fulfilling one of the requisites of Marx's eleventh thesis on Feuerbach: "Philosophers have sought to interpret the world in various ways; the point is to change it." We did not hope, nor did we expect, to be integrated into the prevailing system of economic, political, and cultural power. Notwithstanding the Free University's leftist tilt, we were swept up in the New Left wave of nonsectarianism. We welcomed free market libertarians like Rothbard because we opposed the tendency, all too apparent in the late 1960s, of mainstream higher education to demand homogeneity in political and intellectual standpoints. There were Marxist-Leninists on the "faculty" but also anarchists and libertarians, antistatist socialists like Lynd and myself.

The Free University thrived on the turmoil that constantly raged in its administrative and political councils. In radical democratic fashion, prospective teachers submitted their course proposals, not to the tiny administrative staff, but to the community of students and faculty, which met frequently to decide school policy. So the typical "curriculum" was a melange of ideological orientations, and there was no principle of exclusion save what the community thought was "relevant," a criterion that sometimes masked serious ideological differences. But under pressure of the "new communist movement," which glorified centralism and trashed democracy, the New Left splintered into warring factions. In

1970 the Alternate U, the surviving incarnation of the Free University, imploded.

I ran out of visiting Germans at the New School. I was obliged to take the core courses offered by those trained in post–World War Two American sociology. Apart from the regrettable pedagogy, I found the content painfully thin. One instructor did nothing in class but read from Max Weber's texts, without inviting discussion or offering commentary. Another, although a much nicer and more open person, was so wrong, in my estimation, that continuing to follow his course would have elicited constant disagreements and hostility. Within weeks of the start of the second semester, I was contemplating switching from sociology to political economy. But since I already had a fairly good grounding in Marx, Keynes, and their followers, I was not inclined, at age thirty-seven, to go over familiar ground in order to earn a Ph.D., so with some trepidation, I quietly left.

I found an answer to this academic crisis in a unique program called the Union Graduate School, which afforded people like me the opportunity to earn a Ph.D. on the basis of writing and other evidence of academic competence. The school accepted my publications record, the courses I took, my life achievements, and best of all, my thesis on technology and its implications for labor, which was later incorporated into my book *Science as Power*. I worked with permanent core faculty and adjuncts, but did not attend classes. The school was in the accreditation process when I received my degree in 1975. A few years later it was fully accredited.

In short, I write this book from liminal space. I am neither an insider, never having completed a course of study in an institution of postsecondary education, nor an outsider, since I have worked and been visiting professor in a fair sampling of the range of colleges and universities comprised by the American academic system. As with all of my books, my approach here is critical: I pretend to offer neither a history nor a sociological profile, although there are elements of both between the covers. I draw from my own experience as well as the corpus of research on higher education, and my point of view is by no means tucked into the jargon of science.

My claim is that with only a few partial exceptions, there is little that would qualify as higher learning in the United States. By "higher learning" I mean places where students are broadly and critically exposed to the legacy of Western intellectual culture and to those of the Southern Hemisphere and the East. It is not only that the preponderance of under-graduate curricula, except for specialist majors, ignore China, India, Latin America, and Africa and the literatures and histories of America's racialized minorities and women. The typical college graduate generally leaves without having encountered, in more than a thin survey, European and American philosophy and literature. My intention in writing this book is not to reform the existing system, for I am not at all persuaded that it is possible. For those who would do something different, perhaps these ideas might inspire innovation.

THE KNOWLEDGE FACTORY

CHAPTER 1 KNOWLEDGE FACTORIES

1

THIS IS A BOOK ABOUT "higher" learning and its teaching in America. It is becoming harder to find a place where learning, as opposed to "education" and "training," is the main goal. Training prepares the student in knowledges that constitute an occupation or a particular set of skills. For the most part, graduate schools train students to enter a profession. Education prepares the student to take her place in society in a manner consistent with its values and beliefs. Whatever content the school delivers, the point is to help the student adapt to the prevailing order, not assimilate its values in terms of her own priorities and interests. Education is successful when the student identifies with social and cultural authorities.

The United States of America spends more on primary, secondary, and postsecondary schooling than any other nation in the world. Once limited, for most, to some ten years, formal schooling beyond high school is now the norm for a large percentage of American students. At the end of the twentieth century, about half of those who enter elementary school and more than three-fifths of those who complete high school attend some postsecondary institution. In articles, classes, and public talks over the years, I have used the term "postsecondary" rather than "higher" to describe what U.S. colleges and universities do. The reason is that for as long as I have been teaching in these systems, I have observed only rare instances of "higher" learning, especially in the humanities and the social sciences. For the most part, undergraduate education in the United States may achieve what a decent secondary school was expected to deliver fifty years ago. In turn, with the exception of the thesis or dissertation stage in a candidate's schooling, graduate education aspires to no more than what used to distinguish a good undergraduate degree, and often falls short of the mark. Postsecondary education is rapidly becoming mandatory, if not in legal terms, in practically every other. If present trends persist—a question I intend to address in this book—most Americans will soon spend an average of eighteen to twenty years in school, which implies that a considerable number attend school for a lot longer.

On the eve of World War Two, some 1.5 million students attended postsecondary institutions. In 1941, at a time when the labor force was about 50 million, the proportion of the potential working population attending postsecondary schools was about 3 percent. From 1945 to 1965, college and university enrollments, consisting mostly of young adults of working age, grew by 300 percent while the economy advanced 200 percent. In the next thirty years, enrollments grew by two and a half times while the economy doubled; college attendance has maintained a steady advance in the half century since the war while the rate of economic growth slowed considerably after 1969. By 1991, 61 percent of high school graduates entered some kind of postsecondary school. In 1997, the proportion of college students to the adult population had risen to 13 percent, more than four times what it was in 1941. Of a work force of some 114 million, more than 15 million people of working age were enrolled in an institution of "higher" learning. Of that 15 million, almost 10 million were full-time students. Since more than 80 percent of students entering high school now graduate, that means about half of America's eighteen-year-olds are enrolled in a college or university.[1] Seventy percent of American students are enrolled in public schools, so funding the basic operations of postsecondary institutions constitutes a major government expenditure. Added to the billions spent on public universities are the annual congressional appropriations for research—nonmilitary as well as military—to private and public research universities. It is thus no wonder that "higher" education has become a contentious item in federal and state budgets and the budgets of millions of Americans.

These are astounding statistics. It means that nearly 10 percent of the adult population under age sixty-five is enrolled in a vocational, technical, or liberal arts college and millions of others have already earned postsecondary credentials. Compare this enormous enrollment to virtually any other advanced industrial society. France, Germany, and Italy enroll less than 4 percent of the population in higher education, and enrollments in the United Kingdom are only slightly higher.

The questions leap out: Why in America do we place such a high value on college? Why is college rapidly becoming an imperative for most young people and for a substantial number of "mature" students—those entering at age thirty or older—as well? What are the implications for the growth of higher education for American politics and culture? What does "higher education" mean for its students and their families? Do burgeoning enrollments signify a more educated population? Or are they due to the fact that, more and more, even many elite schools offer vocational programs? If the latter, does this emphasis subvert the historic function of universities as the guardians, even the gatekeepers, of Western or national culture? Can universities maintain their role as political unifiers of an increasingly diverse population by providing the basic guidelines for what constitutes "citizenship" in the contemporary social world? Or, as some have claimed, is higher education for sale and destined to be reduced to a series of advanced and intermediate training schools?

Critics of American society and its culture have expended a great deal of print attacking schools. According to one of the most common critiques, many schools are not merely neutral institutions that transmit skills and intellectual knowledge; they are highly politicized. In David Nasaw's phrase, students are "schooled to order."[2] Schools rob students of their individuality and, instead, train kids to become cogs in the corporate capitalist machine. In elementary and secondary schools, the curriculum is oriented to patriotism, obedience, and above all, to the prevailing morality—the "work ethic," "family values," and citizenship

—which equates virtue with responsibility to something called the "community." Of course, the community is not to be equated with the neighborhood but to the nation-state. The visibility of the education system may be measured by the degree to which schools contribute to the stability of the social order by helping students to know their place within it and their responsibility to maintain it. The key to whether schools work is whether kids hold these truths to be self-evident and endowed by their creator.

This rough model of the function of school in society is only slightly at variance with another take: that at the secondary and postsecondary levels, the role of the humanities is to articulate, in the public sphere as much as the classroom, the essential elements of national culture. If the student is to situate himself in society, it is by means of imbibing those knowledges that mark him as a national subject. Some recent writing on higher education insists that the process of social and cultural formation is effected, in the main, through literature rather than through history and philosophy.[3] Certainly the social sciences, which are usually viewed as "debunking" disciplines, cannot fulfill this socializing function, for in their classical modes, they are preeminently critical rather than positive.

It is worth noting that, at least in the last thirty years, the relationship between literature and the social sciences has been reversed: since the war the social sciences are, to a great extent, policy sciences and, with the single exception of anthropology, have largely lost their critical character. In contrast, having been deprived of their socializing function by the relative decline of the nation-state after the 1960s, both citizenship and its concomitant, national culture, have receded. What is left for literature is criticism and theory, two endeavors whose utility is constantly questioned by technoscience.

The social sciences have increasingly veered toward the natural sciences in their self-conscious subordination to the prevailing order. Their preoccupation with questions of research methods by which to measure public opinion have made them part of the barometric orientation of American politics. Social scientists have become the technicians of social control, providing the scientific legitimacy for social, education, military, and other areas of policy. With few exceptions, the garden-variety social scientists—sociologists, economists, and political scientists—are the intellectual servants of power. Like natural scientists, they are prone to follow the money. Among the social science disciplines, economists are virtually tied at the hip to corporate and government bureaucracies. If the others have not yet enjoyed this intimacy, for many practitioners, it is a condition devoutly to be wished.

2

Sometime in the nineteenth century, philosophy was replaced by literature in the quest for national identity. For one thing, after Immanuel Kant, the sciences were philosophy's chief preoccupation, and in the process of their incorporation, philosophy, excepting ethics, lost its taste for speculation (today even ethics is ordinarily framed in logical discourse). Novels and poems came to typify what Matthew Arnold called the "best that has been thought and said," at least in the West.[4] What the state and most educators wanted was to imbue the student's imagination with what it was to be English, American, or French. Literature was best suited to this task because, unlike philosophy and history, which were international in scope and were assimilated into the sciences, literature was essentially national. You can read the works of, say, Dostoevsky, Flaubert, or Mann in translation, but as everyone knows, something is always missing—chiefly, the sense of place, that is, the specificity of the vernacular of which particular cultures are made. Even the most deft attempts to situate characters in their own cultural context, such as can be found in the work of Dickens, Thackeray, and Trollope, never quite overcome the distance experienced by almost any foreign reader, even the relentless cosmopolitan. Otherwise, how to explain the chasm that separates Constance Garnett's Victorian translations of Dostoevsky, for example, from the more colloquial renditions of Andrew McAndrew or Avram Yarmolinsky. As much as Garnett, later translators have beckoned implied readers to assimilate this modern Russian writer to their own discursive system.

National/cultural assimilation takes on a special significance in the United States, which since the 1830s has presented the educational system with successive immigrant waves, whose integration, I suggest, is its main historical function. At every level of the educational hierarchy, the task is the same for all groups; only the curriculum differs. The degree to which schools enable students and faculty to explore the many dimensions of the dominant culture depend on whether their clientele is the elite or the plebes, whether they are educating an intellectual leadership, the business class, the political class, or those destined to function in technical categories. In fact, as many studies have demonstrated, acculturation to the old Arnoldian ideal is most successful in the upper reaches of the education system. College-educated people tend to vote conservative (and more often), are more aware of their obligations to the state, and routinely observe the tenets of basic morality, except, perhaps, in business.

This picture has been subjected to scrutiny by many writers. Bill Readings finds that the university in the United States is "in ruins" chiefly because globalization has undermined any solid sense of the nation. Besides, he argues, we have never had a genuine national culture. Consequently, the university has become virtually identical with the transnational corporations (TNCs) that serve as a kind of surrogate state. Didactic slogans are thus no longer linked to traditional national identities such as citizenship and patriotism, which are really two sides of the same coin. Rather, as universities have become corporate in their structure as well as in their curriculum, they advance the indeterminate goal of "excellence" to which the TNCs are pledged.[5]

Paul Willis and Pierre Bourdieu have fashioned versions of the role of school in society that differ sharply from the traditional socialization model.[6] Willis shows how working-class youth attending a British comprehensive high school define themselves by means of a tacit rebellion against the curriculum and the values that underlie it, especially the promise, if they observe its rituals, of social mobility. They reject the curriculum and become dropouts or, if they stay through to their diploma, manage to elude most of the requirements that might qualify them for university or college admission. So for working-class youth, high school is usually a terminal degree. In the 1960s and 1970s, the time of Willis's ethnography, the "lads" go off to the local factory or, more often in those years of massive deindustrialization of areas such as England's Midlands, are consigned to the ranks of the long-term unemployed.

According to Willis, the rebellion is buttressed by a working-class subculture in which education, rather than being an opportunity to gain access to a better life, is seen as little more than a sorting machine that separates those who buy in from the traditional class-based community. Willis's study undermines the commonly held, largely middle-class assumption, that "making it," even when it entails buying "in"—when the individual trades one uniform for another—is reasonable and those who fail to measure up may be judged irrational or simply incapable of learning what they need to know. For he demonstrates an all too obscure truth: some people choose not to accumulate the required "cultural capital" (Bourdieu's term) needed to surmount class destiny.

Claiming that cultural capital is equivalent to economic capital, Bourdieu replaces, but does not refute, the theory of socialization common to Western social science. Socialization requires children to internalize the socially prescribed values they must adopt in work, family, and nation as personal goals. Their individual and collective identities are intertwined with school performance and with linguistic codes appropriate to certain economic niches. Basil Bernstein has distinguished between elaborated and restricted linguistic codes and has insisted that they correlate with and are functional to class-based linguistic communities.[7] Bernstein's argument has been profoundly misunderstood to mean that the "real is rational" and that the working class is somehow genetically inferior. What he is saying is that most industrial workers speak in the restricted code, not because they are less intelligent but because the context within which the speech act occurs does not require the use of big words or complex syntax.

But for Bourdieu, the acquisition of an elaborated linguistic code is, perhaps, the primary form of cultural capital upon which all intellectually legitimate knowledge depends. Regardless of whether they attain a postsecondary credential, no student who has failed to acquire the elaborated code is able to accumulate knowledge that is equated with cultural capital. So while it is arguable that going to college is the necessary condition for accumulating cultural capital, it is by no means sufficient. Although there are millions who now attend and millions more who have graduated an institution of postsecondary schooling, many lack the elementary presupposition of professional marketability, to be well-spoken and culturally glib.

Students who put their collective noses to the grindstone do so because the consequences of refusing cultural capital accumulation are grave. They learn to use academic discourse, primarily because it is the repository of the elaborated code and, for graduate students, part of the tools of the trade. If a grasp of national culture, obedience to the nation-state, citizenship education (who the president is, who the leaders of Congress are, how many senators and representatives there are), and so forth are calculated as quantities of cultural capital, it does not matter whether the student believes in these values or not. She learns that a specific regime of knowledge—social, intellectual, or technical—is a ticket to jobs and goods. Thus even those who publicly scorn education as a form of capital accumulation are constrained to participate in reproducing prescribed knowledges at various levels of the educational hierarchy lest they, too, be forced into the job market on unfavorable terms. In the end, the practical relation between the labor market and schooling tends to temper and ultimately defeat the critics of schooling.

For better or for worse, the social world upon which most working-class kids once made their decision whether to buy in or not has all but disappeared in most advanced capitalist societies. In many heavily industrialized regions of the United States, Germany, Britain, and France, well-paid unionized factory jobs have disappeared more rapidly than did the agricultural work they replaced. Deindustrialized cities and towns that have escaped utter destitution have done so because they have transformed themselves into regional financial centers, tourist attractions, and (when they are near research universities) laboratories and small-scale production sites for computers and other high technology products. Absent these conversions, some U.S. urban areas have fallen into abject disrepair in ways that are unimaginable in Europe. Lacking jobs, they have lost population, and their shrinking tax base is unable to support vital services such as schools and recreation or infrastructure such as street, bridge, and road repair, clean water and clean air. In this environment, the best options for a high school graduate are, in descending order, jobs in the police and fire departments, post office worker, prison guard, the armed forces and clerical work, or low-level technical and administrative jobs in local government. Failing this, most young men, especially those who do not graduate or have general diplomas, are condemned to nonunion construction in the residential sector of the industry, where wages range from six to nine dollars an hour, or about a third to half of union scale. Even public sector roadwork often requires a high school diploma. Young women who have not completed high school have few choices other than to become retail clerks earning wages that hover around legal minimums. Many who choose to enter postsecondary educational institutions know that successful completion of their course of study qualifies them to leave town. They are products of one of the important functions of local colleges: export of credentialed workers.

Postsecondary education is no longer the exclusive province of privileged, bright middle-class students or the "deserving" poor. For a clear majority, entering college is as much an imperative as high school was after World War One, and this state of affairs is directly traceable to the absence of real economic alternatives. The narrowing of employment options is reflected by the fact that in the United States, where in 1997 more than 83 percent of those entering high school graduated, 62 percent of graduates go on to college, half of them in community colleges.[8]

The reasons that college attendance has become virtually compulsory for most graduates reduce to two: First, many young adults are pushed into college by anxious parents with firsthand knowledge of the sea change that has afflicted the job market. They know that there are few good factory jobs and even fewer well-paying service jobs, and that most of the others offered to high school graduates are low paid and dead-end. Second, and most important, whatever the major and although it does not ensure a decent living, a college degree provides the minimum qualification to enter the market for a large variety of jobs, even if many are temporary and contingent.

Still, as I will later demonstrate, the rebellion against the curriculum has now shifted to higher education. Many students attend classes but do not accumulate significant quantities of cultural capital, in part because they recognize they are badly prepared and have no strategy for overcoming their perceived deficits. And since college-level preparatory programs designed to make them cultural-capital ready are disappearing, the main function of college attendance is to delay entrance into the uncertain job market.

Although a considerable minority still rebel against the curriculum, thereby selecting to remain on the lower rungs of the working class, it no longer follows that successful completion of the associate's or baccalaureate degree signifies entrance into the middle class. Most postsecondary graduates enter the labor market as knowledge and administrative workers. They become computer technicians, programmers, and repairpersons, subprofessionals in social work and nursing, elementary and secondary school teachers—"sub" because their jobs do not ordinarily entail genuine autonomy in the performance of their work even if they require a formal license. Or they become line administrators—a notch above word processors and other clerical workers—in government and nonprofit social service agencies. Business and accounting majors can, with a B.A., become managers or auditors for small firms. And a much larger group gets jobs as "management trainees" for large chains of every description, especially in the retail food, department store, and clothing industries. A small number, mainly from Ivy League and other elite schools, enter publishing and other communications companies as assistants, editors, and production designers, at starting salaries that are substantially below those of teachers, whose own salaries have stagnated in the last twenty years. Some of these professionals advance more or less rapidly within communications and entertainment companies. Many of those who don't make it decide to go to law school, join the computer-programming trend, or try to make a living by freelancing.

With the exception of some specialties, primarily in the health and the computer fields, for which scientific and technical knowledge remains a prerequisite, a liberal arts, business, or administration degree provides no special qualifications that relieve the employer of the obligation to train. Most employers say they want school-leavers to have a degree, be able to read and write, follow oral and written instructions, and be fairly articulate. From their perspective, the B.A. signifies that the candidate can tolerate boredom and knows how to follow rules, probably the most important lesson in postsecondary education. Whether she has picked up other pieces of substantive knowledge is a matter of complete indifference, although in order to fulfill curriculum requirements the student has to be able to make sense of a large number of texts, at least for the period she is in class.

Judging by the small numbers who were in love with their subjects or who were dedicated learners for reason of compulsion or ambition, I used to think that most students had no idea why they were in college beyond the widely shared sense among several generations of young adults that on the other side was the abyss. Now I am pretty sure most students understand that to play the job game they need a degree, even if their expectations are often buffeted by the market's vicissitudes. From their friends and parents, they know how little a terminal high school diploma will buy. Yet they have little idea what they want to "study." In most cases, their choices of major and minor fields are informed (no, dictated) by a rudimentary understanding of the nature of the job market rather than by intellectual curiosity, let alone intellectual passion.

3

The contemporary American mass higher education system is barely sixty years old. Its resemblance to the earlier model, in which college was mainly a finishing school for children of the upper middle class and of the very rich or for training teachers and members of the clergy, is purely formal. Although this function still describes a small minority, most colleges and universities are part of an academic system in American society whose success is measured by, among other criteria, how much it contributes to the economy. Among the values that economists try to calculate is the central contribution of postsecondary education to what one economist terms the production and distribution of "human capital."[9] Another no less influential perspective shows that universities are the main sites of intellectual knowledge, much of which is embodied in the machinery that enhances labor productivity in traditional industries. This knowledge also leads to the invention of new products for the marketplace, is applied to military uses, and perhaps the most of all, generates new domains of scientifically based human endeavor, some of which, such as communications and information, have had enormous commercial and cultural implications.

Far from the image of an ivory tower where, monk-like, scholars ponder the stars and other distant things, the universities tend to mirror the rest of society. Some have become big businesses, employing thousands and collecting millions in tuition fees, receiving grants from government and private sources, and, for a select few, raising billions in huge endowments. In some cities and towns, the resident private university or college is the area's largest landlord, housing students and faculty and, in some instances, collecting rents for ordinary or slum dwellings. With these funds, the universities construct buildings, help pay their CEOs (presidents) handsomely, and retain a small army of administrators and fundraisers. Whereas smaller, less prestigious institutions often dedicate limited recruitment dollars to athletics or use their resources to repair buildings and grounds, in recent years larger universities have put their money toward attracting academic superstars, for whom they pay two or three times the salaries of ordinary professors.

A considerable number of towns and small cities are economically dependent upon their local university or college. Unless the town is lucky enough to have bagged a prison or state mental institution, the university may be the largest employer for all occupational categories. Blue-collar and clerical workers and professionals of all sorts earn their living there, and while the pay is often below that offered by the private sector, generally the work is more steady. Most universities and colleges are legally "nonprofit," so they pay no direct taxes. On the contrary, the local political jurisdiction in fact subsidizes the college or university by maintaining streets around the campus, taking main responsibility for police and fire services (even when the campus has its own police), and providing other amenities.

The university is the only way some professors can pursue esoteric knowledge, that is, scholarship that has few or no practical uses. This is especially true for natural scientists and humanists whose focus is on theoretical or historical issues. Surely, except for those working in the applied fields of medical and business ethics, for example, philosophers cannot expect to make a living in the private sector. But for the preponderance of the professoriate, research and scholarship are no longer, as they once were, performed as a "vocation" in the religious sense. In keeping with the desacralization of their profession, academics call what they do a "job." For the overwhelming majority, a postsecondary teaching job does not pay particularly well. In 1999, starting assistant professors averaged $34,000 a year, and full professors $68,000 a year, about the same salary as engineers and computer programmers.[10] Although their salaries are comparable to associates in middle-sized and small law firms in cities outside the major metropolitan regions, full professors on the average earn far less than both starting attorneys in large corporate law firms and salaried physicians in group practices or hospitals.

After completing undergraduate schooling, the typical graduate student requires six to eight more years to complete his Ph.D. work, during the course of which he may accumulate as much as $150,000 in debt, to cover tuition, the costs of acquiring knowledge such as books and computers, and living expenses. Leaving aside lost income during this period, faculty salaries are scandalously low, even for those teaching in professional schools, where salaries are considerably higher than those of the arts and sciences. Faced with budget cuts and declining research income, in recent years many postsecondary institutions have reduced their complement of full-time professors. In many instances, adjuncts teach as much as 40 percent of the courses. In community colleges and a substantial portion of private and public four-year colleges, the figure reaches as high as 60 percent, sometimes more.

Yet thousands of the best and brightest of America's students scramble for the relatively few full-time jobs in their chosen discipline. In fields such as English, anthropology, history, linguistics, and physics, the job market in four-year colleges and research universities has shrunk to near vanishing point. As a consequence, thousands of qualified graduates accept adjunct positions where, in the main, they enjoy no job security, few or no benefits, and are not paid for holding office hours or attending meetings. Many qualified teachers with Ph.D.'s and graduate students who are close to completing their degrees, support themselves by teaching four to six courses a semester in two or more institutions. At $1,500 to $2,000 a course, if they teach summer school they may earn as much as a beginning assistant professor, but without the chance of tenure. Ironically, the more they teach, the less their chance of finishing their dissertations or, if successfully completed, of transforming a thesis into a book or series of articles—a prerequisite in some disciplines for one to be seriously considered for a full-time position.

Why do some choose academic professions rather than more remunerative occupations in business or in technosciences such as molecular biology or computer science, where there have been frequent shortages of qualified, credentialed people? The answers, in these times, are culturally startling: some people abhor corporate life and don't care about making more money than they need to live in reasonable comfort, and they enjoy reading, writing, research, and teaching. But contrary to the ceaseless harping of right-wing ideologues that the professoriate is engaged in practicing a scam at the public's expense, academic life is not easy for the majority. Many academics don't mind working hard—the typical teaching load in public and many private four-year institutions of postsecondary education is nine to fifteen hours a week in the classroom, each of which requires an equal amount of preparation to do a conscientious job. Language, math, and science teachers spend many evenings grading papers, and many colleges require frequent publications from social science and humanities faculty as well. Most faculty attend regular department meetings two or three days a month. Under these circumstances, faculty must literally steal time to perform research and writing. While critics on the right may be gleeful about this state of affairs because the scholarship opposes their philosophical and political perspectives, and while others have dismissed the life of the mind as wasteful of human resources that could be put to more practical uses, the heavy teaching loads in the current academic job market are inimical to the formation of critical intellectuals, let alone traditional scholars.

Except in a small number of disciplines, notably economics, accountancy, and some legal specializations where private sector employment is often more lucrative, academic hiring is a buyer's market. Indeed, as universities continue to grant more degrees than the academic market can bear, hurdles such as having a degree "in hand" in order to apply for a job become more common. In addition, candidates are expected to have published in refereed journals, or better yet with a university press. Except in unusual cases, job applicants who have been out of graduate school for five years or more suffer tacit discrimination. Many departments prefer to hire newly minted Ph.D. candidates rather than experienced part-time teachers, who might not as easily "fit in" to department "culture." For the older candidate, the employment barrier is nearly prohibitive, unless she has been trained in a technical field such as nursing, where until recently there was a labor shortage. But now nursing is under siege from changes in the health care system, and applicants for academic teaching jobs are often required to have a Ph.D. in nursing, still a relatively rare degree in this profession.

The case of nursing illustrates a major shift in the significance of academic credentials since the enrollment explosion of the first thirty years after the war. With the advent of the GI Bill and the emergence of knowledge work among the characteristic domains of the American occupational structure, the postwar academic system began to experience shortages in qualified instructors. Until the late 1960s, many schools were pleased to hire teachers who did not have Ph.D.'s, especially in technical fields such as nursing, but also in some social sciences and humanities disciplines. Even today, most community college instructors do not have doctorates. But as academic salaries went up and tenure became a near universal reward for scholarship, academic teaching work became more attractive, and many schools rushed to offer Ph.D. and master's programs to meet the demand. By the mid-1970s the boom was over, and thousands of fully credentialed academics discovered that most of the good jobs had disappeared.

CHAPTER 2

HIGHER EDUCATION OR HIGHER TRAINING?

1

AT THE END OF THE 1930s, the most sophisticated pole of higher education was represented by perhaps a dozen full-scale state universities. California, for example, supported a world-class school at Berkeley, which largely conformed to the objectives for universities set in 1907 by Columbia professor J. R. Wheeler and to which many subscribe today: "to preserve and transmit liberal culture; to share useful knowledge with the populace at large; to serve as an agent of beneficial social change in a burgeoning industrial and commercial order; and to serve as a center for disinterested inquiry and the production of new knowledge through research and scholarly writing."[1] Whatever the University of California's merit as a preserver of traditional liberal culture or as an agent of social change, the sharply honed focus of this and similar schools was to serve as a center for the production of new knowledge, especially for private corporations and, later, the federal government's rearmament program.

Harvard, Yale, Columbia, Princeton, Stanford, Chicago, and a scattering of southern schools such as Duke and Vanderbilt remained among the select private universities offering a broad range of graduate degrees.

Columbia and Harvard were organized by Protestant denominations during pre-Revolutionary times, but only during the industrializing era did their affluent alumni contribute enough money to enable them to evolve into universities, in the contemporary meaning of the concept. In the nineteenth century, just as the emergence of the public library was closely associated with the contributions of the steel magnate Andrew Carnegie, and a wide range of philanthropic concerns from health care to American social science were supported by Rockefeller oil interests, most of the major private universities were founded by leading rail and manufacturing capitalists as monuments to their wealth and largesse.

In the main, however, until World War Two, most students attended some twelve hundred two- and four-year private colleges, many of which were under the tutelage of Protestant denominations or Catholic sects such as the Jesuits and Vincentians. It was only at the turn of the twentieth century that the emerging industrial business class began to send their male progeny to college in order to acquire some cultural polish before bringing them into the family business or into the task of managing its fortune. Gradually, as universities assumed functions as sites of scientific knowledge production, postsecondary institutions became secularized.

At the dawn of the industrializing era, which in the United States began about 1850, a few educators and the prominent industrialists they assiduously and brazenly courted, envisioned the expansion of higher education to serve the emerging requirements of industry for trained personnel and for new scientific knowledge. But, as always, the federal government had to be enlisted to realize their dreams. In 1862, President Abraham Lincoln signed legislation to facilitate public higher education by offering grants of tracts of federally owned lands to states that agreed to establish institutions of research and instruction devoted to the production and transmission of scientific and technical knowledge. But the so-called land-grant colleges did not immediately flower. Public response to this program, especially in agricultural states, was often less than enthusiastic. In Missouri and Ohio, for example, farmers did not buy the argument that they needed education to put their farms on a "scientific" basis. Besides, the American scientific establishment was still much too weak to fill these newly established schools with competent faculty.

By 1900, the university-corporate complex was in full bloom. The two aspects of this relationship, that universities adopt the business ethic and more directly serve business by training cadres for industry was well described by contemporary observers John Jay Chapman and Thorstein Veblen. Writing in 1909, Chapman declared, "The men who stand for education and scholarship have the ideals of business men. They are in truth business men. The men who control [universities] today are very little else than business men." Veblen "detected the hand of business control dominating every aspect of the modern university," including the "prominence given to intercollegiate athletics" and "vocational instruction."[2]

Published in 1918, Veblen's rant against the vocationalization of education and the transformation of universities into teaching machines already signaled that the American university model differed in fundamental respects from that of Europe. Noting the habit of industrial moguls such as Leland Stanford, the Rockefellers, and others to use universities to build "monuments" to their wealth and power, he deplored as well the tendency of even the grandest universities to transform the professoriate into "schoolmasters" by obliging them to teach undergraduate classes. For Veblen, the true function of postsecondary institutions was "higher learning," embodied in the work of research and scholarship. In his magisterial commentary on the vastly expanded postsecondary system after the Civil War, he found very little higher learning going on. Rather, he observed that most professors were engaged in transmitting knowledge of all sorts and more particularly in training young people for specialized occupations for the corporate job markets.[3]

Veblen's prescription for overcoming this sad state of affairs was to rigorously separate graduate schools from undergraduate schools and vocational programs. In his view, graduate education consisted in an apprenticeship to a research professor. The professor was best comprehended as a mentor working with a small number of fully funded assistants. In turn, the dissertation, according to Veblen, represented the *summa* of the individual's and the group's achievement. On the other side, Veblen did not oppose the college, but insisted that its function had to be rigorously distinguished from vocational training. Its role was to build on secondary education to prepare students to become genuine knowledge producers in the human and natural sciences and to remain critics of society. Needless to say, his jeremiad has never failed to inspire some students and professors, but for entirely understandable reasons, old and parvenu money continues to flow into the universities. Monuments are still being built as living memorials to these donors, and the critical role of higher education erodes with every passing year.

Although technological invention was important throughout the industrializing era, most corporations did not perceive the need for the systematic application of science to production until the turn of the twentieth century. So, contrary to myths about the role of land-grant colleges in advancing American scientific and technological capabilities, educators who wished to expand public sector higher education in collaboration with industry found the going rough for many years. Some midwestern universities—including Illinois, Michigan, and Indiana—were early starters in this enterprise and did succeed in attracting leading eastern-educated academics such as John Dewey, George Herbert Mead, and a number of natural scientists to their faculties. But in many states, until the years immediately prior to World War Two, the public institutions of postsecondary education were confined to teacher-training or normal schools. For example, under the restraining influence of Columbia's board of trustees and its administration, New York had no real public university until after World War Two, but the state government supported an extensive network of teacher-training and technical colleges, subsuming their administrative coordination under the State University of New York.

The turn-of-the-century scientific and technological revolution—principally the discovery of industrial uses for electromagnetism, for chemistry, and for geology—required an expanded coterie of scientists and engineers. The emergence of electricity for communications and as a source of energy; the development of the internal combustion engine, which generated enormous demand for oil; and the explosion of uses for chemicals in a wide range of products, from steel to cosmetics and drugs, placed science at the center of industry. Corporations such as General Electric, American Telephone and Telegraph, Hercules Powder—later called DuPont—a leading producer of war materiel, and the Rockefeller-controlled Standard Oil employed a good portion of the small cohort of native-born scientists and mathematicians. Federal government organizations, such as the Geological and Meteorological Surveys, both of which had strong links to commercial and industrial interests, hired most of the rest.

Even as skilled mechanics had been recruited a generation earlier from England, Scotland, and Germany to jump-start America's fledg-

ling textile, shoe, and metalworking factories, the shortages of trained
native-born candidates induced some companies to seek out trained scientists from Europe. Some were offered high salaries and the opportunity to build their own research laboratories. For example, the German
chemist Charles Steinmetz was asked by General Electric to develop the
first corporate laboratory at its Schenectady, New York, headquarters
and AT & T established a huge research facility in New Jersey, in part
to counter Thomas Edison's own Menlo Park lab. The practice of attracting European and other foreign scientists was especially important
during and following World War Two and, with the collapse of the Soviet
Union and the destruction of its awesome scientific establishment, has
continued to this day.

Veblen's commentary on higher learning coincided with the beginning of World War One, during the course of which universities consolidated as premier sites for the production of useful knowledge. That war
was, perhaps, the first truly technologically driven war. Although some
combatants still rode horses, and mules were used to transport equipment to the front lines, it was the first motorized war. Both sides made extensive use of trucks and trains to carry soldiers and materiel and deployed the recently developed airplane for reconnaissance, bombing,
and transportation. Naval power, one of the earliest technologies of warfare, became far more advanced with the general employment of subma-
rines and engine-driven ships of various kinds, and artillery and ordinary weapons were vastly improved. Egregiously, the war witnessed the
widespread deployment of chemical weapons, a testament to the usefulness of natural sciences. Needless to say, when compared to World War
Two and contemporary technologized warfare, World War One's use
of the sciences was rudimentary and fairly restricted. But it represented
a dramatic shift in the nature of warfare; while millions of troops were
still deployed on the battlefield, science and technology also performed a
major role.

The two world wars were as important as industry for promoting scientific and technological discovery and invention and were crucial in the
further development of industrial and commercial sectors. Although
many war-linked products were highly specialized, the scientific research that underlay their invention and development became a key element of postwar economic growth. Contrary to the widely held myth of
the superiority of the American private enterprise system, some indus-

trialists were acutely aware that government sponsorship of often frustrating and costly research and development could save them billions. They were pleased to turn over such expenditures to the state and to the tax system that supported it. As the new war loomed in the mid-1930s, the question of where research and development would take place was fairly quickly resolved: in the division of intellectual labor, private and public universities were assigned the tasks of performing fundamental, that is, "useless" knowledge production, but also of figuring out how to transform basic research into applications for the war effort. Except for atomic weapons, where for security reasons the government reserved research, development, and a large portion of production to itself, the private sector would build the ships, tanks, and trucks and produce the weaponry.

For most Americans, the 1930s were a time of terrible insecurity and searing trauma—marked by falling wages and salaries, more than 30 percent unemployment, and for many, near starvation. Yet throughout the decade, under the impetus of government contracts, many universities expanded their research functions, built new facilities to house them, and hired new science and engineering faculty and staff. State universities, such as University of California at Berkeley and the Big Ten schools, were primed for this new role, but it took some persuasion for the relatively hidebound Ivy League institutions to agree to change their culture to accommodate government interests as war loomed. By 1938 most were on board, and some, like Princeton, were to play an enormous role in the basic discoveries that led to the development of the atomic bomb.

Plagued by the Depression-era collapse of large sections of the middle class who were unable to send their children to college because they could no longer afford tuition, many private colleges closed their doors or merged with sister schools in order to share the misery. While public colleges and universities suffered budget cuts, in most cases they were better able to weather the economic storms. Unencumbered by either a large-scale tenure system (which did not take root until the war) or union contracts (which were nonexistent in education except for some groups of maintenance workers), administrators responded to reduced income by freezing or cutting faculty salaries and postponing needed repairs to buildings and grounds. Since for qualified young people going to school was preferable to unemployment, few public colleges experienced unwanted reductions in student enrollment. On the contrary, faced with the clamor of middle-class students whose parents could no longer afford private schools and with rising demands for higher education among poorer youngsters whose job market options had disappeared, many public colleges raised admission criteria.

During this period, postsecondary schools assumed one of their most important, but largely hidden, functions—absorbing a significant fraction of unemployed professionals and technical specialists, especially intellectuals whose discontent, the Roosevelt administration feared, might spill over into the general population. After the work of the first New Deal—stabilizing the banking system, establishing a labor relations system geared to raising production and profits, and securing America's international markets—a key task was to subordinate and otherwise mollify labor. The National Industrial Recovery Act of 1933 contained a weak provision ensuring labor's right to organize unions of its own choosing, but the lack of enforcement against employer abuses led to widespread criticism and worker insurgency. Responding to threats of a mass labor upsurge in the mining, needle, transportation, and auto trades, the Wagner Act (1935) finally put teeth into the union promise.

The substantial federal arts programs, which employed thousands of writers, painters, and theater people, attracted less comment, although particularly in the large cities, they were clearly a response to the radicalization that had overtaken many intellectuals. In this period, public higher education served a similar function. When the decade of fairly cautious social reform was ended by the overwhelming imperatives of war preparations and war, the university's ideological role, as compared to its direct scientific and technical role, decisively shifted. The country needed knowledge and trained technical employees for the war effort and officers for the exploding military. Many colleges were offered government grants to institute short-term training programs for civilians in various technological domains, especially engineering. My father attended Manhattan College and worked as a civilian employee for the Army Corps of Engineers, where, as a civil engineering technician, he helped build Idlewild (Kennedy) Airport, modernize Floyd Bennett Field, a major military installation, and the Plattsburgh, New York, airport.

2

New York City was the leader in the small, but important municipal college movement. Its public colleges prospered on condition they did not compete with Columbia and New York University in graduate studies. There were five publicly supported free colleges: City, established in 1847 as a men's school; Hunter, its "sister" school; and later, the coeducational Brooklyn, Queens, and New York City Technical Colleges. These schools had key responsibility for teacher training, but City was also a leading engineering school and had one of the first major scientific undergraduate programs.

The cascade of memoirs and other accounts of life in City College that have appeared in the last twenty-five years point to a paradox: According to most who spent time there, the quality of instruction and the distinction of its faculty were questionable. At the same time, many Nobel Prize winners are counted among its alumni, as well as an outsized coterie of public intellectuals, academic leaders in the humanities and the social sciences, and a fair number of prominent artists and businessmen. How to explain this discrepancy? The answer seems to be the presence of economically impoverished, but culturally ambitious, Jews, who dominated its student body from the turn of the century to about 1960. Without City, few would have been able to attend any postsecondary institution. The availability of a free public college provided a means to advance their desire to become literary and political intellectuals, scientists, and engineers. But with the exception of the rare teacher like the fabled Morris Raphael Cohen—the object of adoration for many—neither the curriculum or the pedagogy distinguished City from a plethora of private competitors.

Like the Lower East Side, which elected socialists to the state legislature and to Congress, and the Jewish labor movement, which constituted some of the few mass industrial unions before the 1930s, City was a hotbed of radical politics from the turn of the century. During World War One, the young and precocious Sidney Hook was active in a campus-based antiwar movement and spent the early 1920s ensconced in campus socialist politics. A decade before the appearance of the fabled New York Intellectuals, radical students congregated in the famous lunchroom alcoves where discussions of diverse topics raged: the Bolshevik revolution, contemporary political issues such as the Sacco and Vanzetti case, avant-garde culture, literature, and philosophy. While the food was lousy, the debates were enough to satisfy the intellectual hunger of their participants.

Irving Howe's remembrance is fairly typical of those who attended City in the 1930s:

> City College was a wonderful place in those years, at least for young radicals, but not because it was a wonderful faculty. Most of the teaching was mediocre and only after I myself became a professor did I understand why. Teaching schedules were punitively high: a fifteen hour load, if taken with any seriousness, meant a sixty hour week, and that left no time for reading or intellectual growth. Still there were some great teachers like Morris Raphael Cohen and some gifted ones like Abraham Edel.

Howe reports that Cohen's class was an exercise in intellectual terror, Edel's an exemplar of the much revered but virtually unpracticed Socratic method. But in his "alleged 'subject,' English, the teaching at City College was quite poor."[4] Howe's judgment was echoed, for other disciplines, by several of his contemporaries—Harvard professors Nathan Glazer and Daniel Bell, and one of the leading neoconservative intellectuals, Irving Kristol, later a professor at NYU—all of them self-described revolutionary socialists at the time.

Howe confesses he received mediocre grades, largely owing to the one-year calculus requirement. But I suspect that, as with so many of his contemporaries—except perhaps the science and engineering students, who could scarcely spare the time for a liberal education, let alone politics—his real schooling occurred in the campus political wars conducted, without pause, among communists, socialists, and liberals (at City College there were few, if any, admitted conservatives) and in the Marxist study groups that were intrinsic to student political life. In the service of their positions in the conflicts, students like Howe were obliged to become good debaters, skilled literary polemicists, and at least in relation to Marxist theory, competent scholars.

Yet despite disparaging what they learned in the classroom, they were not disposed to dwell in the world of their fathers—the garment, leather, and food-processing factories of the Lower East Side and Williamsburgh. If Howe, Bell, and others of their generation occasionally worked in factories or commercial offices, it was only to keep their bodies together while they prepared for some kind of intellectual work. They were, perhaps, the first generation of immigrant children who had the opportunity to escape manual and low-level service labor. But unlike their would-be successors today, few expected to enroll in graduate schools in order to take their place in the professoriate. Instead, the many factions of the campus Left were their university.

These students were to become the future writers and editors of the many small radical publications of the 1930s and 1940s, notably *Partisan Review*, whose editors and writers represented a veritable reunion of older City graduates, including Sidney Hook; *Politics*, perhaps the best radical publication of the era, for which Howe served as assistant editor under Dwight Macdonald; and *Labor Action*, whose editorial group included the historian Hal Draper, later a U Cal librarian, and Howe himself. Some City graduates ended up in the trade union movement, which until 1950 was hospitable to all manner of socialists; others went into social work and secondary school teaching when these were hotbeds of radical-led union activity. A few, like the disillusioned former student movement leaders Joseph Lash and James Wechsler, became journalists for the liberal press. And City became the main training ground for many of the communists who wrote and edited the *Daily Worker*, the *New Masses*, and other Party publications. It was only in the 1950s and 1960s that some of these erstwhile radicals found their way into college teaching. At a time when the main qualification in some institutions was that the candidate have a Ph.D. and a steady heartbeat, these veteran radical publicists who had disdained advanced degrees on ideological grounds had some difficulty persuading prospective colleagues that their journalistic achievements were the intellectual equivalent of academic scholarship.

Yet with only a B.A. in hand, in the 1940s Howe published studies of the American Communist Party, a biography of the labor leader Walter Reuther, and a mountain of articles for literary and political magazines. After fifteen years of low-paying jobs editing radical journals, in the early 1950s Howe caught on and got a teaching position at Brandeis. A few years later, Bell, who had been a *Fortune* staff writer after his postwar disillusionment with left politics, was hired as professor at Columbia after Robert Merton, the *éminence grise* of the sociology department, asked him to assemble his 1950s "end of ideology" pieces as a Ph.D. dissertation. *Partisan Review* (*PR*) founder Philip Rahv, who never went to college, eventually got a professor's job. But others, such the poet Delmore Schwartz, a staunch anticommunist and *PR* favorite, were not as fortunate. Years of adjunct teaching and pleading failed to gain him a permanent job. Many who, for its hidebound mediocrity, once held the academy in contempt found no secure positions from which to make a steady living in their middle and elder years. Journalism and teaching were the only options that permitted them to remain active writers.

The emergence of a large number of intellectuals from working-class, rural, and other economically modest or poor backgrounds was, to a large degree, an unintended consequence of the growth of the mostly free public higher education. They were beneficiaries of the broad objectives of liberal education: while students should specialize in their upper-division classes, in their first two years they should also be exposed to the humanistic canons in literature and philosophy. Engineers should read Shakespeare or at least know the plays' plots; and humanists should be subject, for a time, to the rigors of math and physics. And at a time when the twelve hundred private colleges in the United States—still the nearly exclusive province of the rich, well-born, or religiously oriented—had little or no incentive to broaden the curriculum to scientific and technical subjects, the public colleges were skimming the working and lower middle classes for talent that would otherwise have been unavailable. Outside the domains of medicine, the ministry, and law, which have always been upper-middle-class professions, it was left to these "others" to inhabit the relatively new, uncertain niches of science, engineering, and architecture.

As paid occupations, science and engineering are, in the main, developments of the twentieth century. Thus, despite the dedication of people like Townsend Harris, City's founder, to find and educate bright students who might not ordinarily have pursued a university degree, the "mission" of City College and a scattering of state universities to bring "unconventional" students into higher education was determined primarily by the need to train them for professions in which the traditional upper-middle-class student was either unprepared or uninterested.

Certainly, there were other philanthropic motivations and, in the cases of John D. Rockefeller and Andrew Carnegie, religious conviction. But in the antibusiness zeitgeist that spanned the first four decades of the twentieth century, these motives became entangled with an acute sense of public relations. In other words, the expansion of public postsecondary education had a solid basis in labor market considerations. That budding intellectuals like Hook, Howe, and Bell were afforded access to these institutions attests to one of the most important features of the labor market: it is in the employers' interest to have an excess of qualified labor available, a fact not lost on the most practical of educational leaders. In contrast to the high wages offered skilled European mechanics in the nineteenth century, wages for intellectual labor of all sorts were relatively low in this period. Employers welcomed the plentiful supply of trained knowledge workers and were even willing to donate funds to the colleges and universities that trained them. Besides, those not inclined or good enough to perform well in science and math could become schoolteachers, low-level administrators, and social workers. In sum, the fact that City and other public colleges graduated some remarkable writers and thinkers is a product of their outreach to many who would otherwise have ended up driving taxis or pressing pants.

Nevertheless, there was never any question of making the city's colleges "open admissions" schools. Access to state-run schools was, and remains, limited to the "deserving" poor. If anything, public schools had higher standards than most private colleges, which were tuition-driven and, for this reason, frequently made the checkbook a leading prerequisite for admission. From the legislators' perspective, public colleges were an investment in the economic well-being of their states and municipalities. Although there were some who shared the vision of liberal educators that higher education should enhance the national culture or serve the state's broad social interests, technical and vocational training, not broad intellectual preparation, was the point of supporting public higher education. So there was no unambiguous democratic purpose in the maintenance of these institutions, especially in terms of any invocation to be "agents of social change." Instead, publicly funded colleges were integral to the strategy of economic development. If the business of government is business, so should be the business of public higher education.

3

As World War Two drew to a close, government policymakers became preoccupied with providing servicemen and -women the means to negotiate what was generally considered to be a period of difficult "readjustment" to civilian life. Economists wondered openly whether the economy would be supple enough to absorb the avalanche of returning veterans. With the end of the war, postsecondary institutions were called upon to participate in the massive government effort to find a way to address what most economists believed the almost inevitable postwar economic bust. With government subsidies to individuals and to institutions, higher education became a major solution for many who might have become unemployed after their discharge from military service. Some spoke darkly of the resumption of the Depression, or at least of a severe recession during the transition from wartime to peacetime economy.

At the initiative of President Roosevelt, Congress enacted a series of veterans benefits, including low-interest housing loans and short-term income support. The Servicemen's Readjustment Act (popularly known as the GI Bill of Rights) was perhaps the most enduring. Among its core provisions were job-placement and counseling services for World War Two veterans, as well as payments for tuition, books, and living expenses for up to four years of schooling. According to "Statutes at Large," an official government publication, the purpose of the GI Bill "was not only to help individual servicemen to readjust to civilian life but also to prevent a huge glut of the labor market, as some 10 million or more persons were rapidly demobilized at the end of World War Two." After the bill was signed by the president on June 22, 1944, Congress passed amendments increasing tuition payments beyond the original five hundred dollars a year and increased living expenses for up to sixty-five dollars a month for single veterans and up to ninety dollars for veterans with dependents. In addition, unemployed veterans were entitled to compensation of twenty dollars a week for fifty-two weeks. In the wake of the severe postwar housing shortage, in selected areas of the country the Veterans Administration built temporary housing for school-bound veterans and their families. Within a few years, two million veterans had returned to school, a million and half to colleges and universities.

Together with the National Defense Education Act passed by Congress in the wake of the successful Russian launching of Sputnik thirteen years later, the GI Bill of Rights was the boldest and most far-reaching social program of the postwar era. An example of the kind of social engineering that later became the target of conservative counterattack, these powerful interventions passed with overwhelming majorities on both sides of Congress. They jump-started the housing industry by making long-term loans available to returning veterans at low interest rates, doubled the number of students in American higher education, and within two decades spurred the doubling of the number of colleges and universities, an explosion that gave further impetus to the construction industry. These changes also made the professoriate a major profession, of comparable stature with medicine and law and with numbers that equaled and then exceeded the number of accountants.

The GI Bill permanently changed the nature and social makeup of higher education's student body. Colleges and universities do not welcome all high school graduates and, since 1945, have never ceased their complaints about the appearance of students whose profile departs sharply from the traditional upper-middle-class clientele of private institutions. Despite these trepidations, however, Harvard, Yale, and Stanford have never turned down government money. Vast sums in the form of stipends, student loans, and outright grants have been made not only to financially needy students but also to those whose academic achievement merited income-blind scholarships, awarded, in the main, under the National Defense Education Act.

Perhaps equally important was the role that higher education now played in cushioning the effects of recessions, job-destroying technological change, and the frequent shifts and restructuring in the American economy. When, in the 1990s, Americans were asked to view with pride the discrepancy between this country's 5 percent unemployment rate and the double digits that plagued western European economies, what the media, politicians, and self-satisfied economists forgot to mention is that in 1995 ten million Americans of working age were full-time students, about 9 percent of the nonagricultural workforce compared to 2–4 percent in most European societies. In addition, another five million working-age Americans are enrolled as part-time students.[5] Since the United States Bureau of Labor Statistics counts part-time employees as if they were full-time, it is only proper to consider part-time students as if they were full-time. In any given semester, one of seven working Americans, or 13 percent of the workforce, attends some institution of higher education. Thanks, in part, to higher education, jobless statistics in America are consistently lower than any other major advanced industrial society except Japan.

Now, I am not claiming the only role of higher education is to defer the entrance of millions of younger Americans into a chronically glutted labor market. Nor do I see postsecondary institutions as mere aging vats, existing largely to impart flavor and mellowness to their product. Plainly, a considerable portion, if not remotely a majority, of students legitimately acquire occupationally specific knowledge under the auspices of postsecondary schooling. And it may be plausibly argued that, in the wake of the failure of secondary education to equip students with basic writing and reading ability (where this means more than "skills," connoting genuine facility with language), postsecondary institutions of all types have an important role to play. In this sense, even many so-called elite colleges are, in part, remedial. Certainly, the interlock between licensing agencies and professional schools and programs is sufficiently tight to foreclose alternative routes, so that for the growing number of students who are bound for a profession, both the baccalaureate and an advanced degree are entrance requirements.

For example, prospective teachers, therapists, nurses, and physicians must complete a prescribed course of study and accumulate a definite number of credits in their chosen field in order to practice their professions. And, by statute as much as bylaws, higher education institutions increasingly require the candidate for professor to possess a Ph.D. prior to employment or on penalty of dismissal to complete its requirements within a designated period. Whether these courses transmit knowledge that is directly applicable to one's chosen practice is debatable and shall be discussed later in this book. What is not subject to dispute is that, as the social makeup of the academy has changed since the war, the liberal arts undergraduate degree has suffered partial eclipse, except for the small—and shrinking—number of students aiming for academic careers in the humanities and the social sciences.

A common complaint of employers is that nearly all those entering the workplace with a liberal arts degree and most who have graduated with specialized degrees in the sciences and technical fields are not "job ready"; they still require on-the-job training. Even the best laid plans of educational administrators and planners to transform the curriculum from a general liberal arts model to one that may require the student to perform an "internship" in "real world settings" have not overcome the imperfect fit between school and work. Generally acknowledged is the fact that, from the student's perspective, the most important function of the bachelor's degree is to give her or him the credential with which to enter the market on somewhat more favorable terms than earlier school leavers. In the last quarter century, the United States economy has lost some nine million relatively well paid factory jobs. Under these circumstances, many students and their parents have gotten the message that a college education is a necessity in the newly restructured job market. Many students enroll in postsecondary education because there is no better place to go if they are unwilling to accept near minimum-wage jobs, especially in food service. Even if the curriculum prepares students for no particular occupation, steady school attendance is a mark of a disciplined and reliable employee and may be the most important credential.

More than forty years ago, when the present higher education boom was in its energetic youth, the Carnegie Foundation and some top university administrators became concerned that the elite status of the "research" universities—the narrow layer of institutions that had been designated, or elevated themselves, to fulfill state and corporate requirements for knowledge production in order to fight World War Two and the Cold War—was threatened by the changing nature of higher education in American society. Some educators were alarmed by the consequences of the GI Bill. Even before the first baby boomers attained college age, postsecondary enrollments doubled in the decade ending in 1950 and, toward 1960, promised to double again, to six million students. Clark Kerr, an industrial relations specialist and president of the University of California at Berkeley, perhaps the country's premier public research university, studied the problem with a view to preserving the integrity of the few, anointed top schools.

In his influential book *The Uses of the University,* first published in 1963, Kerr laid out the essential premises for contemporary university reform: "The basic reality, for the university, is the widespread recognition that new knowledge is the most important factor in economic and social growth. We are just now perceiving that the university's invisible product, knowledge, may be the most powerful single element in our culture, affecting the rise and fall of professions and even of social classes, of regions and even of nations."[6]

By "university," Kerr meant to include the approximately 125 research institutions in higher education. In his definition, if institutions calling themselves universities fail to produce socially and economically useful new knowledge, they are not true universities. Most transmit knowledge and produce knowledge that corresponds to the "ancient" disciplines of theology, medicine, law, and scholarship. But "new" knowledge is virtually identical to scientific research and development. Kerr was not opposed to teaching, the main transmission belt of knowledge to students and to the general population; nor was he disrespectful of ancient pursuits. But, while arguing for researchers to participate in all aspects of university life, including teaching, he emphasized the need to demarcate and privilege those who perform the most vital of these functions, knowledge production. Their course loads should be relatively light, and the "multiversity" should provide them with the resources necessary to their work.

Kerr recognized that the system of American postsecondary education had no choice but to expand to accommodate a host of postwar changes. A growing population of children needed more public school teachers and administrators; industry needed scientific and technical personnel; the military, which was never demobilized after the war, required people with the knowledge to develop, produce, and operate sophisticated weaponry; the country's growing health industries demanded every kind of scientific and medical specialist; and the universities and colleges needed more professors and instructors to teach the hordes of new, and from the prewar perspective, "unconventional" students (read working class). The solution he proposed aimed to prevent the watering down of the research institutions, for it was upon their shoulders, and only peripherally the others', that America's future rested.

Kerr argued that the academic system should be organized into two tiers. The top tier would be devoted to research, in which graduate study held pride of place and undergraduates would primarily be trained in scientific and highly advanced technical knowledge. In these schools, faculty would have smaller course loads but be expected to perform research, publish their results, and advise and employ graduate students. Standards for undergraduate admissions would take into account the mission of the university to produce knowledge and to educate knowledge producers. Like Harvard president James Bryant Conant, who made a crucial plea after the Soviet Sputnik flight in 1957, Kerr urged that these research universities place greater emphasis on science and mathematics. In this regime, the student was viewed as an apprentice researcher at both the undergraduate and graduate levels, at least for science and math majors.

The second tier was to be reserved for the training of technical personnel and for providing a general education for them. Teachers would not be expected to perform as much research (in the community colleges, none at all), but in consideration of their primary duties as knowledge transmitters rather than knowledge producers, they would have larger course loads. Admission standards would not be so stringent as to exclude reasonably competent students and thereby deprive industry and government of trained technical employees.

In proposing this fundamental codification and restructuring of the academic system, Kerr not only found the formula for protecting the first-tier research university, but reconceptualized its broad social function. Despite its already fixed character as a knowledge factory in practice (he called it the knowledge "industry"), few had articulated the transformation. Most educational theorists remained mired in the old debates about the "mission" of the university.

Stated briefly, Kant and his acolytes had delineated the issue most clearly. Far from conceiving German universities in the mythic strokes of a "community" of scholars, Fichte and Humboldt, the leading figures in the dialogue, suggested instead that it represented, respectively, the unity of the nation-state and the fount of national culture. In the first formulation, the university has to train the political elite of society; in the second, its main function is to provide an intellectual elite, which, if one follows its platonic origins, might amount to the same thing. The Prussian state bureaucracies of the nineteenth century were filled with historians, economists, and philosophers trained at leading universities. Ideally, some of those educated in the Great Tradition would become the leaders of a unified German nation, which, before Bismarck, remained a fervently held, but distant goal.

However, Kerr apparently laid this old conversation to rest. If the highest mission of universities is to serve society, what greater achievement than to provide the knowledge required to assure general prosperity by advancing the scientific and technological revolution and "freedom"—read America's world dominance—and the scientific and technical personnel required to produce it. In a backhanded gesture, Kerr allowed that researchers should have a general education; how else would they know the underlying values of the new technoscientific civilization they were destined to serve and even to lead? But for the Berkeley chancellor, there was no question that the humanities must recognize their secondary place in the new university order. They could uphold the values of Western civilization by teaching literature and history, but their role was clearly a subordinate one.

It is to Clark Kerr that we owe the greatest debt for advancing the cause of student power, which cut its teeth on university reform as much as civil rights, and remains one of the crucial and often ignored features of the cultural and political upheaval of the 1960s. For it was on his watch that, only a year after he enunciated the doctrine of the multiversity and of its key role as knowledge producer, the Free Speech movement at Berkeley was born. Kerr's line, repeated in books, reports, public speeches, and many other venues, was that the development of science and technology was in the universal interest. The university was a workshop of technical progress, and student politics had no place in it. As it turned out, Kerr's book was not only a powerful ideological statement; it was a prescription for an educational policy banning "outside" political groups on campus.

Responding to a sit-in at Berkeley's Sproul Hall on 30 September 1964 protesting this policy, the university administration suspended eight graduate students including the charismatic Mario Savio for "violating the University Policy on Use of Facilities." Immediately after the dean of the Graduate Division, Sanford Ellsberg, announced the suspensions, Savio spoke to a rally, connecting Ellsberg's statement to Kerr's "recent book on the multiversity":

> President Kerr has referred to the University as a factory; a knowledge factory—that's his words—engaged in the knowledge industry. And, just like any factory, or in any industry—again his words—you have a certain product. The product is you. Well, not really you. And not really me. The products are those people who wouldn't join in our protest. They go in one side, as kind of rough-cut adolescents, and they come out the other side, pretty smooth. . . . They're dependent upon the University. They're product. And they're prepared to leave the University, to go out and become members of other organizations—various businesses, usually—which they are dependent upon in the same way. And, never at any time is provision made for their taking their places as free men!

Savio then went on to contrast the ideal that freedom means being able to express "your individuality" with the outcome of the multiversity:

> You've got to be a part; part of a machine. Now, every now and then, the machine doesn't work. One of the parts breaks down. And in the case of a normal regular machine you throw that part out; throw it out and you re-

place it. Well, this machine, this factory here, this multiversity, its parts are human beings. And, sometimes when *they* go out of commission, they don't simply break down, but they really gum up the whole works![7]

Characteristically, Kerr saw no reason to revise his earlier judgments in the light of student protests. Indeed, in a later edition of his book, Kerr argues in the chapter "Reconsideration after the Revolts" that the trend toward the integration of the university and society is both irreversible and desirable. Since the days of the Free Speech movement and despite the activities of its successors all over the country and the world, students and other educational reformers have been unable to change what Kerr regards as a "conservative" institution. If anything, having opened this "Pandora's Box," he finds the university has grown even closer to "city hall." Yet, he insists, while extending their role as professional servants to business and government power, universities can still remain critics of the "status quo" and enter into "productive conflict" with society. Kerr's optimism in this regard springs from his conviction that the multiversity guarantees "pluralistic" higher education, in which diverse and even conflictual constituencies can live side by side.

What Kerr and many others mean by "pluralism," however, is not always clear. Of course, if the investigator wants to find difference, conflict, and diversity within universities and colleges, the evidence is ample enough to justify a conclusion similar to Kerr's, just as the interested observer can find dissent in the polity in the face of the growing convergence of political parties. But Kerr goes further than simply noting that there are various constituencies whose interests sometimes rub against the grain of the academic mainstream. Having posited the production of useful knowledge as the core of the university's mission—where "useful" means that it makes a contribution to economic and social "growth"— there can be little doubt that he privileges the scientific and technical disciplines over the older tradition of scholarship. Thus, even if he is prepared to acknowledge the value of humanistic scholarship as what I would term an "ornament," he certainly does not see it as the meat and potatoes of the university. The ubiquitous Harold Bloom undoubtedly adds to the luster of Yale and NYU, and Columbia gains much needed legitimacy from Edward Said's role as a public intellectual. But if the university is chiefly a knowledge factory, the degree to which it benefits from the work of these literary stars may be measured against the institutional requirement to acquire the material capital that is the stuff of science and technology.

Savio's speech is a reminder that once a vibrant student movement challenged the university to provide the space for "expressive individuality." And some still persist in trying to produce space for difference, debate, and even dissent in universities. But the tendency to view the institution as a knowledge factory may have reached such proportions that, for many, there is little to be gained in trying to operate within its walls. Just as in the face of mechanization and standardized production methods, factory workers have had to take what they can and run, students, many staff, and most faculty have learned that the university is a production site in which criticism of the status quo narrows with each passing year.

4

The 1970s brought a profound change in America's economic and political environment and, by the latter half the decade, in its social and cultural atmosphere as well. Signaled by the energy crisis and near runaway inflation generated by Richard Nixon's virtual abrogation of the Bretton Woods Agreement, the dollar began to float against other currencies. By the end of the 1970s, the long wave of America's postwar prosperity ended as Europe and Japan challenged U.S. economic dominance in world markets. Apart from the still considerable military budget, much of it financed by debt accumulation, global economic growth stagnated after 1975. Capital flight to lower-wage areas of the globe, mergers and acquisitions and the acceleration of technological innovation, led to permanent job losses in America's leading manufacturing industries. After 1980, the automobile industry, once a bellwether, had shed a third of its employees; steel jobs were cut by two-thirds; and the leading production industries, textiles and apparel, lost a million workers, or half their payrolls. In the 1980s and 1990s, mergers and acquisitions accelerated in nearly all major production sectors and in financial services. After the collapse of the Soviet Union and the effective end of the Cold War era, military buildup (although not the Cold War itself), military budgets contracted in relative but not absolute terms and with this decline, research funds to physics and chemistry suffered deep reductions.

Biology has done somewhat better in an era when health has become an obsession and the applications of molecular biology to medicine, agriculture, and criminal justice industries have proliferated. Sales of health care and its products of all sorts soared and with this explosion came an increase in the flow of research funds, especially to molecular biology and molecular physics and their twin, genetic engineering. Today the human genome project, where scientists collect DNA data of the entire population, is the largest federally funded science program. Some universities have received hundreds of millions in grant money from the National Science Foundation, the National Institutes of Health and, more recently, have entered into patent arrangements with private corporations to produce artificial organisms for agriculture and medicine. In return for funds to finance genetic research and production, faculty at schools such as MIT have agreed to share or surrender patent ownership to donors.

Now, faculty and administrators in leading research universities have shifted some of their attention from the government—which still provides considerable support—to private corporations. At the same time, it is no longer difficult to discover that officials and faculty of these institutions rush to tailor their intellectual and cultural capital to the needs of these corporations. Where once Kerr's theoretical and historical ruminations were controversial, by the 1990s it was not so much to city hall to which universities glanced but to the corporate boardrooms. University presidents resemble CEOs and sit on a number of corporate boards of directors. For example W. Ann Reynolds, now president of the University of Alabama at Birmingham, an emerging research university, was, when chancellor of the City University of New York, a member of about a dozen corporate boards, many of them on the list of the Fortune 500. There are similar crossovers between the university and the military, but in recent years, for purposes of building their endowments as much as for making agreements to receive funds for research, the "university-corporate complex" is at the center.

As the GI Bill effectively ended when President Nixon professionalized the armed forces, the Soviet Union came apart, and successive budget deficits and conservative politics reduced tuition and other forms of aid, students from working-class and lower-middle-class backgrounds have returned to the "no fooling around" mode of higher education. In contrast to the 1960s when NDEA and other grant and loans programs enabled many to linger in literature, history, or philosophy, they have no time for anything but a job-savvy credential. Even many whose economic position once permitted them to view college as an interlude between childhood and adult life now feel the pressure to conform to the school-to-work orientation that pervades large sections of academia. Many responded to the growing economic uncertainty by shifting their interests. Enrollments in business and pre-law programs boomed in the 1980s and 1990s as the number of liberal arts majors shrank. In these years, except for the still sizeable computer science and pre-med student body, to be a native-born American and a science major became an oxymoron.

Only scholars and intellectuals who allowed themselves to experience the heady years of the Cold War educational expansion as more than a temporary cornucopia of resources can plausibly conclude, with critic Bill Readings, that the university is in "ruins"—which implies it once was whole—or that open minds have recently "closed." In the 1980s, University of Chicago philosopher Allan Bloom was disturbed by what he believed was the surrender of the private elite universities to the philistines and the bureaucrats. Where, he asked, will the Great Traditions of Western Thought be preserved? Who will carry the torch of moral education to which his intellectual mentors, political philosopher Leo Strauss and Plato, had beckoned? In a time of rampant commercialism, Bloom believed only a select handful of institutions could be entrusted with the task. What bothered Bloom and his latter-day acolytes was not that vocationalization had swept the lower tiers of colleges and universities. Let state schools train teachers, nurses, stock exchange traders, and low-level administrators. For him, the problem was that technical education had invaded the precincts of privilege. The undergraduate curriculum had been invaded by the "multiculturalists" and "postmodernists"(read "ultra" democrats) who demanded of the professor as much as the student a measure of political correctness that, in his view, had no place in an institution of higher learning.

Later in this book I shall have occasion to explore Bloom's and other conservatives' views on the crisis of higher education. For now it is enough to note the distinction he and others make between schooling and education, between institutions devoted to technical knowledge and those which can be expected, but only putatively, to attend to "the goal of human completeness."

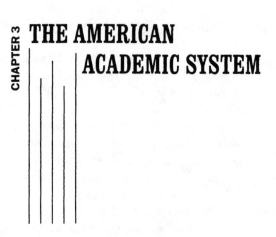

CHAPTER 3 THE AMERICAN ACADEMIC SYSTEM

1

FAR FROM BEING the home of scholars engaged in the disinterested pursuit of truth, for the last sixty years the academic system of American society has been geared to practical ends, the production of useful knowledge in the first place, and since the end of the war, supplying the vast but segmented market for intellectual labor. In fact, at the top of the pyramid, the leading research universities have little to do with their presumed primary mission, education. The knowledge machine that was mobilized during the war was not dismantled; rather, it became the key adjunct to the permanent military economy of the Cold War.

Needless to say, universities and colleges are by no means identical in their functions. As we have seen, for James Bryant Conant of Harvard, Clark Kerr, and their colleagues in the emerging corporate university culture, the main task of the research university was to become a knowledge factory. Its scientific/technological discoveries and inventions would be directed toward the means and the ends of economic growth and of Cold War public policy. As Vannevar Bush, the federal administration's first science advisor, had suggested earlier in the context of the urgent tasks of World War Two, the federal government would be obliged to provide financial support to a relatively small group of leading schools to produce the knowledge demanded by the multiple tasks of the interventionist state. Rather than relying on freestanding research institutions, the strategy adopted by France, the Soviet Union, and other European powers, Bush insisted that universities would serve as sites of knowledge creation. This choice owed a great deal to the American tradition of land-grant colleges and to the need to mount a major research effort in a short period of time. The universities already had much of the talent and some of the facilities required to move rapidly.

Of course, there would be room for artistic and intellectual culture, but not everywhere in the academic system. Only the leading schools would provide space for the esoteric knowledge generated by humanists; after all, even a technological civilization like the United States needed its ornaments. The main task of the public four-year and community colleges would be to transmit technical knowledge to future employees of the U.S. labor market. These distinctions can be traced on the loose hierarchical grid that has defined the vast expansion of colleges and universities since the end of World War Two, prodded by the differential demands of the U.S. economy, the military establishment, and theorists like Conant and Kerr.

At the top of this grid are two tiers of research universities, both dedicated to the production of knowledge. Their products are destined for use in economic and social domains, chiefly corporations and the state, especially the military "Research 1" universities that have taken primary responsibility for basic research in the natural sciences and for knowledge required for the formulation of state policy, chiefly in foreign affairs and social areas. Harvard's Kennedy School of Government, Princeton's Woodrow Wilson School, Columbia's International Affairs building (which houses many area studies centers linked to U.S. foreign policy), as well as centers devoted to public policy in a vast array of domains in nearly all major universities, are clearly sources for such knowledge. But they also supply a high- and middle-level cadre for the executive branches of national and state governments.

The recruitment of academics for government service predates the development of the research university. Woodrow Wilson was a leading American historian and taught at Princeton before running for New Jersey governor. Franklin Roosevelt's so-called brain trust during his first term included Harvard's Rexford Guy Tugwell, and academic economists and several other professors occupied lesser positions. Of course, the government agency known as the President's Council of Economic Advisors, established by the Full Employment Act of 1946, consists mainly of leading academic economists.

But it was not until the Kennedy administration that academics came into their own in government service. Historian Arthur Schlesinger Jr. of Harvard was a special presidential advisor; historian George McGovern ran Kennedy's politically important Food for Peace program, which, under the sign of humanitarian aid, absorbed considerable portions of the chronic agricultural surplus; and McGeorge Bundy served with Kennedy and Johnson in several high posts. By the time Johnson left office in 1969, the integration of academia and the state at the level of personnel was nearly complete; hundreds of professors regularly entered and left key posts in Washington and thousands more served at the state and local level. George Shultz, an academic economist, served three Republican presidents as secretary of labor, secretary of the treasury, and secretary of state. Zbigniew Brzezinski, Jimmy Carter's national security advisor, was a political science professor at Columbia, and Henry Kissinger held the same position at Harvard before becoming Richard Nixon's advisor, later secretary of state.

The Cold War brought into existence new disciplines linked to managerial and research activities in government service. Generally grouped under the rubric "policy sciences," departments and graduate programs in leading universities were established to provide dedicated and relatively narrowly trained professionals and managers for government departments. Although loosely connected to political science, their theoretical basis was grounded not in philosophy but in the recently developed areas of organizational theory, public policy analysis, and the political science field of American government that is typically treated in the discipline as a force of nature. In the 1950s and 1960s, the demand for graduates of these programs grew sufficiently large to prompt the organization of Schools of Public Administration and Public Policy.

Research 1 embraces a relatively small group of institutions. Some, but not all, Ivy League universities are members, notably Harvard, Yale, Princeton, and Columbia, and are joined by several elite private schools such as Johns Hopkins, Massachusetts Institute of Technology, Cal Tech, Stanford, and Chicago. The state universities among this group include five universities in the University of California system, Berkeley, UCLA, Davis, San Diego, and Irvine; five Big Ten schools, Michigan, Minnesota, Wisconsin, Illinois, and Indiana; Penn State and the University of Texas. The second-tier research group, Research 2, is much larger and includes most of the other Ivies such as Brown and Penn; many state universities, especially SUNY's Stonybrook, Albany, Buffalo, and Binghamton campuses, CUNY Graduate School, Washington, Oregon, and Virginia; Purdue, Michigan State, and Iowa in the Big Ten; the University of California's San Francisco and Santa Barbara campuses; and some leading private universities such as Emory, Washington University of Saint Louis, Duke, and Vanderbilt. These institutions perform basic and applied research but, generally, do not pursue Big Science, the term applied to those activities that require massive amounts of machinery and a large number of trained scientists.

Propelled by the huge federal research and development budgets, chiefly emanating from the Pentagon and then from the National Institutes of Health and the National Science Foundation, many private research universities were in fact, if not legally, adjunct institutions of government. While some had ample private endowments, they owed most of the expansion of their student enrollments, their faculties, and their facilities to the provision of public funds. Thanks to these funds, it was no longer necessary for a talented student of modest financial means to forego elite schooling. Under the National Defense Education Act, graduate students in the humanities as well as the sciences were able to obtain scholarships and fellowships that financed four or five years of their training; and sympathetic administrators held out some funds for conferences and research projects in the human sciences that would not otherwise have been available.

Since World War Two, universities have nearly monopolized natural and social scientific knowledge production as knowledge has become the key productive force. While major corporations retain considerable scientific and technical staffs that, with some exceptions, conventionally produce practical applications of theoretical and applied sciences, the responsibility for generating "new" knowledge remains, despite recent draconian cuts in research budgets, the domain of leading research universities. In effect, the state assumes the costs of research intended for use in privately held production and services through contracts let by, among other federal agencies, the Department of Defense, the National Science

Foundation, and the National Institutes for Health to "private" as well as public universities. Indeed, in many of the so-called private schools, income from federal grants has, for much of the last sixty years, equaled and even exceeded income from endowments and tuition. Private universities like to call themselves a public "trust," but it might be more accurate to observe that they live off of the public trough. The Federal Departments of Agriculture, Labor, Commerce, Interior, Transportation, and Justice remain important sources of research funds, despite Congress's recent cost-cutting rampage.

Before the 1980s, much of the "new" knowledge was in areas such as theoretical physics and biology and had little or no immediate use; in effect, the Pentagon subsidized this basic research because national science policy recognized the importance of failure as a vital ingredient of eventual success. But the tendency over the past two decades has been to punish the failures that inevitably accompany theoretical and experimental reflection. Congress and the White House now require that government grants be more dedicated, that is, earmarked for practical, especially commodity, applications. This policy has tended to discourage pure or "useless" research. America's leading magazine of the natural science professions, *Science,* chronicles on a weekly basis both the reconfiguration of research toward industrial uses and the fears of scientists that, because of the precipitous decline of public funding in relative terms, the scientific enterprise is itself in jeopardy. In view of the enormous role that expensive machine technology plays in everyday research in physics and biology, the virtual end of funding for nondedicated work, especially for theory, threatens to cripple U.S. basic science.

For example, funds are rapidly drying up for research in theoretical physics, especially in high-energy particle physics, but also in astronomy, cosmology, and other more esoteric endeavors. In 1994, Congress refused to appropriate funds for a $3 billion superconductor to conduct research in fundamental particle physics, in part because legislators were unable to find compelling practical justification for the expenditure. Scientists' arguments cited the urgent need to find the fundamental building blocks of matter, which, for congressional committees, was unconvincing. Few could see the "pork barrel" payoffs, and others, steeped in anti-intellectualism or anti-science sentiments, simply refused.

To be sure, solid state physics has a ready source of research money in communications and information corporations. And the vast majority of funds for biological studies are devoted to producing new organisms for use in medicine, agriculture, and more speculative uses, such as the notorious goals of eugenics. In this respect, private pharmaceutical corporations have entered into patent arrangements with relevant academic departments; in return for patent ownership or patent sharing, the corporations have donated substantial sums to university scientists to offset losses of government funds.

From 1945 to the early 1980s, Congress appropriated, with almost no dissent, the R and D expenditures associated with "defense," which, as we have seen, included substantial support for the biological and human sciences. This was the period of enormous expansion for research universities, their faculties and staff, and their graduate enrollments. But the combined effects of the uncertain economic climate signaled by the recessions of 1982–83 and 1989–92 and, later, the collapse of the Soviet Union contributed to the rise of conservative skepticism of all things modern, including "useless" science and critical thinking. In the emerging "free market," anti–big government political climate, research funds for projects not directed to specific product applications were mercilessly cut.

Suddenly, the universities came under close scrutiny from the press as well as the federal government. While, formerly, federal oversight was sufficiently loose to permit administrators considerable flexibility in allocations of grants, in the post–Cold War era they had to justify their expenditures. (A Stanford president resigned when auditors found he had overcharged granting agencies in order to help support general university programs.) And increasingly science had to justify itself on commercial and other practical criteria. In this environment, many academic researchers scrambled to make arrangements with private corporations.

In the post–Cold War era, biology, engineering, and chemistry have, at least in funding terms, replaced physics as the growth natural sciences. If aggregate research funds have held up in the 1990s, the composition of support has shifted from physical to biological research. In the 1980s, top research universities began to enter into long-term contracts with corporations. For example, Harvard Medical School formed an alliance with DuPont, MIT with Exxon and Grace, Washington University with Monsanto, Yale with Bristol Myers. In 1988, impending corporate arrangements provoked a lively discussion among the MIT faculty, some of whom feared that the university would severely compromise its autonomy if it became dependent on corporate support. Media phrases like "the selling of science" and "gene merchants" peppered the debate. But fearing further losses of government funds, the majority either greeted the new arrangements with relief or rationalized these relationships as necessary to preserve the enterprises of scientific discovery and invention. By 1988, led by Harvard's sixty-nine corporate relationships, Stanford's forty, and MIT's thirty-five, research universities had entered into an average of twenty-two research and patent connections with private sector companies. This trend has accelerated in the 1990s; today, the university biology and biochemistry departments that fail to forge agreements with private firms cannot hope to maintain their status as important sites of scientific research.[1]

But American research universities had their roots in the selling of science, and that association has defined such institutions for more than a century. Recall, the land-grant colleges of the post–Civil War period were organized to assist agriculture and production industries by providing knowledge and the trained scientists and technicians to help farmers and employers make their business more efficient. Their broad education functions were almost an afterthought in light of these economic goals. It was not until well into the twentieth century, under the impact of the government's rearmament program after 1938, that "basic" science became truly legitimate in state schools. Large-scale scientific work has always thrived on government support; scientists lived off the military for most of the postwar period and, on this consideration, found few reasons to object when private corporations offered research funds. After all, many government contracts were tied to dedicated applications as well.

So the furor over privatization has been more a reflection of liberal guilt than of the scruples of scientists themselves. For example, when some physicists who had worked on the Manhattan Project attempted, after the war, to win their colleagues to a political program of halting research, development, and production of nuclear weapons, most of their colleagues were indifferent to their pleas. They remained complicit in the Cold War military program, if not out of patriotic conviction, then in the belief that the scientific enterprise needed it. And while a somewhat larger coterie of specialists gathered to protest the use of their work by the defense apparatus during the Vietnam War, their efforts never managed to attract the majority of scientists, engineers, and computer programmers who remained wedded, if sometimes uneasily, to the military. Although most scholars in history, philosophy, and literature were unaware of the degree to which their work was dependent upon military grants, they, too, had reason to be grateful, for much of their own funded research would have been starved without the Pentagon's largesse.

The technocratic regime requires no special legitimacy; through the provision of science-based technology, it provides its own justification. Technology presents itself as inherently "useful" for meeting an infinite variety of human purposes. Anyone who challenges the value of this knowledge and invention is immediately labeled a Luddite, literally, an obstacle to "progress." In Kerr's and Fritz Machlup's discussions of knowledge industries, the role of the humanities and the non-policy social sciences in producing knowledge that may be politically and ideologically significant, but has little commercial utility, is given short shrift.[2] By thrusting "research" to the center of the university's mission, Kerr foresaw, and helped shape, its technocratic future. To a large extent, his vision turned out to be dominant. Indeed, in private as well as state universities, considerable funds for the human sciences and the costs of graduate student support were, and still are, siphoned from huge military and product-oriented research grants. So the tendency of humanistic scholars to distance themselves and their work from science and technology may well be an exercise in self-deception. We are all implicated in the fruits of the techno-university, even critics and opponents.

There is a striking correlation between leading universities that produce knowledge for military and economic purposes and those engaged in the production of what might be termed "cultural" knowledge and, by way of their graduate programs, the cultural elite. While the human sciences (the combination of the humanities and social sciences) have in general received less support in recent years at research universities—Columbia comes immediately to mind—in many fields, these institutions boast prominent mainstream scholars and intellectuals on their faculties. They have used their considerable endowments, both private and public, and their traditional luster, to attract many of the most celebrated and influential critical intellectuals, like Columbia's Edward Said and Gayatri Spivak and Duke's Fredric Jameson. Harvard, Yale, Stanford, Princeton, and Duke lead in literature and cultural and social theory, although no individual department—except, perhaps, Harvard's philosophy department and its African American program, Yale and

Duke's literature departments and their collective economics faculties—is a clear leader in its discipline. In contrast to the years immediately following World War Two, when Harvard, Berkeley, and Columbia virtually dominated the social sciences, even the "best" universities have generally mediocre departments of sociology, anthropology, and political science, which survive more on a given university's prestige than on the intellectual influence of its faculty.

By the 1990s, many administrators of top-tier private schools were pronouncing a new era of austerity, even of crisis. Having relied principally on government funds to sustain their extensive research activities, these universities needed a new strategy to sustain their leadership. On the one hand, as we have seen, at the cost of surrendering even more of their autonomy than had been demanded by the federal government, they were prompted to develop relationships with the private sector, a move that, given the compromises of the last sixty years, barely detained them. Yet some administrators were concerned that public criticism of these relationships might hurt the image of the research university as an autonomous institution that operated in, but was not of, the world of power.

On the other hand, in order to replenish their physical plants and especially their faculties, which when all is said and done remains the key to maintaining elite standing, these universities embarked on a permanent program of adding to their endowments. This entailed building monuments to generous industrialists, financiers, and real estate moguls. But endowment drives and other accelerated fundraising activities, as well as the tendency for more administrative centralization, added to the university staffs at a faster rate than they added faculty. By 1998 Harvard had accumulated some $13 billion, and twenty other universities had raised more than $1 billion. NYU, long in the shadows of the leading schools, raised itself to prominence by raising more than $2 billion, largely from New York's largest landlords and developers. Some of the money was used to attract mainstream scholars with national reputations and also to bring in more junior and up-and-coming scholars in midcareer to revitalize weaker departments.

At the same time, most research universities were facing an era of "hard" choices. Some, like Columbia, decided that they should no longer expect to remain "full service" institutions. In his introduction to *The Research University in a Time of Discontent,* an important collection of essays on the future of research universities by various leaders of these institutions, Columbia's provost, Jonathan Cole, argues: "If research universities can no longer cover all areas of knowledge, then each university will have to determine those areas in which it has comparative advantages in developing and maintaining true distinction. It will also have to judge which are the core areas of knowledge, the areas of such importance to the future of knowledge that any great research university, to be defined as such, will have to demonstrate excellence in them."[3]

During Cole's watch, Columbia has closed its geography and linguistics departments and its School of Library Service, once a national leader in this field. Cole allows that these were painful choices but insists that programs, no matter how distinguished, that do not fit the definition of the university's core "mission," or that are not at the cusp of knowledge as defined by the university, have to go. Plainly, given the waning "paradigm" of government-university cooperation, and the specific demands of private firms, none of these commercially marginal fields can be expected to survive unless it has independent sources of funds. Cole reports that in 1993–94, Columbia's annual revenues from patents and licenses rose from roughly "$4 million to $24 million in the [previous] five years." Cole anticipates that this figure will rise to an annual return of $75 million within a decade.[4] Although he maintains that the university should emulate the efficient business practices of corporations in making financial decisions, Cole cautions against adopting the corporate hierarchical structures that permit such decisions to be made rapidly. But neither should the university be ruled exclusively by the faculty. "Ownership" of the research university is invested, he argues, in a collaborative process between administration and faculty. Yet in a "time of discontent," there is no doubt that top administrators are growing impatient with faculty recalcitrance, even hesitation, and want more "flexibility" to speed the shift to making the university more compatible with corporate needs.

Although Cole may wish to keep his distance from corporate culture, his summary of the new problems facing research universities is replete with references to categories of neoclassical economics. Financial and "human" capital are crucial problems for the university; it must act on the basis of "excellence," the mantra of administrators and writers who desperately search for a new "mission" to replace the gatekeeping function that marked earlier periods. In Cole's lexicon, "excellence" is an indeterminate concept that may signify little more than, in his words, "comparative advantages"—a euphemism for competitive position, a basic theme of conservative economic thinking—and thus closely related to "revenues" and other signals of profit and loss. Indeed, he is worried about the "uncertainties" that are bound to accompany the university's shift from reliance on government to private research funds. Among these is the "balance" between economics and science, particularly between "neutrality" in science and entrepreneurship by faculty members who have been freed to seek market opportunities. Indeed, this balance is further undermined by the fact that universities increasingly hold equity in the companies with whom they have forged patent and license deals. Together, according to Cole, these arrangements might compromise the scientist's "dedication to a neutral position regarding the outcome of scientific experiments."

As a sociologist of science, Cole worries about the changing "normative structure of science," especially its commitment to what his teacher Robert K. Merton calls "disinterestedness" and to "communism," that is, to the open sharing of knowledge with members of the larger scientific community. He knows that the private agreements between research scientists and corporations usually entail holding knowledge as property that might not be easily available to colleagues in the scientific community. AS MIT biology professor Jonathan King has reported, many who deliver papers concerning scientific research at scholarly meetings may omit information on patent grounds, thereby closing intellectual communication. Cole is worried, but not deterred, in his conviction that the research university is on a course of decisive change in which the private business sector plays a major role in guiding university policies and priorities.[5]

Another contributor to the volume, Walter E. Massey, provost and vice-president of the University of California, has fewer qualms about the close alliance of research universities with the great industrial corporations. While insisting that the "primary mission of the university is to educate" not only American-born students but many from around the world, he is proud of the place of research universities in economic and technological development: "The institutions have played key roles in the economic and social development of the United States. They have contributed to the founding of many of our great traditional industries and have made the United States highly competitive in new technological areas such as semiconductors and microelectronics and the world leader in industries that depend upon the frontiers of research, such as biotechnology and pharmaceuticals."[6]

Yet, despite this panegyric to their achievements, officials of these universities fret about their future. Public research universities are expected to do more with less. Private university administrators may have more options, but they feel similarly constrained. Donald Kennedy, Stanford's president emeritus, is concerned that, at a time when these institutions are called upon to make hard choices, they lack the structural centralization to act decisively. "Perhaps the most important [differences between universities and the private corporate sector] in our present context is that the intellectual direction and even the leadership of the divisions is not controlled by the center—the teaching and knowledge gathering missions of the institution depend entirely on local divisions within which there is little or no management culture of the traditional corporate kind." That is, there is little or no "accountability" to the center and, in turn, the center cannot direct the various departments to take one or another direction. Kennedy deplores "inertia" by faculty and administration, who by exercising their prerogatives resist giving the institution more flexibility to respond to new situations and new demands. According to Kennedy, fiscal limitations require administrators, particularly presidents and provosts, to make choices concerning which disciplines will receive resources and which won't. The constant threat of losing funds wreaks havoc on departmental morale. For example, Kennedy cites a 1991 speech by Leon Lederman, incoming president of the National Academy of Science and "a distinguished physicist." Lederman had reported that in the current university climate scientists exhibit a "depth of despair and discouragement that I have not experienced in my forty years in science."[7]

But for both Cole and Kennedy, the faculty is simply too turf-minded and discipline-oriented to make the hard choices that must be made in the reallocation of resources. In some cases, these decisions entail shutting down departments entirely, and then there is the ongoing task of keeping the others on their toes for entrepreneurial openings. The privileged few that are likely to prosper in the new environment for research institutions are those that can remain on the cusp of "knowledge gathering" and show some capacity to reach beyond the university's walls, mainly to the corporate sector. While many presidents and provosts vehemently deny that they are pushing the research university to become more corporate, their insistent message is that the old regime of faculty governance must be severely modified, if not entirely abandoned, to adjust to their new partnerships. They complain that some faculty do not understand the new situation, and are holding back the urgent task of moving the institution into the uncertain, but promising, future of corporate sponsorship. As one reads the essays in *The Research University in a Time of Discontent*, a consensus emerges around Clark Kerr's fundamental philosophy that the university is constituted and must remain a source of knowledge that serves the corporate order and, more broadly, the national interest in economic growth. Indeed, the notion that the university has a critical as well as research function has disappeared from the discourse.

Frank H. T. Rhodes, president of Cornell University, sounds a cautious note of apparent dissent: "I believe it is time to state clearly and firmly that, while research and teaching both contribute to the strength and vitality of the U.S. research university, it is undergraduate teaching, and learning, that is the central task," not for intrinsic reasons but because undergraduate education "supplies the future generation of research specialists and it replenishes the supply of teachers."[8] Not content with jeremiads, Rhodes goes on to spell out what he means by this statement:

> I believe the purpose of an undergraduate education is to develop a person of judgement, discernment, and balance, with professional competence in some specific area. . . . We should strive to produce not only competent engineers, for example, but also engineers who practice their profession with a keen appreciation of social, economic and national environment in which they operate and with a sense of aesthetic scale and human proportion as well as the economic costs and benefits.[9]

In other words, education should strive to produce professionals with a little sensitivity and polish, not only a technical and business sense.

My assessment may, at first glance, appear somewhat harsh. Yet as Rhodes spells out the goals of a student's academic career, not one of his six major points includes the ability to evaluate the knowledge that is transmitted through the curriculum. At best, he argues for "some sensitivity toward the ideas, values, and goals that have shaped society and some sense of moral implications of actions and ideas." The qualifier "some sense" should not be taken lightly, for it implies that the main job of the undergraduate curriculum and its teachers is to transmit received wisdom and analytic and reading and writing skills. Although he calls for rigor in teaching, since no professor will confess they fail to measure up to this goal, it has little significance.

Absent in Rhodes's appeal is a critique of tenure, which in all research universities is awarded almost exclusively to researchers and, in the humanities, to those who publish scholarly articles and books in mainstream journals and presses. I know of no major school that has, or would, award tenure to a brilliant teacher unless the candidate has accumulated the necessary publications. On the other hand, abysmal teachers routinely win tenure if they produce useful knowledge or deliver elegant scholarship. So Rhodes's call to focus on teaching is bereft of a discussion of the practical conditions needed to reach this objective. Although some professors take pride in their undergraduate teaching, most know that promotion, tenure, and salary raises have little or nothing to do with whether they are good teachers, unless, of course, the administration is interested in sinking a candidate who they regard as otherwise objectionable.

The long-festering question of tenure is one of the more contentious issues in research institutions. For more than thirty years, the unstated policy of Research I was to deny tenure to eligible junior faculty. During this period, candidates (generally white males) for the most part reluctantly accepted the procedure according to which the university rigorously observed the review process preparatory for tenure—soliciting letters of support from the candidate, sending materials to outside referees, and, if the department recommended tenure, submitting the dossier to an ad hoc review committee appointed by the president or provost of the university. But everyone knew that the cards were heavily stacked (except the candidate, who had to believe in the process in order to spend as much as six months gathering documents and contacting supporters). Even if he survived the department's vote, he could be turned down by the dean. If by accident he went further, he was almost invariably turned down by the review committee. For candidates who made it through the committee, the last hurdles were the provost and the president, who, unless faced with insuperable legal or political problems, were likely to reverse their own faculty and middle managers. The occasional candidate who rose from assistant to tenured associate professor within a Research

1 institution succeeded because he had insinuated himself into the old boys' club and been accepted as a junior member. In other words, the difference between the successful and the unsuccessful candidate for tenure could not be ascribed to differences in the quality of their research and teaching but in their political skills.

Having spent six years in an Ivy League or other major university, the rejected junior faculty member was obliged to seek employment in a Research 2 university. For example, Fredric Jameson, a Yale Ph.D. in French, failed to win tenure at Harvard and in 1967 took a position at UC-San Diego, where he was awarded tenure. Failing this outcome, a candidate might even be content with accepting an appointment in an elite third-tier college. From this perch, he might hope to gain tenure, write a well-received, even influential book or key article, and win widespread respect in his discipline. In candidates' dreams, a Research 1 institution, even better, an Ivy League university, would one day call them to take their place at the top of the hierarchy. As if to validate the storybook version, after publishing his influential book *Marxism and Form* and many of the articles leading to his standard text *The Political Unconscious,* Jameson was called back to Yale in 1977, and went on to lead Duke's literature program as part of the university's short-lived effort to achieve status as a leading national institution by taking the fast track.

In the 1970s came feminism and the first signs of black academic power, and with these movements, President Richard M. Nixon's accommodation, affirmative action. At all levels of the hierarchy, universities were now obliged to seek and promote racial minorities and women. But the application of the principle of minority and women's representation in the heady reaches of high scholarship has proven to be extremely controversial. As the decade wound down, the first cohort of women, such as Harvard sociologist Theda Skocpol, came up for tenure in the Ivy Leagues. And, simultaneously, a small group of Marxist and other leftist male academics, such as Harvard sociologist Paul Starr, whose widely praised book on the social history of American medicine, surely qualified as influential. Since university administrations and human sciences departments had been sufficiently intimidated by the civil rights movement, many black academics in elite schools sailed through the tenure process in this period. Needless to say, the relative ease by which they achieved this status was, at the time, interpreted by some as an unprincipled compromise of academic standards. Yet in most cases, the victors in these early tenure decisions went on to become major figures in their respective fields, including philosopher Cornel West at Union Theological Seminary, literary critic Houston Baker at Penn, and Henry Louis Gates at Yale.

But women and male radicals did not fare as well. In what became a famous case among social scientists and women academics, Harvard's sociology department turned down Skocpol's tenure bid, even though she was highly regarded in the discipline and had achieved a national reputation for her work on national states and revolutions that belied her junior status. She promptly sued on affirmative action grounds, eventually won the case, but scorning Harvard's offer of tenure, went to Chicago. Finally, however, she did return and was reintegrated into Harvard. As a leftist white male, Starr appealed a similar decision at the department level, was turned down by the administration, and was ultimately fired. (Academics don't like this term, preferring the euphemism "denied tenure.") However, he landed on his feet when he was offered a job at Princeton.

Still, at Columbia and other Ivies, tenure is largely reserved for those faculty who have achieved distinction in the wider academic marketplace and return "home" from triple A institutions as academic stars or, at least, safe bets. With exceptions, these institutions avoid hiring senior professors who, despite their international reputations, are labeled "marginal" or "oppositional" to mainstream scholarship. A case in point is that of historian David Noble, whose critical work on technology earned him the reputation of Luddite. His critical study of engineering education, *America by Design,* and his broad history of machine technology, *The Forces of Production,* both of which challenged the social and political neutrality of technology, have become controversial but widely admired works in the field. Yet after he was denied tenure at MIT, he was unable to find a job except at Drexel, a technical university in Philadelphia. Finally, he was hired at a major Canadian research university, Toronto, but until recently remained effectively excluded from the American research institutions.

Put bluntly, the top tiers of the academic system are, for all intents and purposes, uninterested in intellectuals, except those of the ideological center and right, who, by the way, often attract endowed chairs from conservative foundations. That a major left intellectual such as Noam Chomsky has a tenured appointment at MIT is due, not to his voluminous political writings, but to the fact that he is arguably the world's leading linguist of the postwar era. In short, he is rewarded for his contributions to positive science, which is presumed to be ideology-free. To be sure, philosopher Richard Rorty has become a left-of-center public intellectual. But his Princeton professorship was secured on the basis of his work in technical, analytic philosophy and in pragmatism. Notwithstanding these instances and many more among women, black, Latino, and Asian scholars, the pattern remains similar to the path taken by Edward Said: prove your disciplinarity, then take your stand.

Similarly, tenured biologists Richard Lewontin and Richard Levins of Harvard and Jonathan King of MIT are politically and intellectually active. Lewontin and Levins have published widely read, but controversial, works in the politics and philosophy of science, and King was a leader in the social responsibility movement in science and has written extensively about the relation of biology to society. Yet these achievements are not viewed by their institutions or, indeed, by most of their colleagues as salient to their scientific work. In short, the days when intellectuals and journalists such as Irving Howe and Daniel Bell were recognized within the academy for their political work, even if they held appointments in English and sociology, are over.

2

The third tier of higher education institutions comprises nearly all private and public liberal arts and technical colleges. Whether intended to train elite or plebeian students, these colleges transmit the knowledge produced in research universities. Conventionally, the more elite schools also assume a major responsibility to impart the Western intellectual and moral tradition to students. Of course, the elite liberal arts schools, such as the "Seven Sisters," as well as Wesleyan, Hamilton, Trinity, Mills, Hampshire, Amherst, Bard, Colgate, Haverford, Rhodes, Bucknell, Oberlin, and perhaps another twenty, are in a somewhat different category than the state schools. Their libraries are better endowed, their students generally more affluent, and their facilities more opulent. But although faculties at these colleges teach fewer courses than do their colleagues at state schools, in many instances, their tutorial and advisement responsibilities more than compensate for their reasonable course loads.

All private school faculty conduct considerable academic and often personal counseling sessions with students. Many supervise ten to fifteen senior theses, some of which are of graduate school quality, requiring meticulous attention to the student's research methods and process. Every faculty member is expected to participate in the life of the academic "community" by serving on departmental and collegewide committees, performing administrative tasks connected to running centers, organizing conferences and colloquia series. And many are expected to attend myriad social events and college ceremonies, a sign of their membership in the "community." In some cases, they are not expected to write and perform research after publishing their first book and several articles. Elsewhere, after receiving tenure, if they want to rise in the ranks and in income, they must perform at the level of faculty at research institutions. In other words, even if their jobs are more secure than those of faculty at public schools facing frequent budget cuts, many are destined to remain relatively low-paid and relatively overworked.

Still, with a wealth of applicants for a fairly small number of jobs, four-year colleges and third-tier universities are demanding more publications as a condition of tenure as well as promotion. In the elite four-year schools, institutional standards may exceed the requirement that the candidate produce a book for a university press, a sign that she has submitted work to a peer review process. Some junior faculty terrified of losing the tenure fight have gotten the message that, in the current buyer's market, it is better if their book is published by a leading press linked to a Research 1 university than by a second-tier press. Harvard, Cambridge, Oxford, Chicago, Yale, or Princeton thus carries more clout than Minnesota, Nebraska, Kansas, or SUNY. There are instances where, despite the fact that the "leading" university press is a less aggressive marketer and distributor and may have a slim list in the author's specific field, the candidate feels obliged to violate his literary sensibilities in the hope of avoiding the sack. In more than one case, the book gets lost in the pile because the prestige publisher does not reach its audience.

In contrast to private colleges, where a high proportion of graduates attend graduate schools or enter professions where postgraduate degrees have only recently been regarded as essential, liberal arts majors in public higher education are declining. As job-panic has escalated, public colleges are responding by transforming themselves into vocational and technical schools. Enrollments in business, accounting, education, engineering, and other technical areas, including media technology, have grown at the expense of the arts and sciences. In order to halt and even reverse the plunge, some departments are adding occupational courses and concentrations to their majors, such as social work (sociology), journalism (English), pre-law (political science), management and public administration (economics and political science), and applied math, materials science, and chemistry. Others have been converted into service departments: literature scholars get few opportunities to teach upper-level or honors courses in their particular field of study. Instead, they teach so-called core literature courses to accounting and business majors or, more likely, composition. Philosophers are drawn to domains such as medical and business ethics for nonphilosophers, or else condemned to teach many introductory courses geared to fulfilling a student's "breadth" requirements. History professors may be somewhat more fortunate because their field is still attractive to some pre-law students and the few students who are interested in international relations.

As for the sciences, with the exception of biology, which, as we have seen, has become "hot" in the commercial sense, in many colleges and universities—even research universities—there are virtually no native-born undergraduate physics and math majors. Rather, students are almost invariably Asian or, in some large cities, Russian. The nickname for the University of California–Irvine is "Beijing University," but most students major in computer science and other technical fields. They may be required to take math and physical sciences courses, but see no point in majoring in them because, apart from teaching high school, there are few jobs.

The bottom-tier schools are engaged preeminently in training students to take their places as subprofessionals in the increasingly volatile technoscientific industries. They train computer programmers and technologists in the medical, engineering, chemical and biotechnology, and other industries, and at best pay only rhetorical tribute to critical education. This tier includes the community colleges and two-year technical schools; their main job is to provide technicians to business and industry.

The community college has become increasingly important as an ideological institution insofar as it fulfills, if only in the bureaucratic sense, the promise of higher education for all. Of the fifteen million students enrolled in postsecondary education in 1996, about half were enrolled in two-year colleges. But in contrast to the 1960s and 1970s, when most community college students transferred to four-year colleges, in the last twenty years in the majority of instances, they major in technical fields and earn "terminal" degrees. As financial aid has dried up, drop-out rates in many of these schools have ranged from 40 to 70 percent, largely because students have to go to work to stay in school. Many work during the day, some as much as fifty hours a week, attending evening classes and trying to read and write on weekends.

Given the shrinking demand for entry-level technical employees of all kinds, the community college is moving toward a sharper focus on placement. One of the more widely used techniques of job-finding is to develop required internships with private companies and public agencies for students in the hopes that they might stay on as regular employees after getting, or even while still pursuing, their associate's degree. In many colleges, counselors and "cooperative education" faculty devote considerable time to helping students fill out applications, write resumes, perform well in interview and test situations, and learn how to dress properly.

Many students attend community college because their grades are not high enough to gain admission to public four-year colleges, but a considerable number return to community college to learn a specific occupational skill, such as medical technology, word processing, and computer programming or repair. In many cities and states, the community college fulfills the promise of "open admissions," where any student with a high school diploma or general education diploma (GED) may be admitted. But for many students the promise has turned hollow because the conditions of their schooling—both their life situations and their education—conspire to raise the odds of failure.[10] Because they have frequently perceived high school as a waste of time, they enter community college ill prepared to perform at a college level. Native speakers have never learned how to read and analyze complex texts because they were not qualified to take academic courses in high school. Many non-native speakers find their command of English is not sufficient for most of their course requirements. Hence community colleges offer remedial courses in the hope of enabling a majority of entrants to qualify for college courses.

But, in the 1990s, state and local budget cuts for higher education have trimmed and sometimes threatened to eliminate remedial courses. Where these programs have survived the fiscal knife, colleges have been forced to offer fewer sections, leading to overcrowding in the remaining sections, and to exclude, by techniques of triage, students they consider less likely to succeed. As the 1990s draw to a close, enrollments have not dropped, but dropouts have skyrocketed, especially in large cities, where black, Latino, and Asian students predominate.

3

Neoclassical economics and its latter-day version, neoliberalism or "rational choice" social science, construes consumer choice as the foundation of economic power. When a product fails in the market, it must be replaced. Thus, ultimate sovereignty in the market belongs to the consumer. On this model, universities must maintain high quality in order to attract students to buy their services. But how to measure the quality of educational services? In econometric models, Harvard, Yale, and other Ivy League schools are the best because they have a surfeit of student applicants who are willing to pay a premium for their product. Accordingly, if the quality of the credential, measured in the number of jobs and the salaries offered to recent graduates declines, the consumer will cease to come. The credential, rather than the various standards of academic evaluation, thus becomes the crucial criterion of the worth and standing of a university.

To the traditional academic mind, this account may seem somewhat crude. But the crudeness is the result of the selling of American universities as sources of cultural capital. As universities have blatantly marketed themselves to business as knowledge and human capital producers and to students as employment credentials, only the most devoted champions of the idea of the university as an independent community of scholars can doubt that the academic system corresponds more to the above description than to any other.

By the early 1960s, this new model university was fairly well developed. The major problem remained the faculty. Except in some branches of the natural and social sciences, where scholars were well aware of the degree to which research had become subordinated to practical ends, most humanities faculty remained committed to the precepts of the older model. For at least two decades, they fought a rearguard battle to preserve the humanistic disciplines against encroachments, as administrations transformed the English and philosophy departments in all but a few schools into service departments for a largely technicized curriculum. The humanities as a concept survive only in the first tier of elite universities and a few other private institutions, along with some of the leading state universities. And, of course, the disciplinary associations such as the Modern Language Association (MLA) and their regional affiliates have provided an alternative professional and intellectual life, especially for those whose workplaces offer almost none.

It was in the research universities in the late 1960s that the students mounted their attack on the complicity of the universities with the military and corporations. In the elite universities, graduate students faced the hostility of humanities and social sciences faculties, who still defended the university as one of the few sites of critical thought. Many professors were prepared to allow universities a role in providing knowledge for government and military research in the Cold War era, not only because they were in agreement with U.S. foreign policy, but also because they were persuaded that the university remained committed to academic freedom in a time of conformity.

At Berkeley, faculty opposition to student protests included former socialists and communists. Seymour Martin Lipset, for example, saw campus unrest as more than irresponsible; for him, the protests were an invitation to the Right to intervene, and for this reason, they were dangerous to academic freedom. Like his colleague Lewis Feuer, a philosopher and former Marxist who saw in the student movement a generational revolt directed not only at liberal authority but at the Oedipal figure of the Father, Lipset discerned a definite authoritarian strain in student demands for democratizing the campus. For Lipset, as for many of his colleagues, an alliance with the administration was preferable to supporting the students, who at times appeared to want to dismantle the university rather than seeking reform. Steeped in Cold War fears, many of the liberal professoriate were skeptical of the incipient doctrine of participatory democracy within the universities. Already buffeted by new winds emanating from on high that they were not yet fully prepared to acknowledge, let alone accept, they were deeply hostile to the idea of student academic citizenship.[11]

Clearly, Lipset and Feuer understood student life neither as part of the emerging consumerist and corporatist culture (an analysis they ascribed to paranoia) nor as a potential democratic public sphere. The community of scholars, however diminished, needed defending, not against creeping commercialism, but against the callow mob of violent, radicalized, middle-class brats. The Berkeley Free Speech movement succeeded not only in winning the right to engage in political activity but inspired movements that secured for students, in many places around the country, a measure of academic citizenship. At many universities and colleges, token student representatives were elected to various departmental committees, as well as to boards of trustees. Needless to say, university faculties were not pleased, but the strength of the movement had at least for a time imposed a putative new regime. Administrations hastened to accommodate the new political influence that students, through protest and press visibility, now constituted. Their power on campus would reappear in the 1980s under the sign of political correctness.

Stung and disgusted by liberal professors' resistance to university reform, some who had been radicalized in the student movement left academia to become activists in "social change" movements such as labor, civil rights, and the organized Left. But a considerable number of erstwhile student protesters found their way into the professoriate. In literature and the social sciences—especially English, sociology, and anthropology—they formed radical, Marxist, black, and women's caucuses within the professions and, for a brief period in the late 1970s and early 1980s, managed to terrify the old liberal and conservative faculty. Left and feminist presidents were elected by the MLA, the American Studies Association, and the Anthropology and Sociology Associations, and there were, for a time, strong radical caucuses in political science and economics organizations. Prodded by the influx of younger members bred in student protest, dormant faculty senates and councils bestirred themselves to debate the future of the university. They sanctioned the creation of women's and black and Latino studies programs and departments and, under the impetus of the radicalized student movement, various educational innovations, most visibly in the development of ethnic, women's, American, and cultural studies on many campuses. In a number of instances, the new academic energy was manifest in the emergence of faculty and staff unions, whose leaders had been active in 1960s antiwar protests and, in some cases, were still members of radical organizations. Among these spokesmen were Ernst Benjamin and Wells Keddie of the AAUP's locals at Wayne State and Rutgers; Phil Nicholson of the American Federation of Teachers' local at the large Nassau Community College; William Scheuerman, the president of America's largest union of professors, the United University Professors at SUNY; and many others at campuses across the country.

By the 1980s, the number and the influence of radical faculty in the academy had grown large enough to cause alarm in insurgent intellectual conservative precincts. Roger Kimball, later managing editor of the neoconservative journal *New Criterion*, published a diatribe against what he called "tenured radicals," who, he argued, had infiltrated universities and were effectively subverting their mission for ideological ends.[12] Works by Dinesh D'Souza and Charles Sykes echoed these charges. Sykes's opus *Profscam* argued that the professoriate did not work hard enough, at least in the central activity of teaching courses. While acknowledging that leftists were often among the most prolific academics, he questioned whether their research was worth doing. D'Souza opened a new front against what later became known as "political correctness." Radical professors were not engaged in disinterested scholarship and teaching, but were indoctrinating students to their values and, in the conservatives' view, had forfeited their right to tenure protection. Their values—antiracism, antisexism, and a passionate commitment to more equality—had, in the Reagan era, become defined as "ideological."

Seen in this context, the fiscal crisis of public education has become an occasion for the recentralization of universities and may, perhaps unintentionally, mark the end of the brief period of academic innovation and legitimate dissent begun by junior faculty, especially women and African Americans, in the 1970s. Thirty years after the emergence of student power, the conjunction of the end of the New Deal, Fair Deal, Great Society era in which public goods enjoyed a position of some privilege, governmentality is itself in question. In the 1990s, under a centrist Democratic national administration and conservative local governments, the state's police functions tend to overpower and mediate its diminishing social functions. For the Clinton administration, defending a provision of the welfare state may be undertaken only on condition that it can be combined with a new manifestation of social conservatism. Echoing the famous 1920s Soviet dictum "She who does not work, neither shall she eat," where the shirker is taken to be a slothful single mother, some universities have been told by welfare agencies that students on public assistance will no longer be supported unless their education can be shown to have a vocational outcome. In any case, class attendance is no longer counted as "work" for the purposes of qualifying for a welfare check. Police now routinely patrol urban public high schools and universities as if they were identical with the mean streets of the central cities or, more to the point, tantamount to day-prisons. Educational parsimony in the face of legislative budget cutting has eclipsed the democratization that accompanied the rise of the black freedom and women's movements in the late 1960s.

4

Since the late 1980s, the academic system of American society has undergone another process of profound transformation. But the logic was already established during the "golden age" of the immediate postwar era. Having adopted the framework and the ideology of the large corporation, universities and colleges—private as well as public—are "downsizing" in the name of rising costs and declining or stagnant revenues but have also used budget cuts to effect a decisive power shift from faculty to administration. In multicampus universities such as New York's State and City University systems, the California State University system, and many others, the slogan "academic planning" has been used to remove authority over curricular decisions from the local campus community to the central administration. As the institutions have become more bureaucratized in the past twenty years, presidents and chancellors resemble CEOs rather than academic leaders. For the most part, their grasp of the mission of the university has been articulated in terms of (a) the job market and (b) the stock market. The intellectual mission of the academic system now exists as ornament, that is, as a legitimating mechanism, for a host of more prosaic functions.

The priority of knowledge as instrument over substance places humanities scholars and critics in an ambiguous position. Excepting only the most prominent consensus intellectuals among them, unless their writing and teaching can be situated within the corporate university's ongoing functions, funders and administrators regard them as redundant. As purveyors of "the best that has been thought and said" in the elite undergraduate curriculum, they enjoy a relatively comfortable, but progressively marginal and anxiety-ridden existence, being only too aware that they have lost considerable status in the newly restructured academic system.

Both in their methods and in their understanding of their role in this system, the social sciences have modeled themselves on the natural sciences. Theory no longer has a guiding purpose in the disciplines; it has been relegated to a not very important subdiscipline. The crucial branches are those having to do with policy, those that can be considered state social science. In sociology, criminology has once more emerged as the leading domain; many graduate students interested in academic and research jobs are advised to build a sufficient claim to this field. This transformation is entirely complete in economics and political science, hegemonic but still contested in sociology, but has not (yet) made significant inroads in anthropology, which, in any case, may prove moot because of the crisis created by the loss of (Third World) fields in the postcolonial age.

Public universities—most typically the State University of New York (SUNY), City University of New York (CUNY), the New Jersey and Pennsylvania systems of third-tier state universities, and the California State University (CSU)—have received a clear signal from their respective governors and state legislatures that the moment of mass public higher education is over. Or, if it has not technically ended, the faculty must reconcile itself to becoming managers of ever larger classes typical of Kerr's vision of the multiversity. In a recent decision of its board of trustees—a body of outside appointees, consisting mostly of corporate executives, lawyers, ex-politicians, and "civic" leaders recruited from the philanthropic upper crust and the black and Latino middle class— CUNY has sharply curtailed its open admissions policy. Among other "reforms," it has reduced to one year its commitment to provide remedial courses for academically unprepared students, many of whom are immigrants requiring language training before or concurrent with entering the ordinary academic curriculum. "What the City University and other public systems have done" according to *New York Times* reporter Joseph Berger, "is to shift remediation from four year colleges to two year community colleges. The community colleges are cheaper places for remedial courses because professors are required to teach more hours, classes are larger, and in New York, a greater proportion of tuition payments can be used to pay for remedial classes."[13]

In sum, the university's restructuring means that community colleges have been designated as the solution for a broad range of students requiring an extra boost on the way to credentials. The only problem is that this solution has been designed on the basis of the celebrated Joseph Heller narrative: "We want to help you, but we will set impossible conditions for our helpers." Like a roach motel, the university will let students in, only to release them as intellectual corpses.

Furthermore, following the trend of the private corporate sector, where downsizing has continued even in a time of relative economic growth, local governments have been forced by declining tax revenues to cut their own workforces. In step with the steady march of Congress to dismantle key elements of the welfare state, especially federal aid to education, health care, and social services, the proprietors of state governments have begun to argue that maintaining expanded professional and technical education will only flood the market with unneeded workers. Hence, the drive to raise admission standards in order to restrict enrollments to academically qualified students. The new public university systems' slogan might be "give me your qualified and deserving poor."

These broad changes are already taking their toll on graduate programs. Facing draconian cuts in student aid, many programs are limiting their admissions to the money available to support students. Since many schools are raising teacher workloads, and faculty are required to teach more undergraduate, particularly lower-division courses, many have no time to teach graduate courses. As the number of graduate courses declines, seminars turn into lecture courses and lecture courses become experiments in mass postgraduate education. The core of traditional graduate education, the one-to-one relation between mentor and protégé, is eroding as graduate school more resembles undergraduate college.

The idea of the university has, as does much of our moral and intellectual culture, religious roots. In medieval and Renaissance Europe, the collegium was formed first in the monastery, or among Jews, in the "school," as a community of scholars who together studied the sacred texts and wrote commentaries on them. Their readings became the basis of religious teaching to the general population. In this regime, the college was primarily constituted as a space for the search for knowledge of God, but it also evolved into more secular areas such as science and art.

The early "secular" colleges were similarly constituted. They remained church-sponsored, and church officials assumed the task of maintaining the institution—primarily its buildings and finance. But faculty retained authority over the curriculum and pedagogy. That did not eliminate conflicts between the two governance structures of the college, but lines of authority were far more clearly delineated than now.

Nowadays, our concept of academic freedom is one-dimensional. We understand and generally support the right of an individual faculty member to speak and write according to the dictates of her own conscience, free of legal or administrative sanction. It has become an aspect of speech protected by the spirit and the letter of the First Amendment. The many violations of this meaning of academic freedom, especially denial of tenure to the unconventional, and dismissal and administrative intimidation of dissenters, have been vigorously opposed by the aggrieved professional associations, faculty unions, and civil liberties organizations.

We associate the institution of tenure with the need to protect dissenting faculty from sanction imposed by the public, the administration of the university, and colleagues who might be prone to punish apostates. Before World War Two, however, tenure was rarely awarded to the garden-variety instructor. No less a figure than critic Lionel Trilling held the rank of a untenured instructor at Columbia throughout the 1930s; in 1936 he almost lost his English department job for his Marxism, his Freudian beliefs, and because he was a Jew, and only achieved real job security after the war. In fact, as a practice, tenure is barely a half-century old. It was gradually instituted by most universities after World War Two, when the American Association of University Professors issued a 1940 statement saying that the only way to secure academic freedom was through tenure. But this widely discussed proposal, first enunciated in 1915, is once again under attack.[14] In 1995, the president of the University of Minnesota floated a proposal to abolish tenure; the president of Bennington College actually got rid of it, along with a number of tenured faculty; and prominent colleges—the New School's Eugene Lang College and Hampshire College among many others—do not offer more than multiyear contracts.

The second dimension of academic freedom, the rights of the faculty as a collectivity to retain sovereignty over the educational process, has also been buried with the restructuring. Whether a department or program should be established, expanded, retained, or eliminated; which faculty should be hired or dismissed; how programs and departments will be assigned and workloads and classroom sizes determined are only a few of the crucial decisions affecting schools that have gradually been assumed by administrations and boards of trustees.

In the midst of these changes, nearly all higher education institutions maintain the formal apparatus of faculty sovereignty and have only made tentative gestures, so far, toward challenging prerogatives like ten-

ure and faculty-based academic review. Promotion and tenure committees still deliberate on individual cases. Faculty-administration retrenchment committees still decide on how to reduce staff in times of budget
crisis (within parameters established by the administration and, where
applicable, the union contract). Curriculum committees continue to
approve or refuse new courses or programs. And student affairs committees, now reduced to an aspect of the policing function of the administration, monitor and make discipline decisions on academic and
extra-academic student performance. But in both the public and private
university sectors, power has slowly but surely shifted to administrators,
who retain final determination of nearly all university issues. Faculty
senates and academic committees are really advisory bodies whose recommendations are no longer routinely approved by higher authorities.
Everywhere, departmental and divisional recommendations for tenure
(or its refusal) are subject to reversal by deans and presidents. And curriculum issues are now subordinated to budget considerations, which often
take precedence.

Although cases of individual academic freedom violations may have
received more publicity, it should be evident to all but the most myopic
observer that the worst abuses of the collegium have been in the abrogation of faculty sovereignty by the corporate university. The disparity in
public awareness need not be ascribed to conspiracy or even to evil in-
tent. The centralization of the academic system is a product of what Alan
Trachtenberg has called "the incorporation of America."[15] Just as the
family-owned firm and the craft union or guild have been relegated to a
subordinate existence in the U.S. political economy, so the collegium
occupies a purgatory between the heaven of the corporate university
boardroom and the hell of the huge lecture halls that dominate public
universities. It has a voice with little authority; its crafts—reading, writing, speaking—suffer a wizened existence; and its minions, embattled
and dispirited, have been able to mount only a sporadic, disorganized,
and largely ineffective resistance.

Thus, we can see the steamroller at work. For example, during the
last budget crisis, many CUNY presidents and the chancellor's office ex-
empted professional administrators from the retrenchment plan, and
planted the burden of the layoffs or thinly disguised force-outs on low-
level administrative and clerical staff. The corporate culture was firmly
in place. At many public universities in the past two decades, faculty hir-

ing has been virtually frozen while administrative hiring has experienced a veritable boom. These trends are a measure of the power shift during this period. The question that must be addressed is why and how the faculty lost its sovereignty. Before dealing with this issue, however, one more must be discussed. Does the collegium include students? Is the power shift a violation of their academic freedom?

Symptomatically, we now speak of a corporate "culture," which in the academy signifies a displacement of the old intellectual culture of the sciences, humanities, and the arts. Research and writing goes on, but it becomes increasingly instrumental to the overarching goal of individual survival, let alone advancement, in the academic hierarchy. More to the point, scholarship serves as a means to enhance the coffers and, secondarily, the prestige of the institution. True, the individual who pursues knowledge for its own sake or for human betterment may still perform this work on her own time. But in their official roles, faculty are more than ever urged, cajoled, and even threatened to direct their scholarship and research to the ever-decreasing pots of grant gold on penalty of losing resources such as computer time, assistants, equipment, promotions, and tenure.

In the process, it is no wonder faculty feel like employees rather than members of communities devoted to common intellectual concerns. In consideration of their new, proletarianized status, many have joined unions and converted their faculty senates into adversarial bodies. In their perception, university administrations and legislatures are bosses just like any other. Increasingly, the institutions of faculty control are losing their status and are viewed by administration as, at best, a nuisance whose utility for purposes of legitimation may have (over)reached its limit. While faculty, including adjuncts and teaching assistants, have reevaluated their traditional antipathy to collective action to adjudicate their grievances, they view unions as the unions see themselves—as economic bargaining agents concerned chiefly with salaries, workload, and job security issues. As a result, with some important exceptions, faculties are experiencing a long winter of retreat before the new corporate university.

CHAPTER 4

ACADEMIC LABOR AND THE FUTURE OF HIGHER EDUCATION

1

IN SPRING 1969, I was asked to come to Madison to meet with the leader ship of a new Teaching Assistants Association (TAA) at the University of Wisconsin (UW) and address a meeting of its membership. The two thousand or so graduate teaching assistants wanted help from a quarter other than the official labor movement, which, at the time, was riven by the Vietnam War question as well as many other issues important to stu dents. Besides, many among the fledgling union's leaders and activists were opponents of what they perceived was the prevailing "business" unionism of mainstream labor, that is, its narrow guild orientation. While they wanted to become part of the labor movement, they weren' sure they should affiliate with an established union. As a known indepen dent labor radical with strong ties to the student movement I could be trusted, even though I was over thirty. I suppose the invitation had to do with two of my preoccupations at the time. Throughout the 1960s I had been a full-time union official, first for the Amalgamated Clothing Workers (now UNITE) and then for the Oil, Chemical, and Atomic Workers, where I directed organizing for the Northeast District.

My other credential was my involvement in the antiwar movement. As a leader of the movement (in 1965 I had co-organized the first national coordinating committee against the war) and a columnist for the *Guardian*, then the leading New Left newsweekly, I was well known, at least among activists. During the spring of the previous year, I had been asked to debate the assistant secretary of state for Southeast Asia affairs, Roger Hillsman, on the occasion of the centennial of the university. Maybe five thousand students and faculty, most of them war opponents, heard me excoriate the war and the Johnson administration's role in pursuing it. Hillsman, a very nice person, had to carry the water for the administration's unpopular policy in one of the strongholds of the opposition. I did not have to be particularly effective to win the day.

In my talk to the TAA, I stressed the need to forge a close connection between new social movements and trade unionism, a connection that helped account for the startling and largely unexpected rise of public employee and professional unionism—doctors and attorneys, as well as professors and other teachers. Among the forgotten stories of that much celebrated and excoriated period was the explosive growth of public employee unionism and the birth of a new era of professional unionism as well. By 1975 about five million public, nonprofit, and private sector service employees had joined unions, the same number as the far more heralded movement of industrial workers in the late 1930s.

While the thirty-five years since the mid-1960s have been a period of decline for the independent scholar and intellectual, and for professors, a time of steady deprofessionalization, they have also witnessed the explosive power of the feminist and antiwar movements to change the everyday culture. Nearly all of the leaders associated with the new "white-collar" union movement were sympathizers if not active participants in these social movements. This was especially true of the State County and Municipal Employees, which actively enlisted student, feminist, and antiwar activists to its staff, and the local 1199 Health and Hospital Employees, which was rapidly expanding from its New York origins to become a national union. The equally fast-growing American Federation of Teachers (AFT) benefited from these movements even though the New York local—the heart of the national organization—was led by staunch defenders of the administration's foreign policy who were largely indifferent to feminism. But its president, Al Shanker, and his associates had actively supported mainstream civil rights organizations and were closely allied to A. Philip Randolph, the AFL-CIO's leading black trade unionist.

At the time of the TAA fight for recognition, academic unionism was a relatively rare phenomenon, among faculty as much as among students. By the late 1960s, the AFT had chartered a number of small locals of college and university teachers, but almost none of them had yet won collective bargaining rights. Academic unionism, like teacher unionism generally, was still at the lobbying stage: state legislatures and city councils were the main arena for winning more money for teacher salaries and benefits. TA unionism was virtually unheard of. Indeed, when I arrived at Madison, the TAA officers were still unsure of their ground. They had managed to recruit the vast majority of the assistants, but were not at all confident that the university administration would recognize them as bargaining agents. The administration made now familiar arguments against TA unionism: Their teaching duties were part of their academic program as graduate students. In effect they were professors "in training," not employees. Consequently, they received grants, not salaries.

The TAs were concerned with workload as well as income issues; they were part of the instructional staff of the institution but enjoyed few of the perks of graduate research assistants in the natural sciences. Far from being apprentices, many taught classes with almost no supervision, prepared lessons, graded papers, and provided undergraduates with academic counseling. In the aggregate, they accounted for a considerable portion of undergraduate teaching. When not delivering lectures to large assemblages, the professors were busy performing the research activities for which they were rewarded. For the typical tenured professor at a research university such as UW, undergraduate teaching was a nuisance, if not an actual impediment to professional advancement. Popular teachers among them were often labeled "demagogues" and suffered the envy but also the contempt of their colleagues.

By 1969, it was already clear to most English, philosophy, and history graduate students that halcyon days of plentiful academic teaching jobs were over. The job market had tightened, and most social scientists were beginning to feel the pinch. While jobs in research universities were available for some, a majority of those trained in the humanities could look forward only to teaching in a small state school or community college, or worse, becoming part of the academic proletariat of temporary, contingent, and part-time instructors. In a time of lingering hopes, primary and secondary school teaching, an option widely practiced by Depression-era Ph.D.'s, was still unthinkable. A few years later, even as the full-time job had all but disappeared in history and philosophy, English was making its long march from literary to composition studies. Only a relatively small proportion of graduate students attached to well-known national figures could expect to obtain a research university job, and even then they were often hired, not to teach literature, but to direct composition programs.

In the grim wasteland of the 1970s, university administrations were solving the problem of expanding undergraduate enrollments, not by hiring new full-time faculty, but by increasing class size in lower-division courses and pressing TAs to teach sections of fifty students or more. My son, who entered Rutgers University in 1971, told of attending lower-division courses three hundred strong, addressed weekly by a professor who was never available for office hours. His main contact was the twice-weekly section with a TA. In fact, when I began teaching at Staten Island Community College in 1972, I was surprised to discover that CUNY did not follow suit. My classes and those of my colleagues were relatively small. Recently, of course, my own CUNY graduate students report they are entirely responsible for an introductory sociology class enrolling some eighty students at the Queens and Hunter campuses of the university. They have no TAs or even graders to assist them. Their agony consists in weighing the ethic of giving multiple choice exams, which they believe are travesties of education, or sticking to their guns by assigning frequent essays and spending their evenings and weekends grading papers rather than pursuing their own research or any kind of social life. On neither campus do they receive any official or even much unofficial guidance, since the faculty is busy dealing with its own work overload.

So the formation of the TAA at UW prefigured the growing unease and even anger shared by many of today's graduate students that the encroaching multiversity concept—according to which only the research professor deserves the time to perform the work of knowledge production—has overwhelmed graduate education. From the UW administration's perspective, whatever their collective chances for obtaining a real academic job after graduation, its graduate students were ready sources of teaching labor. In the late 1960s, UW provided fertile ground for a militant response. As veterans of the mass antiwar struggle and of the southern civil rights summer projects, many students had acquired the skills of professional organizers. They knew how to organize and run planning meetings, speak effectively before large audiences, had considerable experience dealing with the administration, and perhaps equally important, knew how to deal with press and television. Moreover, the union idea was not foreign to these students, many of whom were influenced by Marxism or by the independent radicalism of C. Wright Mills and local luminaries such as labor sociologist Maurice Zeitlin, historian Harvey Goldberg, and especially William Appleman Williams, the great figure of American revisionist history. After a strike, the administration recognized the TAA, negotiated a union contract, and promptly started a campaign to decertify it as bargaining agent. Briefly defeated, in the late 1970s the TAA came back. For many of the same reasons that prompted the pioneer Wisconsin TAA battle, teaching or graduate assistant unions emerged in the 1970s and 1980s at, among other schools, the University of Michigan and UC Berkeley, and in the 1990s, at Iowa, the remaining California campuses, and most famously, Yale.

At first glance, the case for self-representation, and especially for unions, among graduate assistants seems self-evident. In the last twenty-five years of relative austerity at all levels of the academic system, salaries have deteriorated in real terms for most research and teaching assistants. Some enjoy fully paid health benefits supplied by the university, but elsewhere an increasing number of grad assistants must contribute to the plan and, in some cases, the university contributes little or nothing to their coverage. As class sizes have grown, the number of assistants has grown more slowly, remained constant, or even diminished, and their section-loads are larger. In many universities "assistants" or teaching "fellows" are, in fact, adjunct instructors because they teach classes unassisted or unadvised by a full-time professor. While a side benefit of such neglect is that these graduate students get good teaching experience and enter the job search with more qualifications, their teaching load frequently delays completion of their dissertations.

But despite the growing gulf between faculty and administration created by the erosion of faculty governance in fact if not in form, professors at many research universities and private schools, especially the Ivies, are in overwhelming numbers indifferent, if not hostile, to the efforts of graduate assistants to organize unions. For example, when a majority of graduate assistants petitioned the Yale administration for recognition of their union in 1995–96, they were rebuffed. The administration contended that, as graduate assistants, they were not employees but "apprentices" working under an experienced professor who would guide their teaching. The Graduate Assistants Association (GAA) countered by pointing out that they, not the professors, did the bulk of undergraduate teaching and were largely unsupervised. Since they had no access to the provisions of the state or national Labor Relations Act, their only recourse, they felt, was to strike.

And strike they did, in the form of what in Europe is known as "administrative blockage," refusing to submit grades at the end of the semester until the administration recognized their union for the purposes of collective bargaining. At strike rallies, some of which I attended, I observed only a handful of Yale faculty in attendance—Michael Denning of American studies, emeritus history professor David Montgomery, and Paul Johnston, an assistant professor of sociology whose pathbreaking book on public employees unionism had recently been published. When I asked about others, I was informed that, while there were faculty supporters who were unable to attend, their numbers were pitifully small. In fact, most faculty were either absent from the fight or, in an alarming number of cases, actively sided with the administration. A leading liberal American historian was rumored to have "turned in" the names of his graduate assistants who participated in the strike.

Most TA and GA unions are in public universities. Among the underlying currents that animated the unusual movement at Yale was the palpable fear among many of its graduate students that, after two decades of downsizing, the tight academic job market might even have caught up with them. They had come to believe that the present anticipated and even foreshadowed the future. Specifically, they suspected that the Yale Ph.D. was not necessarily a ticket to a tenure-track position in a research university or an elite four-year college. Instead, some, especially those in the humanities, saw themselves competing for a shrinking number of slots in public colleges and third-tier universities, where, as likely as not, they would be required to teach composition and other introductory courses or limp along in part-time and contingent jobs.

In fact, the tenure track is quickly fading over the horizon. Increasingly, as senior faculty retire or leave university employment, they are taking their lines with them and their subjects and fields of inquiry are also disappearing. To fill the gap, temporary and contingent faculty jobs are slowly replacing junior-level tenure-track positions. A growing number of Ph.D.'s, especially in the human sciences, are offered one-, two-, three-, and five-year non–tenure track teaching jobs at Ivy League and other research universities. Others are hired as "substitutes," ostensibly a stopgap solution to replace faculty members on leave or those who have recently retired. Some get these jobs to teach introductory courses, but others, in state universities that have experienced downsizing, are hired to teach subjects not covered by the shrinking corps of tenured faculty members. Frequently, the title "clinical professor" is conferred on those to whom the university does not wish to commit itself but who have special "skills" in writing, technology, and professional domains such as journalism, teaching, and psychotherapeutic and social work field supervision. Many of these jobs are renewed on a year-to-year basis with no chance of tenure, and for this reason clinical professors are not subject to the same academic publication standards as those on the tenure track. But this is small comfort in the face of their job insecurity.

By far the preferred method for administrations to fill classrooms is to hire adjunct professors. After all, clinical, substitute, and limited-contract professors usually receive benefits and are almost as expensive as tenure-track faculty. A college can hire five to eight adjuncts for every junior faculty position and typically does not pay them benefits unless they have some form of union rights. Even though many well-qualified Ph.D.'s in the humanities and a substantial number in the social sciences prefer to teach as adjuncts than to become computer programmers or investment counselors, their passion for teaching exacts a heavy price. They are condemned to accept as many as five or six courses or sections each semester at different schools, often at far-flung locations, in order to earn a bare-bones living. Adjuncts cover more than half the courses offered by many four-year and community colleges, just as graduate teaching assistants perform similar functions in the undergraduate curricula of research universities. Yet while the TAs and GAs have been able to form unions of their own, in only a few universities and colleges are adjuncts organized, let alone having a collective agreement with their employer(s). These include Rutgers and New York's Nassau Community College and some others where full-time faculty and staff have separate bargaining agreements. But at CUNY, for example, even though adjuncts are included within the bargaining unit and their hourly wages are set by the agreement, only a minority are eligible for benefits such as health care because most do not work consistently at the same campus.

Adjuncts are, in the main, not paid for holding office hours, although many feel ethically compelled to advise students and do hold them. As one told me, "How can I refuse to meet with students with academic or even personal problems?" Since they usually teach larger introductory courses while full-timers are assigned the upper-division courses or teach graduate courses exclusively, most adjuncts have little time to write and to engage in research. They have more papers to grade and students to advise. Many complain that they work much harder than full-time faculty for less compensation. More to the point, they frequently find themselves on a treadmill. They have no sense of place, so their lives are not stable enough to provide the mental conditions for performing intellectual work. As a result, they can never step off to seek other options. And if they spend five years or more after receiving their Ph.D. performing adjunct teaching, they are frequently regarded by academic job committees as "too old."

The position of the adjunct is analogous to that of a building trades worker, working this month or year at one construction site and next month or year at another. The major difference between the two occupations is that, in this country, because of the extreme mobility and insecurity of the building trades, workers have organized a strong guild to protect their benefits and their wages wherever they work and, traditionally, have some control over the market. So far adjunct professors are, except in the small number of fields marked by labor shortages, at the mercy of those who hire them. Since they are generally unorganized and cannot limit the supply, they are in a poor position to bid up wages, although many colleges and some universities could not function without them. Conspiring, perhaps unwittingly, with the buyers, the humanities and sciences disciplines continue to turn out more Ph.D.'s than the "market" can bear.

In fact, the program of restructuring on university campuses, which entails reducing full-time tenure-track positions in favor of part-time, temporary, and contingent jobs, has literally "fabricated" this situation. The idea of an academic "job market" based on the balance of supply and demand in an openly competitive arena is a fiction whose effect is to persuade the candidate that she simply lost out because of bad luck or lack of talent. The truth is otherwise. While it is entirely possible for a freshly graduated Ph.D. or an adjunct teacher to land a full-time position, it is increasingly rare for a candidate whose advisors are not prominent in their discipline, or at least part of a network of professors in a subfield, to be appointed to a "good" or even a mediocre job. It is still possible to find full-time employment in institutions located in parts of the country far removed from major urban or university centers. In some fields, those willing to move, say, to the Dakotas, Idaho, or several southern states may readily find jobs. In addition, some candidates find appointments in community colleges where workloads resemble those of urban high schools: five days, five courses. However, every writer knows that few books are accepted for publication in leading university and trade presses without an agent or a contact, and the same rule pertains to academic labor.

Basking in the plenitude of qualified and credentialed instructors, many university administrators see the time when they can once again make tenure a rare privilege, awarded only to the most faithful and to those whose services are in great demand. To be sure, it is altogether too early to predict whether the long and heartbreaking fight to establish tenure in American colleges and universities that began at the turn of the twentieth century will have been reversed sometime early in the twenty-first. Yet how else can one interpret the proliferation of graduate assistant and adjunct-taught courses, the emergence of temporary and contingent employment as a characteristic mode of faculty status in many schools, and the concerted effort of university administrations to prune the ranks of tenured professors through buyouts and other retirement incentives? To which must be added the exploding movement of "distance learning," which like the dream of the automatic factory, promises the era of the absent professor. That tenure will not entirely disappear reflects the administrative intention to retain prestigious faculty for both pecuniary and ornamental reasons and the fact that many, if not a majority, of professors in public universities have collective bargaining rights and a union contract protecting tenure. But the Yale graduate assistants, like those in more than thirty other major universities who have formed unions as the best way to address their situation, know better than the established professoriate that the days when they could look forward to a tenure-track job at a first- or second-rank research institution or an elite four-year college are over.

The Yale faculty, among whose number were outstanding feminist, African American, and liberal scholars, were divided in their view of the GAs' demands. Some were adamant that the graduate assistants union was an ill-begotten adventure and reflected the pique of a small number of overprivileged students who were playing at proletarian politics on their way to tenure-track jobs. Others remained silent because, whatever their sympathies, they believed discretion was the better part of valor. These professors were living examples of what the Supreme Court had found in the *Yeshiva* decision, which denied professors at private universities and colleges access to protections of the National Labor Relations Act. Whether their view was accurate or not, Yale faculty identified with the institution, thought themselves to be its decision makers, even managers, and seemed unembarrassed in their scorn or silence, even though silence in the midst of such a momentous event is an embarrassment. Unlike the struggle to establish a union of Yale clerical and maintenance workers several years earlier, where significant elements of the university's constituency, including faculty and parents, had sided with the workers, the grad assistants were essentially isolated. In the end, they found supporters only in the labor movement and among some (but not most) labor intellectuals. Facing intimidation in the form of sanctions that might endanger their graduation and career possibilities, they called off the strike. However, despite its loss, the association has not disappeared and may live to fight another day.

One may speculate further about the reluctance of the elite professoriate to support unionizing efforts at private universities. Recall, these institutions have adopted a policy of not granting tenure to junior faculty. Like old married people who often exhibit the same symptoms because they are condemned to live in the microsociety called the nuclear family, the senior faculty has become more ingrown and given to intramural warfare and incessant bickering. Tenured faculty tend to turn on each other, rather than on the administration, to express their frustrations, except when their discipline, as was Yale's sociology department, is threatened with extinction. True, administrations hire junior faculty, but in most universities and colleges, the nontenured enjoy almost no academic citizenship and no influence on their senior colleagues. Clinging to the often vain hope they will one day join the anointed inner circle, they are admonished to keep their heads down and their noses clean. Rarely are junior faculty members afforded the chance to share with seniors any new ideas they may have developed. If they have the temerity to do so, they are frequently rebuffed because, naturally, most established scholars are busy defending their hard-won turf against the incursions of the multiculturalists, postmodernists, feminists, and other transgressors of the disciplines. Since graduate assistants' unionism qualifies as a new idea and may threaten the sovereignty of the senior faculty, it suffers the same fate. If the full-time junior faculty is disenfranchised, how can even more abject assistants expect better treatment?

Since the activism of the Yale graduate assistants was so rare for an Ivy League institution, the media trained a bright spotlight on it. Working on the assumption that, of all students, those obtaining graduate credentials from Ivy League universities were assured a secure and comfortable future, journalists were puzzled by the Yale struggle no less than was their audience. But Yale's GAA is only the most celebrated instance of a veritable social movement among graduate students that emerged in the 1990s. Yale is symptomatic of the anxiety felt by a generation whose sixties forebears once rebelled against comfort without meaning but today also have genuine and substantiated economic fears. Now, as the corporate university spreads its tentacles, academic work struggles to find its fading quasi-religious mission. Perhaps this, as much as job insecurity, is the impulse behind recent unionization efforts. Not to mention that, according to the GAA, assistants teach 60 percent of the undergraduate courses at Yale.

Among leading public universities, graduate student unions at Michigan, Iowa, Illinois, Indiana, and the nine campuses of the University of California stand out. Some, like the sixteen hundred member Michigan Graduate Employees Organization, have affiliated with the American Federation of Teachers. But since the early 1970s, the United Auto Workers has emerged as a major union among university clerical workers and teaching assistants, especially the six thousand teaching assistants at the University of California. The Iowa TA union affiliated with the small, but aggressive, independent United Electrical Workers. And others, such as the Wisconsin TAA, are linked to the State, County, and Municipal Employees, the country's largest union of public employees. Together eighteen TA unions have collective bargaining rights around the country, and a dozen more are in various stages of attempting to win these rights. In May 1999, graduate assistants at NYU demanded union recognition and filed a petition with the National Labor Relations Board for election.

The most closely watched contest during the 1998–99 academic year was the drive of teaching assistants for union recognition at the University of California. After a decade of organizing on eight of the University of California campuses, TAs voted in a state Public Employees Labor Relations Board election for union representation. In fall 1998, the TAs voted overwhelmingly to strike when the administration refused to recognize and bargain with them. Unlike their colleagues at Yale, many professors support them. In the words of UC Riverside sociologist Edna Bonacich, "Who are we, paternalistically, to tell them they shouldn't have [a union]? The model of an apprentice is someone watching over you, teaching you how to stick the bolt into the nut. It doesn't work that way here. The model is not 'we will teach you how to be a professor.' . . . Being a t.a. is not learning how to teach. It's doing scutwork, a lot of scutwork."[1] Typical of antiunion employer policy over the last fifteen years, the administration warned UCLA department heads that it was their responsibility to keep instruction going and that they might be required to hire "some replacement workers." In late fall 1998, informed by the university administration's hard line, both sides were preparing for the worst. But in an unexpected development, the Democrats captured the statehouse and the Democratic legislative leaders called upon both sides to negotiate. The union promptly suspended the strike pending results of the negotiations, and the administration felt obliged to come to the table. The outcome of the fight would likely influence the fate of TA organizations in dozens of universities around the country. Meanwhile, the parent union, the United Auto Workers, deposited a large check in a California bank to pay strike benefits and, perhaps equally, to impress upon the administration its intention to support the TAs. Finally, in spring 1999, pressure from below as well as from above forced the UC administration to recognize the union, and it began to negotiate a first contract.

2

As university and college enrollments nearly tripled from the end of the 1960s to 1995, the professoriate began to experience a decline in their salaries, working conditions, and status within the institutions. In state schools, budgets had been enrollment-driven, and resources should have grown proportionally. But signaled by the crisis in New York's City University, by the end of the 1970s legislatures and executive authorities throughout the country were placing arbitrary caps on funding for higher education. At first, these de facto cuts were confined to third-tier four-year colleges and universities. But a decade later, even some public research universities, such as New York State's multicampus university and the nine-campus University of California system, were experiencing similar problems. In fact, although the 1990s witnessed no substantial enrollment drops—indeed, the demand for postsecondary education remained buoyant—were years of stagnation in university budgets owing to declining state tax revenues and the drying up of federal funds. The major component of absolute and relative declines in state budget allocations for postsecondary schools was the tax revolt of the 1970s and early 1980s, which almost everywhere focused on and affected state and local expenditures for public goods such as education, health, and social services.

What was widely viewed by pundits and by the universities themselves as a "fiscal crisis" was manufactured in part by such ballot initiatives as California's Proposition 13 and Massachusetts "Prop 2$^1/_2$," each of which placed caps on public spending, including education. As a result, local property taxes tended to rise to meet the budget shortfall or, in poorer communities, school and other services simply began to shrink. Class size grew in elementary and secondary schools, and when teacher unions negotiated salary and benefits increases, the school budget was not indexed to these raises so that some teachers and support staff were laid off, an outcome not seen since the Great Depression. Buffeted by shrinking budgets, public postsecondary schools had no access to property taxes, which are reserved for local school districts. School authorities had no recourse to meet their bulging enrollments but to hire devalued academic labor such as adjuncts and teaching assistants and increase full-time faculty workloads, adding courses and stretching class size.

In order to thin the ranks of the expensive full-time professoriate, state legislatures authorized university administrations to offer senior professors the chance to retire early with beefed-up pensions. Perusing the steady deterioration of facilities, resources, and working conditions, many professors over age fifty-five availed themselves of the bailout. In the process, many academic departments of public colleges and universities were left threadbare. In some cases, they were permitted to hire only adjuncts to fill course sections; in others they were returned between a quarter and a half as many positions as they had lost and had to fill the rest of the sections with part-time teachers.

What was once the hidden curriculum—the subordination of higher education to the needs of capital—has become an open, frank policy of public and private institutions. Where at the turn of the century critic Thorstein Veblen had to adduce strenuous arguments that far from engaging in disinterested "higher learning," American universities were constituted to serve corporations and other vested interests, today leaders of higher education wear the badge of corporate servants proudly. Plagued by rising costs and mounting resistance from their primary "customers"—the corporate term for students—to higher tuition, administrators in higher education at all levels are convinced that the ticket to saving their institutions is to forge closer relations with business. At a time when the corporate mogul has entirely shed the image of villain and has become a popular culture hero, there are good ideological reasons to have taken this turn. But a more practical consideration is that many institutions are strapped for money. Most of the private colleges and universities have small endowments and are experiencing sharpened competition for students. Even if their enrollments remain fairly healthy, lenders are balking at higher tuition rates, and some parents are turning away from non-elite private schools and sending their kids to public colleges.

In the Northeast and on the West Coast, where most public colleges and universities suffer from the chronic academic disease "budget crunch," many administrators are being encouraged by their conservative boards of trustees to seek private funds to supplement shrinking budgets. The less affluent colleges are selling chunks of the curriculum to corporations who are willing to contribute relatively modest sums in order to obtain trained workers; even when no money changes hands, business-university partnerships are good public relations for lobbying the business-minded legislatures. Several New York area two- and four-year colleges have agreed to tailor their curricula to meet the specific requirements of companies such as Bell Atlantic, Consolidated Edison, and other utilities. Most of the associate degrees awarded to company employees are in relatively narrow technical areas, and the colleges confine their "breadth" requirements to composition and history or sociol-

ogy. One example: New York City Technical College, a campus of the
City University of New York, won a National Science Foundation grant
to develop a curriculum for employees of Bell Atlantic. A curriculum tailored to the company's requirements for upgrading employees has been
in operation since 1996. Regular faculty teach in the program for about
150 students each year in both technical and liberal arts subjects. Although there is little new or innovative in the program, the big change is
that by funding and announcing the program as a "model," a prestigious
government agency has sanctioned the subordination of the curriculum
to specific corporate needs. Perhaps equally common in the emerging
privatization of public colleges and universities devoted, primarily, to
teaching is to outsource as many educational and noneducational services as possible.

Queens College president, former State Department functionary
Allen Sessoms, openly acknowledged in an interview that he had embarked on an aggressive program of privatization. He vigorously denied
that the school was being vocationalized in part because "corporations
want high-level liberal arts" graduates, but he did admit that under his
leadership the school would do corporations' bidding. Citing the land-
grant colleges, he said that higher education has always been oriented to
serving business. Among his plans, Sessoms cited establishing an extensive science research program in collaboration with private corporations, the most publicized to date being Queens' recent acquisition of the
famed Pasteur Institute from France. Sessoms also anticipated the construction of privately financed dorms in order to attract a national student body, as well as the establishment of Jewish and Asian studies centers because private donors had been found for them. When asked about
creating black and Latino studies centers and institutes, he responded
that he readily welcomed such programs, provided that donors from
these communities supplied money to support them. In short, Sessoms
has positioned himself as one of the more unabashed prophets of the new
corporate university. In order to facilitate this program, in 1998 Sessoms
announced plans to separate his college from City University and, following a pattern of some major New York State University campuses, to
initiate the University of Queens, a move that, presumably, would give
the institution greater flexibility in starting its own doctoral programs
and raising private funds to finance them.[2]

This transformation comes on the heels of the veritable fire sales in academic natural and social scientific research that followed the decision some seven years ago of MIT faculty to embrace novel arrangements with biotechnology and pharmaceutical corporations. As we have seen, in return for replenishing their depleted research coffers, the faculty agreed that the companies own the patents for new discoveries and inventions. In fact, since the Bush administration, federal science policy has been to encourage these partnerships and to target its own funding toward products rather than basic science. Sciences at the University of California campuses at San Diego and Irvine are dominated by corporate deals, as are many at other state universities. After all, science funds have often supported centers and institutes, conferences and research leaves for the ordinarily impoverished humanities and arts faculties. And as federal funds have shifted from basic and applied to product-oriented R and D activities, many theoretical physicists, for example, have found that they are more like humanists than molecular biologists; they, too, need subventions to support their work.

But from the grave, Soviet Communism struck yet another blow against "disinterested" knowledge. Even before the Cold War officially ended in 1991 and until the blows inflicted by rising right-wing attacks on Big Government, federal money for all sorts of public activities had begun to dry up. When the Soviet Union collapsed, research support took a nosedive. Every president or chancellor of a major university immediately donned CEO clothes and aggressively sought investors from the "private sector." By the mid-1990s, the corporate university had become the standard for nearly all private and public schools. Today a veritable army of consultants, marketing staff, and fundraisers has been marshaled by America's more than three thousand institutions of higher education to attract students, beef up their endowments, and organize partnerships with industry. Needless to say, many corporations and individuals have been more than willing to enter a partnership with colleges and universities, especially if they can reap direct benefits. Many scientists, law and medical professors, and business academics have started private consulting businesses. As one business school professor reported, his department now houses many whose teaching and research duties take second and third place to their small businesses. Those who choose to remain aloof from the new regime risk extinction or marginality.

The results of these changes have only begun to be felt. Every business practice imposed on the private sector is being implemented in U.S.

universities and colleges. For example, mimicking the drive to "flexibility," or "lean" production, where production corporations no longer stockpile parts but bring them to the work site "just in time" to be assembled or processed, higher education leaders are seriously debating a sharp curtailment of tenure and have already converted about half their faculty positions to part-time, contingent, and temporary jobs. These part-time and contingent instructors are available to fill the gaps left by retiring faculty or those on leave. In turn, panicking professional associations are urging that the labor market be severely restricted by closing or cutting back Ph.D. programs. Some, like the Modern Language Association, have pondered developing a new M.A. for composition teaching to replace the Ph.D. for the bulk of language teachers. Many Ph.D. programs have already limited admissions to candidates it can fully fund; in an era of lean fellowships and other forms of student aid, this may end the aspirations of tens of thousands who envision becoming academics. Administrators have justified these proposals on academic as well as business grounds, but few faculty have bought into the arguments that tenure should be reserved for only the most productive scholars or that the expansion of the already burgeoning academic proletariat will assure the university innovation, fresh ideas, and vigor.

The application of accounting principles to academic employment and planning is perhaps the most blatant indication that higher education is going corporate. Cost-benefit and cost containment is, in many schools, the main criterion for perpetuating a traditional department or starting a new program or department. The question administrators-as-cost-accountants ask is whether the department or program pays for itself in terms of tuition, outside funded research and other contributions that do not put stress on the institution's budget. And even as many corporations have moved beyond "zero-based" budgeting—where evaluation no longer assumes an ongoing commitment, but judges the department's viability on a year-to-year basis—higher education has rediscovered it with often calamitous results. Departments and programs are being asked to justify their very existence by showing anticipated as well as past results: in enrollments, in grant money, in contributions to the university's coffers. As we saw in the cases of Columbia's library school and its geography and linguistics departments, the argument that a discipline or line of inquiry might have other justifications for its existence than the "bottom line" seems to have lost its ability to persuade.

Nor are elite private four-year colleges by any means exempt from the trend toward rationalization of their academic programs to meet fiduciary demands. In fall 1997, I gave a talk on the future of academic labor at Hampshire College in western Massachusetts, a private institution of some twelve hundred students, since its founding an innovator in alternative higher education. Although students attend courses, much of the curriculum consists of yearlong individual projects supervised by a faculty member. The requirements are more rigorous than most because the student must write a serious research paper to advance to each of a series of levels. The whole process is capped by a senior thesis; some of the work could qualify at many graduate schools. And Hampshire gives no grades. Unlike many privates' boast of faculty governance, until recently Hampshire's was more than smoke and mirrors.

When I arrived I discovered that at the instigation of the administration and the board of trustees, the school was in the throes of a massive self-evaluation and restructuring and the faculty was up in arms. Despite tuition fees that compare with the Ivies and other elite private liberal arts colleges, but endowment-poor, the administration was pressing for more revenue. Toward this end, it had hired a consultant to market the school's unique features and, in violation of its tradition of faculty governance, embarked on one of the new money-making ploys of contemporary universities—creating centers that will attract donors in whose name or interest the center will serve. One of the earliest ventures was the campus-based Yiddish Studies Center, whose director and staff were quite independent of the faculty.

Lacking a sumptuous endowment, the administration of the 300-student Marlboro College is making moves to force the retirement of its tenured faculty, and other small institutions are desperately trying to raise money in similar ways. Many follow the lead of educational ideologists such as Robert Zemsky of Penn and Chester Finn of the Hudson Institute. Shunning academic criteria, they and other consultants advise their clients in the name of "efficiency" to act like corporations selling products and seek "market niches" as the best way to save themselves. Confidently, they predict "prices" of admission will, in Finn's words, "level off" once the universities commodify their services.

Take the case of New York University. Before the 1980s, NYU was distinguished by its first-rate law and medical schools and a top-ranked clinical psychology program. It also boasted a money-making continu-

ing education program enrolling thousands of students in both nonde-
gree and degree programs, ranging from short-term training in areas
such as real estate to bachelor's degrees. It had a few relatively respectable graduate programs in the social sciences and the humanities, as well
as a considerable number whose national ratings left much to be desired.
But its natural science, business, education, and social work schools were
barely blips on the screen, and its undergraduate college was widely
viewed as the New York branch of the University of Parties and Frater-
nities. Then the entrepreneurial John Brademas was selected to guide
this essentially mediocre, but land rich, institution into the twenty-first
century. A congressman from Indiana, Brademas was among the senior
Democrats defeated in the 1980 Reagan landslide. What commended
him to NYU's board was his long service as chair of the higher education
subcommittee of the House Education and Labor Committee, where he
fought vigorously for more federal support to private and public universities. As a Washington insider and aggressive fundraiser, he was just what
the ailing institution needed.

Upon Brademas's arrival, he made clear his intention to rouse the
university from its torpor. His strategy was to build the endowment by
selling every itch and scratch of the university's vast real estate holdings
to create shrines to its corporate donors, and he offered some existing
schools and programs as bait. Pet-food manufacturer, alternative newspaper owner, and real estate developer Leonard Stern funded a living
memorial to himself and his family, the Stern School of Business. Real
estate mogul Lawrence Tisch had an arts school named for him to supplement the already-established Tisch School of Continuing Education
and a couple of Tisch wings of the medical school. Warner Communications established a school in its own name, and liberal investor Arthur
Carter gave substantial funds to journalism and to other programs. And
for a mere $2 million, lesser donors were invited to endow a chair. Even
less money was required to assure a person's immortality by putting her
or his name on a theater, a museum, or even a bench.

Blessed with the university's Greenwich Village location and, more
to the point, its subsidized apartments, Brademas began to rebuild the
faculty. The costs of this recruitment were paid for by the results of its extensive advertising campaign and superb press relations to recruit students and by the tens of millions Brademas and his staff raised from corporate donors. Like Duke, Virginia, and Pittsburgh, NYU had enough

to buy talent from all over the country. It purchased dozens of academic superstars in almost every field. One senior recruit was given permission to fill six new academic positions to overhaul a troubled sociology department; another was able to hire three new faculty members to infuse fresh blood into the veins of an all but expired American studies program. NYU raided the City University graduate school program to restart its expired philosophy Ph.D. program. Many were hired in the professional schools, which in short order regained national visibility. Lacking minorities, history and journalism were given leave to hire up-and-coming black professors, and the university instantly established centers and programs in African and Asian studies.

The undergraduate program remained a major problem, for as every academic administrator knows, graduate students do not make good donors; it is the undergraduates who cultivate attitudes of love and loyalty for their alma mater and are the mainstays of endowments. NYU's national publicity and recruitment drive focused attention on high schools, where they hoped to attract good, upper-middle-class students to the campus. To this end, the superstars were admonished to teach large lecture courses and upper-division undergraduate seminars as well as their graduate seminars, spurring the renovation of the university's College of Arts and Sciences. By the mid-1990s, NYU's undergraduate school had become a school of "choice" for many high school students.

But the recent experience of Duke University's English department may put a damper on the hopes of those institutions who seek to improve their national standing in highly visible fields of scholarship (and not incidentally boost their endowments as well) by hiring stars. In the late 1980s and early 1990s, Duke's administration was persuaded that the university's profile could be raised by investing a sizeable chunk of its considerable resources in the mass hiring of leading theorists in the highly contentious literary studies domain. Among those recruited to the English department were Frank Lentricchia, whose bitter renunciation of traditional literary studies had propelled him to prominence while he was still a relatively junior professor at Irvine. From Johns Hopkins came Stanley Fish, a nimble debunker of literary canons, who as the newly appointed chair quickly—and aggressively—lured some of the top academic figures in the country to work in the department. Eve Sedgwick, a founder of what became known as "queer" theory, came to Duke, along with Henry Louis Gates, the erstwhile Yale scholar of African American literature, who soon departed for Harvard. Fredric Jameson, the Marxist theorist who developed and ran the graduate literature program, came from UC Santa Cruz; and Barbara Herrnstein Smith, a president of the Modern Language Association, was persuaded to leave Penn.

A decade later, wearied of constant bickering over hiring and promotion issues, battling for money for speakers, and perhaps most of all, realizing that under Fish's leadership the department had little or no genuine procedures for faculty governance, five professors, including Fish himself, announced their departure. The department was put into "a kind of trusteeship" by the administration. According to a *New York Times* report, "As some professors see it, the story is a cautionary tale for universities hoping to emulate Duke's success in building a national reputation by strategically hiring star scholars; they say the department's problems stem in part from resentments that took root because celebrated outsiders failed to become fully integrated into departmental life."[3]

While like professional sports managements the universities want to hire big players in the academic game, they rarely demand of them participation in "departmental life." In fact, apart from offering a handsome salary, striving schools like NYU and Duke often assure the "prospects" that their teaching duties and other responsibilities will be light. Since integration into departmental affairs is voluntary for those at the top of their game and the administration and department chairs rarely welcome too much participation by intellectual heavyweights, these schools shouldn't be surprised that this strategy undermines any sense of community in the departments. The corporatization of the university may be good for the spreadsheet, but it augurs badly for education and learning.

In 1998 and 1999, universities were plagued with another series of scandals associated with their sports programs. Many institutions that value their academic standings were revealed to have relaxed their requirement that athletes maintain passing grades in academic subjects as a condition of remaining on the team. Many outstanding players were failing courses, and in some instances, administrators and coaches put pressure on instructors to give passing grades to athletes who performed almost no academic work. The practice was widespread, and almost no institution with top-rated teams seems to have avoided the trap.

The problem led some commentators to advocate removing the elite division-one college athletes from the academic program, making them professional players rather than maintaining the charade of student status.

Of course, most division one teams have virtually "hired" most, if not all, of their key players. For these schools, sports has many valuable functions. Proceeds from ticket sales comprise a significant contribution to the budgets of some of the smaller schools. More to the point, the athletics program plays an enormous role in building loyalty among students and alumni, which often translates into substantial additions to the endowment. For these and other reasons, sports plays an enormous role in enhancing a school's recruitment efforts, contributing a bit of luster it might not otherwise enjoy, especially on academic merits. Yet for a major research university like Duke, which fields top-ranked women's and men's basketball teams, to acknowledge openly the professional status of its players would present significant problems. The illusion of amateurism has always sustained the efforts of Ivy League and top-ranked private universities. Harvard, Columbia, Brown, and other Ivy League institutions deliberately downgraded their once formidable athletic programs long ago, but many institutions—the University of California and the Big Ten schools are only the most well known—rely heavily on sports to sustain their political as well as, indirectly, their financial support from the state legislatures, many of whose members are alumni.

In 1986, Georgetown and other schools belonging to the National Collegiate Athletic Association (NCAA) responded to criticism by attempting to deflect its insistence that athletes were, in effect, professionals. NCAA Proposition 48 and its later amendment, Proposition 16, required potential athletes to show academic proficiency before being permitted to play in first-year competition and players to be advanced only if they had achieved passing grades in their core courses. Athletes were also expected to have at least minimum test scores in the Scholastic Aptitude Test (SAT). Twelve years later, concerned that colleges were failing to meet minimum standards, the NCAA proposed stiffening the requirements. In the furor that followed, some athletics officials, including the Georgetown basketball coach, claimed that NCAA rules discriminated against blacks and other minorities and asked that restrictions be lifted, on the ground that black and other minority athletes typically attended high schools that prepared them poorly in academic subjects. His claim echoed charges made by, among others, the advocacy organization Fairtest, which observed, "The NCAA's [own] researchers [have] found that the 'use of any single indicator [such as standardized tests] is not psychometrically sound.'" According to Fairtest, the NCAA board had "ignored" this finding with its two propositions imposing restrictions. Nor had the board considered the objections of President Gregory Angrig of the Education Testing Service, who in 1989 stated that the cutoff "is not based on any valid study and was apparently an arbitrary choice that has yet to be explained by anyone." A similar complaint was registered eight years later by a college board vice-president, whose admissions office administered an alternative test.[4]

Finally, in January 1997, two student-athletes filed a lawsuit in Philadelphia charging that the NCAA's Proposition 16 discriminates against African American athletes and violates Title 6 of the Civil Rights Act. Others have argued that it also discriminates on the basis of class, since many white and black working-class students attend academically "challenged" high schools and cannot afford the private tutorials which have become virtually mandatory for many upper-middle-class students. The 820 SAT cutoff score or the 68 ACT minimum was, according to the plaintiffs, "hurting hundreds, if not thousands, of student-athletes . . . who have worked hard in school."[5]

But all this misses the point. Student-athletes are not admitted to major sports institutions to be scholars. They are given money packages by leading schools to play sports, and it is not uncommon for these universities and colleges to invite them to leave school when they are injured or have not performed well. These practices are as old as the practice of semiprofessional college sports. The problem is that higher education has been hoist on its own petard. It needs top-ranked athletes to bring in revenues and build prestige for the school. Many of these athletes are black. Many blacks cannot qualify to play because, under the glare of negative publicity, the trade association of the schools has lifted the bar. In the next decade, some schools are certain to step down reluctantly from the two top divisions of NCAA competition, because as most Ivies have found, maintaining first- or top second-division teams is simply too controversial. But it is likely that many others will find ways to lower the barriers, both to bow to pressure from civil rights suits and because they are willing to take the heat in order to fill the coffers.

Of course, those most hurt by the virtual professionalization of college sports are the players. As the documentary film *Hoop Dreams* (1997) has affectingly shown, for many black youth, basketball and other sports still represent their only hope to find a way out of ghetto and slum neighborhoods. Lacking other prospects, many have staked their youth on the remote chance they will survive the grueling competition of high school sports and find their way into the first two divisions. Needless to say, most who finally are lured to college campuses never make it to varsity teams and never finish their undergraduate degrees.

3

Since 1970, union organizing has been far more successful among faculty, especially at the community college and public university levels, than in virtually any other sector of the work force, except health care. But despite the establishment of faculty unions in private colleges and universities, especially in the New York Metropolitan Area, further unionization has been stymied by the Supreme Court's 1978 *Yeshiva* decision. As I indicated earlier, the Court ruled that faculty in private colleges and universities are not protected by the National Labor Relations Act because they share in academic and other areas of decision making and should be considered part of "management," an excluded category under the act. In contrast, the Court also ruled that, subject to legislative and executive authority, public school professors are employees. The American Federation of Teachers (AFT) is the largest faculty union, but the American Association of University Professors (AAUP) and the National Education Association (NEA) have also organized thousands of college teachers, some, like AFT, in major universities. In fact, during the dismal 1980s, when for the first time since the early years of the Depression, unions as a whole recorded a net loss of membership, faculty and academic unionism became one of the few growth fields in the labor movement.

Today, approximately a quarter of full-time faculty and nonsupervisory professional and administrative staff in U.S. universities and colleges are organized in three unions: AFT, with about 85,000 members; AAUP, with about 22,000 members under contract, although its total membership is about 44,000; and the NEA, with about 20,000 members under contract in postsecondary education. The unions bargain for faculty at some leading universities: AAUP has organized Rutgers and Wayne State; Cal State, the nation's largest with more than twenty campuses, was organized by NEA. AFT represents SUNY faculty, staff, and the health care employees, including physicians at the university's three medical centers, where its affiliate has 22,000 in the bargaining unit, one of the two largest academic unions in the country. CUNY's faculty and staff union is next with about 11,000. AFT represents faculty at Temple, the Pennsylvania State University system of former teachers colleges (not Penn State), most Illinois and California community colleges, and has won collective bargaining for the University of California lab workers. AFT has not yet won collective bargaining rights for faculty, although it does have locals among full-time professors in most of the U Cal campuses. Even in the Midwest, where faculty at the large state universities are not unionized, state and especially community colleges tend to have faculty unions.

Some private colleges and universities, notably Long Island, Hofstra, and Adelphi (AFT) and Saint John's (AAUP), are unionized. TAs are affiliated with unions ranging from the AFT and the Auto Workers to the United Electrical Workers and the Hotel and Restaurant Workers (Yale). Clerical and maintenance workers in universities are organized into many unions, notably the State County and Municipal Employees, the United Auto Workers, and the Service Employees. These employees are not excluded by the notorious *Yeshiva* decision, and so clerical and maintenance unions have made significant inroads in private universities, where they represent employees at such elite institutions as Harvard, Columbia, Yale, and Boston University. Their strength is characteristically concentrated in the Northeast, still the largest bastion of unionism in services, then in California, Michigan, and other Midwest states.

Apart from the private colleges, which faculty union leaders believe are, for the time being, outside the realm of possible unionization, the glaring weakness remains the public research universities. Professors at these institutions enjoy considerably higher salaries than in the third- and fourth-tier institutions and many earn significant outside income as consultants, grant recipients, and writers. These material conditions contribute to the self-image of many professors as independent entrepreneurs or scholars. Apart from the exceptions already noted, faculty at research institutions such as California (Berkeley, UCLA, and others, not to be confused with the California State system), Texas, Penn State, Virginia, and the Big Ten universities generally view themselves as exempt from the imperative of collective action. They are convinced that their professional fate is, for all intents and purposes, a function of their individual talents and achievements. California, as well as many other public universities, rewards faculty by merit, in which publications in certain journals, academically respectable books, and funded research play dominant roles. Even when resources have been cut by state legislatures, most of these faculty members remain indifferent, if not antagonistic to unionism. I suspect this is in part because they fear to admit that their own position, in absolute terms, has deteriorated even if their relative status and working conditions are princely compared to colleagues at state and most private colleges. In fact, the cultural as opposed to the economic position of the elite university professoriate increases in proportion as public colleges and universities suffer vocationalization, faculty and staff reductions, and deteriorating working conditions. Salary stagnation notwithstanding, the status gap between the various tiers of the academic system is widening.

Like teachers in the primary and secondary schools, professors organized unions when they understood that their diminished cultural capital would not sustain their economic and professional positions; that regardless of the pedigree of their graduate and undergraduate degrees, they were being ground down by increasingly arbitrary administrations and vindictive legislatures; that as salaried employees in an unfavorable political and economic climate, they needed the advantages of collective action. More to point, they had to surrender, to a certain degree, professional illusions, especially the pernicious doctrine, inherited from the nineteenth century, of genius and talent as accurate predictors of professional success.

The first move of professors, as trade unionists, was to frame their organizations in the images of conventional business or economistic unionism. Understandably, the more "trade unionist" the faculty, the more antiprofessional. Of course, although unions of professionals were never able to entirely avoid dealing with professional issues—indeed most faculty owe as much loyalty to their discipline as they do to the university—their first responsibility was to assert, against the prevailing wisdom, that professors' interests were closer to those of the labor movement than to management. In this respect CUNY's union is an example of an ideologically moderate leadership that, until recently, steadfastly resisted the concept of merit as a base for salary determinations. To be sure, promotions and tenure were—and remain—the last bastion of the merit system, but at CUNY salary increases within academic rank are awarded on the basis of length of service. In contrast, many other union contracts retain management's right to distribute academic rewards, subject only to the grievance procedure. For example, the State University of New York collective bargaining agreement provides general salary increases, but within academic ranks step increases are awarded strictly on merit as determined by professional and budget committees.

The majority of the professoriate, whether in or out of the unions, have not yet been convinced of the benefits of organization. Trained within professional ideology, most professors in research universities see themselves neither as intellectuals nor as teachers, which in either case would be a politicizing reflection on their social position. Consequently, many union members primarily identify with their professional associations and seek approval from disciplinary colleagues and, ultimately, from the university administration that retains the purse strings, rather than with the class of intellectuals to which they putatively belong. Culturally, they have introjected the values of their discipline; strategically, they tend to behave as the institution wants; and given their profound professional identification, they can never articulate these affiliations as forms of subordination.

The research university faculty may be doing better, but they are not doing particularly well. With diminished funds for research, most are teaching more than ever. Many have been forced to live primarily on their salaries, a change that in some cases has reduced their incomes by as much as half, especially among natural scientists accustomed to deriving part of their income from large grants. Austerity in research funding has been matched by legislative parsimony. Faculty salaries at leading universities have barely kept pace with inflation and are—absent a few thousand chair holders and academic stars, whose incomes, nevertheless, rarely exceed $125,000 a year—modest in comparison to those of their peers in medicine and corporate law. Still, when they look down at their colleagues in nonresearch universities, where in 1998, a full professor earned a median salary of $68,000 a year—much less in the South, rural areas, Catholic schools, and community colleges—their $80–$110,000 a year looks good, if not sumptuous.

There can be little doubt of past union effectiveness in vastly improving faculty and staff salaries, working conditions, and benefits. Until recently, for example, CUNY salaries compared favorably with nearly all major private and public universities and, for a time, were the highest, on average, in the country. But the fiscal crisis of 1975–76 and parallel legislative cutbacks of funds for public universities, combined with faculty reluctance to strike or otherwise take direct action to win its demands, are decisively shifting the balance between public and private universities. Unions still make a difference, but as in manufacturing and many services, today they provide mainly a grievance procedure and a broad range of benefits through the union contract, rather than having substantial impact on salaries or working conditions.

The Professional Staff Congress's active participation in the creation of City College's Center for Worker Education and its collaboration with a major literacy center in New York City, the Consortium for Worker Education, may be exceptions to the rule of labor's noninvolvement in educational innovation. In addition, the union has negotiated a fund to defray some research costs, mostly for social science and humanities professors, by permitting them to temporarily reduce their teaching loads. Yet if recent bipartisan assaults on higher education persist, faculty unions may be obliged to become leading vehicles for counterplanning. Their role will become more urgent if faculty senates, frequently dominated by the most senior professors, who shuttle back and forth from faculty to administration, can no longer muster the political will to oppose downsizing/reorganization programs aimed at vocationalization.

What is less clear is whether unions see themselves as agents in the wider university life. Until now, the fundamental power grab by university administrations has not elicited a strong response by campus unions. Some, like CUNY's Professional Staff Congress (PSC) and SUNY's United University Professions (UUP), have addressed issues of academic planning. UUP thwarted an administration proposal to privatize the SUNY medical schools and medical centers; PSC played an important role in helping to remove several of the system's college presidents who it believed were acting against the interests of faculty and students. In 1995, the union joined in a successful suit against the CUNY board of trustees for its premature declaration of financial exigency before the state budget was completed, declaring that the action was a ploy to force retrenchments and, more important, organizational changes not warranted by the budget situation.

Perhaps AAUP is the most visible of the faculty organizations in the public higher education arena. Before half its members had entered into collective bargaining agreements, it was the leading advocate for faculty on such issues as tenure, academic freedom, and equity in faculty salaries. Its censure/boycott list of universities who violate these principles has no teeth; few even know who is censured. But it does bother university administrations, and from time to time, some actually appear to mend their ways under the glaring light of unfavorable publicity. Moreover, it was the AAUP that, almost alone at first, made the fight to make tenure an institutional imperative, although curiously, it has been relatively slow to respond to its erosion. Still, in contrast to the largely economistic unionism of AFT, AAUP remains singularly dedicated to traditional academic values and loses few opportunities to reassert them in the face of continual assault.

Yet, beyond these and some other instances, faculty unions have found themselves operating in a severely restricted compass; for understandable reasons they have made the sphere of economic bargaining, including job security, their special province. Issues such as the creation of new programs, the elimination of old departments, and major curricular changes are, in a rough division of labor, understood to be the province of the faculty senates and the administration. The president of the Professional Staff Congress defended his inaction in the face of a 1998 board of trustees edict that, in effect, would eliminate open admissions at CUNY by abolishing so-called remedial programs in the university's nine senior colleges by declaring such decisions "management's prerogative."

4

What has been the response of faculty and students to the new regime of educational dismantling? Where there *is* an organized response, it has been confined to resistance. I want to offer CUNY's experience over the past five years as a case study of what is possible, and of what faculty and students have perceived to be the limits of their power. In spring 1995, faculty and student organizations, including PSC, effectively mobilized to oppose the new Republican governor's proposal to cut the university's budget by more than 15 percent and Mayor Giuliani's threat to cut off $20 million from community colleges. Thousands demonstrated, called public meetings, and lobbied legislators in behalf of restoring the budget cuts. At the campus level, some faculty fought administration-sponsored "retrenchment plans," which proposed to eliminate entire departments and programs rather than anticipate across-the-board cuts. In the end, the cuts did result in some department closings and layoffs. But early expectations that some state campuses would be discontinued and the two state university medical centers would be privatized were stopped by the adroit efforts of the UUP and the state's teachers federation, New York State United Teachers (NYSUT), which led an intense legislative lobby.

Even as the coalition opposing the cuts celebrated its partial victory, the governor's budget proposals for SUNY and CUNY in 1996–97 and beyond stepped up the pressure for reorganization and downsizing. While denouncing the proposed cuts, administrations at both universities used the occasion to begin a process of academic planning aimed at sharply reducing many of the liberal arts to service departments for enhanced professional and technical programs. Accelerating tendencies built into both systems, administration plans called for the overt establishment of a few research-oriented campuses while relegating most to vocational roles. And, like other institutions, City University's chancellor allocated a million dollars to begin research development of a distance learning program, which, when it is put on stream, will undoubtedly help reduce the size of the full-time faculty.

On the whole, the educational vista of faculty and students has been limited to preserving the existing state of affairs—especially the much maligned open admissions policy, where students need only present a high school diploma or GED to gain admission to one of CUNY's community college branches. But while resistance is necessary, there is more at stake than the systematic restructuring and selective dismantling of the university. The faculty and its organizations have not been able to generate ideas for a plan that would not only not diminish access but also would radically improve the curriculum, pedagogy, and school governance. Even the most progressive have hesitated to propose anything innovative or even different, fearing that any change will only enhance the administration's drive to further centralization.

As in so many other struggles in this corporate "downsizing" era, the Right has all the ideas and the opposition finds itself backed into a corner: liberals have become conservatives, staunch defenders of the status quo. For example, in the fight to prevent the dismantling of the archaic welfare system, the Left seems to have forgotten its own critique of the cynicism of the welfare bureaucracy; it has now become the most fervent defender of a system it once excoriated. Similarly, educational radicals—not to be confused with the traditional left-liberals, who believe that the main task is to preserve school budgets—once condemned the disciplinary basis of school knowledge as an outmoded, repressive regime. But many now resist any hint of educational reform, on the grounds that such proposals rarely signify the enlargement of resources, but are used by administrations to facilitate consolidation and reduction.

On the run, the liberals have steadfastly refused to enter a serious dialogue with their adversaries. For example, critics howled when CUNY chancellor W. Ann Reynolds announced the College Preparatory Initiative (CPI) in 1993, a program that would force high schools to raise graduation standards by offering serious language, science, and math courses. The critics simply refused to believe that CPI was more than a thinly veiled effort to phase out open admissions. Perhaps they were correct. Yet who can deny urban high schools need significant reform? Those concerned with preserving open admissions might have explored the possibility of joining the chancellor in fighting to upgrade many of New York's high schools' curricula. It would have entailed finding new money for laboratories, hiring math and language teachers, and perhaps equally significant, reforming administrative structures in secondary education.

Educational reformers have successfully argued that the monolithic high schools containing two to four thousand students are inimical to learning. In New York City, some two dozen smaller schools, each enrolling between one hundred fifty and five hundred students, have been established in the last twenty years, most of them since the late 1980s. Some school districts have extended their alternative intermediate schools to high schools, introducing a 7–12 concept for secondary school. And a reluctant, foot-dragging board of education has approved breaking up some existing big high schools that are not working into smaller houses. So far, the results have been encouraging, if inconclusive.

The higher educational democrats are, with exceptions, not part of this movement. Rather they are stuck in a sniping, marginal position, refusing to acknowledge that many New York high schools aren't working. Or even if they agree that students come to CUNY and other large urban university systems without sufficient academic preparation, their deep suspicion of the administration's motives for undertaking reform produces a state of paralysis. The paranoid style of politics is entirely understandable in this environment. Bereft of ideas, the university administration demands of the campuses "academic planning," which, as almost everyone knows, is a euphemism for adapting to the new downsizing programs mandated by the state bond holders, who are, at least symbolically, represented on the board of trustees. Still, we must ask whether it makes sense to deny everything and construct the fight entirely in terms of resistance.

In August 1993, the CUNY administration, at a moment when their plan for top-down academic planning had been almost universally rejected by faculty and students, asked me what would be an alternative. I suggested that a faculty-controlled committee award small grants to groups who would propose and attempt to implement domain, not disciplinary-based, curricula. Each proposal, I suggested, would have to involve faculty from different disciplines and even different campuses. Working with Dean Ronald Berkman of the chancellor's staff, we procured from the Aaron Diamond Foundation enough funds for awarding some fifteen grants over a three-year period. As we developed the program, which we called "New Visions in Undergraduate Education," some faculty warned me of the risks: working with the administration at a time of severe budget crisis would invite the perception that we had simply opened a back door through which the proposals of the Goldstein report, the main incarnation of the administration view, would sneak through. Neither participating faculty—those on the committee and the applicants—nor the administration understood New Visions to be other than what it purported to be: an alternative approach to academic planning. We were not being co-opted. We were aggressively intervening in the crisis, in this case not with protest, but with alternatives.

Tacitly rejecting the either/or of protest and collaboration, members of the committee have protested the governor and mayor's assault on the City University. We have, as individual faculty members, testified, lobbied legislators, and marched before city hall. Some of us have given press and television interviews expressing complete opposition to the prevailing program to gut the institution. We still affirm the virtue of entering the planning process; that a dialogue has not genuinely ensued is a function of our own inability to broaden the approach in the context of the debate, but also the way in which the discourse of crisis has hardened positions on both sides.

Needless to say, the great battle for higher education did not end when, in the face of massive protests, the New York State legislature and the governor scaled back the cuts, and the university's shortfall was closed by raising tuition. Having seen the shutdown of more than a dozen programs in 1995, we can expect new stages in the crisis that might follow slowing economic growth and declining state revenues. Once again facing reduced revenues, produced fundamentally by the legacy of bipartisan tax concessions to business and the wealthy and the recession in the state's economy, the state administration will once again try to slash the budgets for public education—in both lower and higher institutions. Heaving a sigh of regret, the university administration will be forced by these new budgetary calumnies to consider closures of several colleges, retrenching faculty, and closing thousands of courses. Once again, faculty and students will face the choice of whether to protest or find alternative solutions.

A small but dedicated group has joined in sustaining various incarnations of a coalition of faculty and students that has consistently fought the budget cuts. And the groups working on new curricula have not surrendered hope; in some cases, their plans have been realized in new undergraduate programs. But the obstacles are formidable. Many professors are deeply committed to their own disciplines and others to professional and technical education. They are willing to resist reductions that hurt their own programs but are unwilling to entertain new approaches that might entail radically rethinking their own professional and intellectual status. Some, indeed, are in state of deep denial. They hope for renewal on the basis of a new liberal state government, economic growth, or a surge of political support for public goods. And a considerable portion of the most thoughtful and experienced faculty have already left for other universities or have retired rather than suffer the humiliation of watching their ship go down.

The deep question is, of course, power. Most budget shortfalls are the product of the reversal of progressive taxation and of allocation choices rather than reduced revenues. Have the faculty and students effectively surrendered their vision of the community of scholars and accepted their already institutionalized status as employees and consumers? Or is there still hope that in addition to the rituals of resistance—which, it must be admitted, can only slow the steamroller down, not stop it entirely—academic communities will abandon their moralistic, ritualized, paranoid style for a more nuanced, and ultimately strategic, effort to fight for a democratic university? Although a democratic university would include some of the elements of the hard-won open admissions policy, it would also go beyond it to ask some fundamental questions: What is the mission of the university in an era when technological change and economic uncertainty renders most occupational and vocational programs obsolete within a few years? Can faculty and students disengage from the orientation to jobs, jobs, jobs, and to a corporate culture to found our own? The answers to these questions are ineluctably linked to other issues: Does the political will exist? Who are the agents? What is the program? Beyond rage, lurks a new approach. Whether we will stumble on it before we have been locked into antinomical and ultimately futile positions remains to be seen.

For academic unions there can be no question of reversing the de facto end of mass public higher education through collective bargaining. Having successfully shown that the professoriate in some academic precincts can act like traditional trade unionists without seriously damaging their academic integrity or standing, the unions are now faced with the awesome task of becoming institutions of alternatives as well as of resistance. In short, they are challenged to accept responsibility for the academic system rather than remaining representatives of specific interests of faculty and staff within the university's technocratic boundaries. The challenge is to become agents of a new educational imagination—that is, to join with others in counterplanning that aims both to retain mass higher education as a right and to suggest what education is in the postwelfare, postregulation, postexpansion era.

CHAPTER 5

WHO GETS IN, WHO'S LEFT OUT OF COLLEGES AND UNIVERSITIES?

1

NO CONTROVERSY in postsecondary education has produced more heat in recent years than who should be admitted to colleges and universities. College entrance has become an issue in an era of what might be described as "mass" higher education, for more than 60 percent of all high school graduates now enter these institutions, most of them in the public schools. According to some statistics, 46 percent of those who enter college have failed one or more sections of placement or admissions tests. That half of all students in postsecondary schools attend community colleges, mostly in vocational and technical programs, has not deterred the critics' contention that many who attend both two- and four-year institutions should not be there. Some critics favor restricting all college admissions to those who, in addition to holding a high school diploma or a GED, are able to read and calculate at a tenth- or eleventh-grade level. When measured by standard tests, students should be able to write discursively and grammatically at some length, and know how to produce a research paper. Needless to say, this standard would exclude many students past and present, in all manner of postsecondary institutions. In fact, underlying the controversy is the sometimes tacit, and often overt, argument that college is not for everybody and should not be a "right." In the public institutions where tuition is much lower than in private schools, although it still provides as much as 80 percent of school budgets, only those who have achieved academic competence should be afforded the privilege of higher education.

The pro-standards arguments are directed, almost exclusively, to public colleges and universities, which account for nearly 70 percent of all enrollments.[1] Unstated, but implied, is that if students and their families can afford elevated tuition fees, and if private schools choose to provide remedial services, as most of them do for the less well prepared, these are not appropriate matters of public concern and should not be objects of public inquiry. If, say, small- and medium-sized third-tier private institutions wish to make a checkbook, a secondary school credential, and a heartbeat the major standards of admission, this is their business. What concerns the public—read conservatives—is whether hard-earned tax dollars should be spent on students who require considerable help to get through the early years of college and who may not be able to complete a four-year curriculum in less than seven or eight years.

The complaint that most high school graduates are poorly prepared for postsecondary education has been used to argue for raising admission standards at public universities. Skeptical of grade point averages, some critics have insisted as part of this demand that remedial courses, especially for students who fall short on standardized aptitude and achievement tests, should not count toward the college degree or should be discontinued entirely, at least in four-year institutions. In these times of chronic budget constraints, "raising standards" may constitute a convenient ideology for current and future downsizing. We have already seen declines in enrollments in some public university and college systems, and as policies such as open admissions and affirmative action come under increasing attack, there is a strong prospect of a steamroller effect. The likely gainers will be third-tier private institutions.

Whatever the intrinsic merits of proposals to raise admission standards, there are some unexamined assumptions underlying the cry for restrictions. One is that, somehow, public policy went awry after the war when millions of young people who would not ordinarily have attended college were not only admitted, but were eagerly recruited by many schools. Given this gross error, which, as we have seen, can be traced to the GI Bill, standardized tests in reading and math are viewed as the best and the most valid sorting device to protect the integrity and the value of credentials earned in our cherished schools of higher learning. Measures such as writing and speaking, recommendations of teachers and other mentors, and other qualifications occupy the margins or, as in the case of interviews, are ruled out on the grounds that they are open to bias. Standardized tests exclude discursive competencies of all sorts. Generally, the admitting institution has no idea of the applicant's verbal skills on paper, let alone in speech. Similarly, income-blind criteria of admission are, in the post–affirmative action moment, replacing the idea that economic, as well as racial and ethnic, diversity may enrich academic and student life. In short, the broad prejudice of the new academic gatekeepers is that higher learning should be reserved to the paying elite, those who have the money to take college preparatory courses that train them in techniques of test taking, and the select coterie of "deserving" poor who have miraculously succeeded in rising, like cream, to the top.

The "access" debate has elicited an avalanche of charges and countercharges. Even when acknowledging no willful malice on the part of educational administrators, conservative education experts, and skeptical legislators, many liberal and black educators and activists contend that the effect of higher admission standards has already been to reduce the participation of blacks and other minorities in higher education. Following the 1997 decision of the California regents to discontinue affirmative action criteria for admission to the University of California's nine campuses, minority freshman enrollment plunged by 75 percent. Although by 1999, UC campuses reported a nearly full restoration of minority enrollment, the Berkeley campus lagged seriously, and the statistics do not tell us much about the composition of the minorities who were admitted, particularly how many black men were among the cohort. In the last five years of the 1990s, national enrollment of black students in postsecondary education has declined from 9 to 7 percent of the student population, and there has been an even steeper fall in black male enrollments. Some argue that higher standards merely reinforce the prevailing inequality at the elementary and secondary school levels. Many point to the relative deprivation of resources and equipment, to the erosion of well-appointed and safe school buildings in urban elementary and secondary schools, and to the lack of enriched cultural programs. Unless national policy works to reverse failures at these levels, the demand to raise standards is tantamount to a policy of wholesale class and racial exclusions.

Indeed, growing gaps in teacher salaries between cities and suburbs, not to mention the pervasive differential per capita spending on public education between more affluent suburbs and poorer city districts, lend credence to these contentions. For example, in 1996, New York City spent about seven thousand dollars for each of the system's students while an affluent New York suburb, Scarsdale, spent about nineteen thousand dollars per student in the same year. In addition, in affluent suburban districts throughout the country, as well as in middle-class schools in the city, parents are asked to contribute money to supplement deficiencies in state funding. In our daughter's high school, a New York City public school that requires an academic entrance exam, the bottom line contribution is in excess of $250 a year. In addition, parents are expected to volunteer time to supplement the public budget. Of course, parents in poorer schools can afford neither the time nor the money to raise the quality and quantity of educational resources. Still, when our daughter attended one of New York's elite public intermediate schools, more than half her classmates failed the earth science Regents' exam when their science teacher, already far behind the curriculum schedule, left in the middle of the year to have a baby. This school has the highest reading scores of any intermediate school in the system, 94 percent at grade level or above. But burdened by a succession of substitute teachers, the class as a whole performed in the exam at a dramatically low level. Imagine how students in less well-endowed schools performed on this examination. Since passing the Regents' exams is a condition for entrance into some of the city's highly ranked high schools, had our daughter failed, she would have been obliged to join many of her classmates in summer school.

There can be little quarrel with those who link the educational deficits of many college students to the physical and intellectual conditions in high schools. In many cities such as New York, Philadelphia, Los Angeles, and Detroit, state-mandated requirements for academic diplomas in languages, sciences, and mathematics cannot be fulfilled because of teacher shortages, the absence of science laboratories, and an antiquated infrastructure. Where, as in New York, the Regents' or other capstone examinations are given as part of the academic diploma requirements, students attending forty of the city's one hundred high schools are virtually unable to pass science and math examinations. Their schools simply do not offer science courses such as physics, laboratory-based biology, and chemistry or, in mathematics, trigonometry. In a third of urban schools in cities such as New York, Philadelphia, Atlanta, and Los Angeles, students are not afforded the opportunity for advanced placement courses.

So it is not necessarily a reflection of a student's ability when he fails to pass the mathematics part of the placement exam, the most common cause of remedial work at New York's City University, the branches of the California State University system, and other public universities. Nor can the growing number of students from immigrant families be faulted for poor reading skills and English comprehension. Most secondary schools simply do not offer adequate language programs for these students. Still, conservative critics of public higher education insist that these are problems that should be handled elsewhere. They argue that, otherwise, what can only be described as the thirteenth and fourteenth grades of high school masquerade as "higher" education. Similarly, they claim, four-year colleges are not the place to assist students whose first language is not English. Such services are best delivered in community colleges or, better, in special privately administered institutes, which might receive public funds in the form of vouchers, or in continuing education. In any case, none of these programs should carry college credit.

One of the consequences of their lack of preparation by America's high schools is that many students must devote an increasing portion of their college careers to catching up to what they have failed to learn elsewhere. Even in the three hundred so-called elite universities and colleges, a sizeable minority of students experience some difficulty mastering the curriculum because of reading and writing problems, regardless of their scores on standardized tests and high grade point averages. It turns out that grade inflation, an acknowledged national problem, is frequently more rampant in research universities and elite four-year institutions than in many public colleges, a phenomenon that is only puzzling to those who ignore the weight of power, money, and prestige in determining "standards." We have seen that in the two tiers of research universities, most lower-division teaching is performed by graduate students and, in some institutions, by adjuncts as well. In these schools, seeing no rewards for teaching, the full-time faculty has little or no time for undergraduates. Indeed, in some cases, they tend to treat graduate students who are not available to work on their own research projects with disdain. In many of institutions, students are often encouraged to play to their strengths, that is, to specialize early in their academic careers. In which case, they may never learn how to read critically or write an essay, even with a minimum degree of elegance. For example, in research universities with a heavy technology emphasis, such as MIT, Carnegie Mellon, and Pittsburgh, it is not uncommon for a freshman to take, almost exclusively, science and technology courses, with perhaps a single humanities course in each of her first two semesters.

Lacking the protections of prestige and power, many third-tier college faculty in the humanities find themselves teaching basic reading and writing rather than literature, history, and philosophy. Lacking majors in their respective fields, science and math professors are relegated to teaching introductory courses to business and other vocational majors. As for the social sciences, since the 1960s boom in student interest in "social problems" such as poverty, peace and war, and politics, the number of undergraduate majors throughout the academic system in sociology, political science, and anthropology has plummeted. The decline has been disastrous for social science faculties in many third-tier schools. Except for economics, which is closely tied to business, social science programs have been transformed into service departments even in elite four-year colleges. Since, in many instances, the number of social science majors is too small to support a large number of upper-division courses, the discipline survives on the classic "breadth" requirement of the core curriculum. In some cases, required courses for majors have to be canceled for lack of enrollment. Under these circumstances, everywhere one finds at least some faculty pleased to accept incentives for early retirement; seeking administration jobs in order to be relieved of the classroom; taking refuge in grant-driven research; or devoting most of their energies to avocations, some of which become small businesses.

For these reasons, any proposal to raise admissions standards in public institutions that does not address the general crisis in education is bound to be viewed by those who have historically been excluded from higher education as one more instance of racial and class discrimination. More specifically, it will be seen as a ploy to reassert the doctrine that "college" is a privilege reserved for the few. Although in my opinion, critics are right to argue that it is time to halt the process of shifting the burden of educational failure upward, the question is what to do in the meantime. One perspective suggests that if colleges and universities simply refuse to remain complicit in educational failure and halt remedial programs, secondary schools will be forced to raise their own quality of curriculum and instruction.

Forced by what? We are in midst of at least a quarter century of severe budget constraint in public education. What the critics of mass higher education have failed to address is how their proposals dovetail with the current ideology of "smaller" government, a euphemism for privatization of health and education and other public goods. The condition for raising standards at many secondary schools, even by conservatives' own lights, is massive infusions of funds, not the least of which would be spent on recruiting science and math teachers, a program that inevitably entails raising starting salaries and providing the physical materials for effective pedagogy. Funds would help reduce class size, as well as the number of sections required of teachers. If critics of public education were serious, they would advocate reducing classroom hours in most urban schools from the current twenty-five a week to fifteen or twenty hours, the standard practice in some affluent suburban school districts. Teachers would have more time for preparation, individual tutorials, and curriculum planning and writing. And many teachers burnt out by the education wars desperately need renewal. In-service programs to upgrade knowledge and to revoke the authoritarian pedagogies that have resulted from the primary classroom focus on alleviating discipline problems in many schools would have to be initiated.

In this respect, the conservatives are right: liberals often stop at throwing money at the problem. Major revisions of curriculum and pedagogy are needed. I will reserve a fuller discussion of this question for chapter 7. For now it is enough to ask, Are critics of open admissions and other inclusive policies in higher education prepared to make the political and intellectual commitment to raise the ante at all levels of schooling? Are they ready to demand that elementary and secondary schools be funded, not by property taxes, which produce much of the discriminatory gap, but by progressive state income taxes? Or, as their opponents suspect, is their assault on public higher education directed to another agenda?

In Vermont, the state legislature took the radical step of attempting to equalize funding between affluent and poorer districts by redistributing state funds raised through taxation. But instead of raising the bottom to the level of the more affluent, the legislature and the governor chose to depress the top, a measure that, in 1998, justifiably provoked protests among middle-class parents and some educators. Here we have an illustration of cockeyed populism run amok. In the larger educational scheme, the problem of equality pales by comparison with the problem of learning. It is arguable that nearly all schools—private and public, poor or affluent—suffer from intellectual, if not fiscal, deprivation, for it does not follow that money can buy more than an adequate school system, even if it is the best available. If some children receive the best mediocre education a system can offer, why can't all children share in the mediocrity? To push decent schools down simply exacerbates conflict between the economically deprived and the intellectually deprived, when the fight should be to transform all schools into good schools.

It may be argued that since "college isn't for everybody," the standards should be raised even if high schools are not urgently upgraded. In either eventuality, the result will be to swell the official jobless rolls, invite protest, and hence more street repression by police and other authorities. In some cities such as New York, Philadelphia, and Los Angeles, where official unemployment remains chronically twice the national average— three times in minority communities, six times for black men—sharp cutbacks in enrollments are likely to have a snowball effect. Some public schools will be obliged to reduce faculty and staff employment and contract out their facilities, and in multischool systems, some branches may shut down. In towns where the university or college is the main employer, raising admissions barriers might provoke a major economic crisis analogous to the closing of a large industrial plant or a military installation.

Another result of policies to bar unprepared students from public colleges is to beef up enrollments in some private third-tier schools. For example, early indications are that the board of trustees' mandate to end remedial programs in four-year branches of New York's City University has resulted in a 17 percent rise in applications for admission at Long Island University and similar increases in nearby Adelphi and Hofstra Universities. The unintended consequence of this policy has been to restore some of the luster to CUNY colleges such as Hunter, Queens, Brooklyn, and Baruch, whose admission standards are significantly higher than those of their private competitors. According to a recent study, Brooklyn is the college of choice for students who have also applied to these competitors. The problem is, besides Columbia and NYU, the combined enrollments of CUNY's private competitors in the New York Metropolitan Area is only a third that of City University, and for many students, tuition remains prohibitive. Consequently, after just a few years of restrictive admissions policies, a growing number of prospective college students are forced on an already overburdened job market.

This leaves the community colleges as the remaining "open admissions" institution for those holding a high school credential. However, even in these schools remedial programs dominate the first two years of many students' curriculum, and even longer for those assigned to "English as a Second Language" programs. Many are unable to take college-level courses until their third year. With a sixty-credit graduation requirement and burdened by the need to hold down full- or part-time jobs, it is not surprising that many attend school for five or six years in order to complete the requirements for the associate degree.

As the community colleges emerged in the 1950s and 1960s, more than half of the students were enrolled in liberal arts programs designed to enable them to transfer to four-year institutions. When I taught at Staten Island Community College in the 1970s, the transfer programs were still a major aspect of the college's mission. But, Steven Brint and Jerome Karabel have shown, these were also years of increasing vocationalization of community colleges, as administrators, prompted by the onset of severe budget constraints and by their own perception that a vocational curriculum was their best survival strategy, desperately sought an economically viable niche for their embattled institutions.[2] By the 1980s and 1990s, the liberal arts were consigned to the few breadth requirements as many of the community colleges became almost completely dedicated to vocational and technical training. Most now focus on "school-to-work" approaches to curriculum, a pattern that, perhaps surprisingly, is characteristic of some technical and scientific universities such as Carnegie Mellon, New Jersey Institute of Technology, and Stevens Technical Institute. Once more than half of community college graduates went on to seek baccalaureate degrees. By 1996, only 28 percent of graduates transferred to four-year institutions; for the remainder, the associate degree was considered "terminal." But fewer than half of all community college students graduate. And even among those who remain in the liberal arts throughout their associate degree schooling, few are able to study beyond the introductory stages because more advanced offerings are severely limited. Adjuncts teach more than 50 percent of course sections, compared to 40 percent in four-year schools; in some, the number is as high as 70 percent.

In many of these schools, the quality of technical programs has, until recently, been relatively high. In the past thirty years, community colleges have provided training for most technical categories in the health field, especially nurses; bookkeepers and other office/technical personnel; computer technicians such as entry-level programmers, repair technicians, and word processing operators; and lab technicians. They have recently negotiated relationships with telephone, airline, and utility companies and agencies of the federal government for programs tailored to the specific needs of the company or agency. For example, the Northeast's largest telephone company, Bell Atlantic, and the unions have negotiated, through the collective bargaining agreement, one paid day a week for employees to attend community colleges. But despite a few humanities and social sciences courses, the bulk of the curriculum is devoted to upgrading students' skills in order to qualify for supervisory and advanced technical positions. And on the theory that placing students in companies for work experience will enhance their employability, a growing number of community colleges offer internships and instruction in work and "job-finding" skills.

One of the central problems facing these schools is how to keep abreast of rapidly changing technologies and job structures. For example, given that the half-life of a PC operating system (and increasingly programming languages) is less than five years, it is difficult to keep the school-to-work curriculum relevant. Faculty knowledges must be constantly refreshed and adjuncts with up-to-date information hired to teach courses, and since hardware and software companies thrive on planned obsolescence, equipment must frequently be replaced. If the changes are incremental rather than revolutionary, many schools can manage to keep their heads above water. But if the changes entail large expenditures on education and equipment, hemmed in by budget constraints, some inevitably find themselves unable to credibly sustain the job orientation of their curriculum. As a result, no less than universities, community colleges are rushing to make arrangements with corporations that conveniently require their services and to privatize themselves further by raising tuition.

In the health field, the challenge is far more extreme. With the emergence, since the mid-1980s, of health maintenance organizations (HMOs) as the core service providers of the health care industry, some professional and technical occupations are disappearing and new occupations are being created owing to hospital closings, technological innovation in many testing areas, and job redesign. One of the more telling changes is the disappearance of the registered nurse as a profession, once at the heart of the patient care system. New titles such as the physician's assistant (PA), reflecting the partial removal of the doctor from direct performance of many medical procedures, are gradually replacing the RN. Although some of the education and training is similar, the PA has far more latitude than the RN. As jobs for registered nurses disappear, or more precisely, as the RN increasingly becomes an administrator rather than a service provider, some schools have closed their nursing programs. But since the PA and the RN degrees increasingly entail bachelor's and even graduate training, the community college is unable to upgrade its own program without affiliation arrangements with a four-year college or university. As a result, more of them are offering what amount to transfer programs in health professions.

Ironically, the more specialized the knowledge, the more vulnerable is its bearer to the vicissitudes of the job market. At a time of rapid shifts in the job scene, high-level general education—arguably the best preparation for the new types of knowledge work dominating the upper and middle ends of the occupational structure—is declining, not only in the community colleges but in many four-year schools as well. Undergraduates are choosing accountancy, business administration, medical technology, computer science, and technology, even as these fields undergo profound changes that render some skills obsolete and require of labor more versatility than at any time in recent memory.

The truth is, many educators are prone to follow paths suggested by the privatizers who have assiduously urged them to tailor the curriculum to the labor market and to the corporations that control it. They are surrendering larger portions of the curriculum to corporations, which, in return for faculty and administration collaboration, guarantee a steady flow of paying students. As the curriculum becomes defined by its commercial and industrial outcomes, some corporations get what they want—a narrowly trained work force—but the students are less free to explore wider options. Even as management claims that it wants more versatility and broader cultural knowledge in its professional and technical workforce, programs and courses that could provide the student with these qualifications continue to shrink because college administrators have read the political and the economic situation badly.

2

Until the 1930s, it was relatively rare for most students of working-class and rural origins to finish high school, and many who achieved it had general or vocational diplomas that did not qualify them for college. In fact, many students were stuck in the eighth grade and ended their school careers without entering high school. Thus, the pool of working-class and lower-middle-class students able to qualify for college admission was tiny. When my father graduated from a New York City high school in 1923, for example, few of his classmates hoped to enter college. Almost none had the money for private college tuition, and only a few had good-enough grades to qualify for New York's single tuition-free higher education institution, City College. My father entered New York University on a basketball scholarship, and only a small number of high school athletes were afforded similar opportunities elsewhere. He attended NYU for a year and mainly studied journalism, still coded today as a vocational program. As soon as he got an offer to work on a local newspaper, he quit.

By the 1920s, most states mandated school attendance until age sixteen, but many youths dropped out at fourteen, the minimum age for obtaining working papers, and finished their required school program at night. The Depression altered this situation for many students. Since, by the late 1920s, work was hard to find, many stayed in school who would have entered factories, transportation, or construction trades. During the Depression, young workers between ages sixteen and twenty-five had a significantly easier time in the job market than older workers. For this reason, although more students were completing high school, it remained the exception rather than the rule. With their parents unable to find jobs, often younger people who found work assumed the main responsibility for supporting their families. Not until the late 1950s did as many as half who entered high school graduate.

The growing number of high school graduates in the post–World War Two era is attributable to two distinct influences: the restoration of the family wage, which permitted parents to encourage their children to finish school rather than seek full-time employment, and the shortage of well-paying industrial and service jobs in the late 1950s and 1960s. In-

deed, by the late 1950s, politicians and other policymakers took note of
the emergence of youth gangs, the concomitant rise of petty crime, not
only in the cities but in the suburbs, resulting from the ubiquitous growth
of unemployment among youth. The problem was deemed so serious
that, years prior to the so-called antipoverty crusade of the 1960s, Congress passed "depressed areas" legislation. Among other provisions, this
program poured federal funds into road building and other job-creating
infrastructure projects in mining, textile, and farm areas, although it
benefited few in urban ghettoes and slums. Spurred by the Cold War–
inspired National Defense Education Act, the 1960s witnessed a dramatic increase in federal aid to education and to training.

By 1958 much of the astounding postwar boom was spent. In the
wake of the recessionary tendencies in the American economy, demonstrated by the 1958–59 and 1961–62 recessions and technologically
induced job shortages, educational and political authorities initiated a
campaign to urge youth to remain in school. The allusion in these campaigns to the growing unemployment among young workers was hardly
ambiguous, but consistent with American ideology, the new emphasis on
finishing high school was invariably linked to improved chances of land-
ing a good job. Furthermore, while joblessness among young people
transcended race and gender, social policy tended to focus on alleviating
black and Latino youth unemployment in an effort to forestall urban dis-
ruptions. But this solution served mainly to intensify racial hostility, giving credence to the charge that federal policy favored racial minorities to
the detriment of those coded as "white."

By the mid-1960s, as the expanded war economy generated by Vietnam gradually drew many experienced industrial workers back into relatively well paid jobs, the problem of youth unemployment had become
even more visible. Many observers believed the persistence of youth joblessness, which was typically twice the rate of unemployment in the general labor force (three or four times among black and Latino youth),
would prove "intractable" unless the government intervened to provide
young people with marketable skills. As a consequence, the federal government established antipoverty programs for virtually every major
urban black and Latino neighborhood in the country and, in the rural
agricultural and industrial areas, among white youth as well. But the
emphasis had shifted from job creation to education and training. Run

by social welfare professionals, particularly social workers, psychologists, and teachers, public and private nonprofit organizations provided tens of thousands of youths and a growing population of welfare recipients with a wide range of services. In Harlem and the Lower East Side of New York, on Chicago's South Side, in Oakland, Newark, and many other cities, these programs included literacy training, job training, and sometimes courses leading to high school diplomas. In very few cases did these agencies focus on creating jobs. In fact, the most notable effect of antipoverty programs was to have provided new employment opportunities for professionals, a growing army of "indigenous" administrators, noncredentialed social workers, and community organizers. Perhaps the most successful training programs were those for education and health paraprofessionals.

The basic assumption behind antipoverty programs was that youth unemployment and "welfare" dependency were produced by moral turpitude, by a culture of poverty that precluded a collective work ethic, and, in more liberal explanations, by the lack of education and training. Radical and left-liberal critics disputed these assumptions. According to their perspective, unemployment and underemployment—that many qualified people worked at low-paying jobs well below their abilities and credentials—was largely a structural feature of the economy, which for various reasons chronically produced fewer jobs than job seekers. Whether the argument was Keynesian or Marxist, there was more than enough evidence that, even in a period of postwar economic boom, the jobless rate remained greater than growth rates. Even in the 1960s, when many accepted the presumption of permanent boom, a small group of critics insisted that the effect of technological change, mergers and acquisitions, and capital flight would, at an accelerating rate, continue to destroy unionized and other well-paid factory jobs.

In fact, the greatest achievement of the antipoverty programs was not to solve youth joblessness, but to create a new black and Latino middle class. Many who were hired by the antipoverty agencies as counselors and low-level administrators found they needed credentials to move up the ladder to professional and managerial jobs. With few exceptions, they enrolled in education, public administration, social work, and liberal arts graduate and undergraduate programs and became the first generation of working-class minority students to attend institutions of mass higher education. By the 1970s and 1980s, their children were attending college in large numbers, joined by a new coterie of Vietnam War veterans and a relatively large number of urban high school graduates.

Several historical streams came together to drive expanded enrollments. In the first place, higher education had become a leading demand of the civil rights and feminist movements. The dramatic and highly publicized occupation of CUNY chancellor Albert Bowker's office by Latino and black students in 1969 was followed by similar actions in other cities, stimulating the implementation of open enrollment policies around the country, some of which had already been on the drawing boards. Colleges and universities were also under pressure to open their doors to the rush of new "unconventional" students, who in earlier periods would have been summarily rejected on either academic or financial grounds. The influx of older students was prompted by the rapidly expanding service labor force where credentials were required for many entry-level jobs and, as we have seen, by the relative decline of industrial jobs. Just as high schools had always provided a holding pen for the surplus labor force, postsecondary schools were now called upon to perform similar functions. The near open admissions policies of many state schools were supported by federal funds for student aid, school construction, and research grants. But higher education was enlisted as well to assume the costs of education and training of many occupations in the exploding public bureaucracies and knowledge industries. The corporations and public agencies that once shouldered these responsibilities were delighted to transfer them to mostly state-supported schools.

Thus, the vocationalization of higher education became a leading theme of the 1960s. But far from constituting a "new" policy, students' future employment had always been the primary mission of public schools, albeit one shrouded in the aura of the liberal arts. In order to accommodate what educational leaders perceived to be the practical demands of their new constituencies, they instituted thousands of undergraduate programs in social work, health careers, public administration, and management. In some instances, these were added to existing social science departments; in others, new departments and schools were added to colleges and universities and, in many cases, overwhelmed the traditional liberal arts.

In short, the irony of postwar higher education reform has been to swell the enrollments and expand faculty and physical plants just as all signs point to a systematic downgrading of education and learning. David Lavin and David Hyllegard have shown in their study of employment outcomes for CUNY graduates up to 1987 that associate's and bachelor's degrees are important for many who would otherwise have been condemned to a lower income by their lack of college credentials.[3] But although Lavin and Hyllegard have demonstrated that the CUNY degrees have been effective sources of cultural capital, this historical development tells us little about the relationship between higher income and the specific curriculum offered by the colleges. There is little doubt that academic credentials remain an important sorting device in a chronically oversupplied labor market, and that for most prospective candidates for administrative, professional, technical, and commercial positions it is better to have a degree than not to have one. In 1998 the Commerce Department reported that, in the previous year, bachelor's degree holders still earned about twice the annual incomes of those with only high school diplomas. And an advanced degree will, on the average, provide one and a half times the income of bachelor's degrees. The rising rate of graduation at all of these levels is bound to raise the ante on degree holders. The problem is, now that a postsecondary credential is rapidly replacing the high school diploma and the apprenticeship as a universal sign of minimum candidature, we are rapidly approaching the time when comparative advantages require one or more master's degrees, in some instances, even a Ph.D.

What do the credentials of higher education convey? Does a degree signal that the successful candidate commands wide knowledge of artistic, scientific, or political culture? Or is it a fair indicator of detailed knowledge in a specific field? In a buyer's market, the degree simplifies the employer's task by automatically disqualifying a large number of applicants. It also allows the remaining applicant pool to be differentiated according to the presumed value of their cultural capital, that is, measured and ranked by the status of the school from which the degree was earned, as opposed to by what the job seeker may actually know.

For example, while the basic requirement to practice law is to pass a bar examination—the same for Harvard and Podunk U graduates—not all attorneys who pass the bar are selected by large corporate law firms for the entry-level position of associate. The leading firms choose their associates from among applicants with degrees awarded by a very few schools and, from them, may select only those who are ranked by the *Law*

Review, signifying they ha⋅ ⋅ ⋅ ned the top of their class. With the production of attorneys saturating the market—except in the poorly paid, relatively small field of public interest or advocacy law—even middle-sized firms have their pick among mid-ranked and top graduates of the leading law schools. Many graduating attorneys from less well ranked institutions are scrambling for the remaining jobs and even face unemployment in some regions of the country. Similar evidence may be adduced for physicians, accountants, starting stockbrokers, and managers with advanced degrees in business. When the postsecondary degree becomes the norm, new hurdles appear that subvert its temporary advantage in the job markets.

From this perspective, the arguments for restoring standards reveal less about racism than about the declining value of higher education as cultural capital. This poses a challenge for education populists. They have demanded that the cultural capital that can be accumulated in postsecondary schools be available to working-class students, women, and minorities, but they have left unexamined the fact that higher education is an economic and cultural marker that retains its value only if it is a scarce commodity. It has taken more than fifty years for higher education to become the new educational norm. But as a normative degree, it has been progressively transformed into a minimum requirement rather than, in itself, a marketable credential. In light of the inevitable ranking of colleges and universities on the basis of criteria like research facilities, faculty reputations, endowment size, and position in the system of economic and cultural power, even if the academic system retains its mass character, it will not succeed in leveling the playing field.

What we can expect in the next several decades is that advanced degrees will replace the B.A. as the new standard for most good service and professional jobs. But in terms of the acquisition of critically appropriated knowledge and intellectual capacities, what, exactly, do advanced credentials signify? In many cases very little, for most graduate education is a type of boot camp. Even more than undergraduate schooling, students are there to learn the tools of their trade. If the now hidden, now open curriculum of undergraduate education is job preparation, in graduate schools there is no pretense. Even in academic disciplines in the sciences and the humanities, whether the student managed to obtain some general education or not is irrelevant. In graduate school, students are expected to undergo an apprenticeship that, in its broad sense, entails learning the vocabularies of the field, its latest fashions, and in the humanities and social sciences, learning how to write a book, treatise, or "study" on a specific topic.

So where does this leave Diane Ravitch and other critics concerned with overcoming the deficits of our three-tier system? Looking to some European education systems, they wish to impose standards as a meritocratic basis for school admissions. While merit systems do not pretend that all people are equal, they do claim that theirs is the only sure method of ensuring equality of opportunity. Presumably, if national standards were to be adopted at all levels of schooling, by the time students entered postsecondary education, only those who had demonstrated excellence at earlier stages would be admitted. The state might establish vocational and technical schools for others. In this way, the value of the academic college degree would be restored because only those who deserved to attend college would be afforded the opportunity. And those who did not make the grade would have only themselves to blame—provided elementary and secondary schools taught an identical curriculum, had the same level of funding regardless of the economic position of families of students, and paid similar salaries to teachers so that competition between districts would lose its economic dimension.

In a meritocratic system of higher education, all schools would not be equal; students would gain access to research institutions strictly on grades and examinations. Four-year liberal arts and technical colleges would be available to those students who met lesser criteria, but in any case, a minimum standard of competence would be presumed. Although in most European countries movement between the tiers is limited, U.S. state policy would specify conditions for transfer in order to provide incentives for excellence and, equally important, to ensure that society would not be deprived of talented people whose earlier academic records were less than luminous.

But there is a glitch of no small proportions in this scenario. Virtually all European universities are state run; the few private schools have been permitted to stand as a concession to the Catholic Church. Moreover, except in Great Britain, where recent Conservative governments have instituted tuition, most European universities are tuition-free. Students pay only the normal costs associated with participation: books, room and board, and most important, deferral of the income they would have earned if they had entered the labor force as full-time workers. In contrast, American higher education began as an assortment of church-sponsored private colleges, which, because they became the customary finishing schools of the business and intellectual elites, were never displaced by public universities. They require tuition and, privately run, are free to select their students on a variety of criteria beyond scholarship, including nepotism and cronyism. Until fairly recently, some were even permitted by law to select students on the basis of race, religious belief, and gender. Discriminatory legal barriers against both minorities and women have come down, and in the last quarter century some leading universities have tried to mitigate income-restrictive practices by raising more scholarship money, tightening admission requirements, and undertaking minority recruitment. But, however significant, these measures cannot erase the bare fact that privatization is a barrier against the creation of a meritocratic system.

For meritocratic objectives to be reached, America would have to adopt national standards at every level of education, as well as a progressive tax system that would equalize school funding. Public authority would have to purchase leading private educational institutions and abolish the tuition system, which enforces differential opportunities based on the ability to pay. Under these conditions, although populists would remain discontented because an educational hierarchy would be retained and, depending on the definition of standards, a large number of students would still be excluded from higher education, many of the privileges of wealth and position would be somewhat mitigated.

The prospects of instituting a meritocracy in our education system are as realistic as the populist hope of reversing the devaluing effects of its current inequities. True, despite the fierce attacks on public higher education, the fact that virtually anybody with a high school diploma can get into some college may not change. But the likelihood that upon successful completion, this credential will level the playing field upon which to compete for good jobs is nil. Under conditions of scarcity, corporations and other bureaucracies require that universities remain efficient sorting devices to limit the pool of possible choices as much as they draw commercially useful knowledge from university and corporate-sponsored research. And, as I have argued, as college attendance has become common practice rather than a privilege reserved for the few, the role of higher education as an effective means of keeping a substantial section of the labor force off the market for full-time employment is bound to grow.

3

The standards/access war comes at a time when good jobs in America are disappearing. There is still a lot of work but few jobs, if by that term we mean steady employment carrying pension, health, vacation, and other benefits. Forget the talk about how the economy is humming, about how the stock market is doing, about the official jobless rate still hovering at 5 percent a year. On the street, almost every young person and a mounting army of middle-aged victims of corporate downsizing know that talk of "careers" and secure professional, technical, and managerial jobs is constantly undermined by layoffs. In 1998, as the media crowed about relatively low official joblessness, seven hundred thousand employees who were among the best-paid in America were handed pink slips by some of the largest Fortune 500 corporations. Most were caught in the vise of mergers and acquisitions, themselves caused by the world economic crunch—overproduction, sagging profits, and job-destroying technological change. But, perhaps equally important, American capitalism has entered the era—one hesitates to call it an epoch—of the normalization of temporary, part-time, and contingent employment.

True, many of those laid off are rehired by the same company as "consultants," a term that has come to signify that they are paid by the hour, day, or week and have no benefits such as pensions and health insurance. After six months or a year of looking, others may find work in their fields, but they are often less well paid than in their previous positions, and in smaller companies whose prospects are more uncertain. Many older employees find work in retail services where incomes average about three hundred dollars a week. There are thus grounds for believing that, like the spotted owl, the good job is an endangered species in most walks of American economic life.

But as in the academic labor market, one of the salient outcomes of college and university schooling is to expand the pool of qualified, credentialed knowledge labor, even though today most fields are chronically oversupplied and hence undervalued. Seen in this context, raising the hurdles of admission might eventually lead to labor shortages in some fields and would improve the cash value of professional and technical degrees. The problem is not that a college degree will not, for some time to come, improve the relative economic position of its recipients. Its benefits are still obvious in an era when wages for a growing proportion of factory workers and for uncredentialed service employees are sinking, in some cases, to near minimum levels. The problem is the comparative advantages of postsecondary schooling for the student and her family, at a time when its economic rewards do not adequately compensate for its costs. As tuition and other expenses for all manner of schools soar and real incomes—money compensation measured by the inflation rate—remain stationary, even graduate schools are beginning to experience the enrollment squeeze.

Take a few examples. In major metropolitan regions, entry-level social workers with master's degrees earn about $30,000 a year on the average, while those with bachelor's degrees start at $22,000. So far, the credential vindicates the value of more schooling. But since the cost of full-time attendance at graduate school is, in many instances, in excess of $30,000 a year for a two-year program, the successful graduate faces a huge debt accumulation unless salaries move up rapidly in her first few years of employment. She may owe as much as $90,000 without an immediate prospect of earning enough to pay it back and pay rent at the same time. For this reason, facing labor shortages of fully qualified staff and budget cuts that make it impossible to raise starting salaries, many institutions have taken to hiring less-qualified people to perform direct services to clients. Pressured by the imperative of paying back student loans, more social workers with master's degrees are becoming supervisors after just a few years on the line and many never have enough experience to assist line workers to perform their jobs well.

In the 1990s, the cost of a five-year program of medical school and internship is about a quarter million dollars. Today most newly credentialed physicians have only about a 33 percent chance of ever owning their own practice. For the two-thirds who earn salaries rather than fees, paying back student loans has become a prolonged process. Even though medical school enrollments have not declined in absolute terms, the economic costs of remaining salaried labor has discouraged many from entering the profession. So enrollments have stagnated. At the same time, facing increased job competition, some engineering schools have closed and the remaining middle-ranked institutions are scrambling for students. Whereas in the 1970s and 1980s there were five jobs for every certified public accountant, by the late 1990s demand had caught up with supply. In 1998, there was one job for each qualified candidate. As a result of mergers, the largest firms in the field require fewer employees and therefore select only graduates of the leading schools for entry-level positions. Even middle-sized firms are merging and the number of self-employed accountants continues to shrink. In the largest firms in medicine, law, and accountancy, 5 percent of associates will be selected for partnership. Meanwhile the firm gets some of the most dedicated years of a young professional's life. She works sixty to seventy hours a week and does not hesitate to give up weekends to the job. For the 95 percent who leave after five years, most will land on their feet, but almost invariably they will not enjoy the same income and prestige as they did in the large firm.

If what I have argued in the first section of this book is right, the end of an academic system devoted to providing masses of qualified labor for corporate America is near. In the foreseeable future a limited number of schools will continue to perform this function, more or less efficiently. As for the rest, many institutions are educational bureaucracies in search of a mission that might justify their collective existence. As mass schooling comes under increasing pressure from the bean counters and educational conservatives, some earlier formulations may rise to the surface. The classical expectation—enunciated eloquently by Thomas Jefferson, Frederick Douglass, John Dewey, and more recently, by the civil rights and feminist movements—that in addition to economic opportunity, education may help usher in a more democratic society has, for the time being, passed from the debate. In the vanishing, what will have been lost is a critical citizenry capable of governing itself. And the specifically *academic* mission of higher education—to produce and transmit knowledge that helps society by enriching the self—already relegated to the back burner, is rapidly being consigned to history by the corporatization of American colleges and universities. As I have argued, knowledge production and transmission must now justify itself in terms of its economic value or risk oblivion.

But the discourse informing the current debate about higher education remains on the surface of things because, in the American way, it tends to address symptoms and not underlying political and ideological currents and economic forces. What remains to be asked is, Have all schools submitted to the prevailing zeitgeist, or are there places of resistance? Are there currently any alternatives to the current direction of higher education, which, as we have seen, increasingly treats students and their families as customers and subordinates the academic programs of colleges and universities to the marketplace? Or must we pick up the threads of a fallen loom and reweave the garment anew? The next chapters address two overarching questions: What are the prevailing trends in the undergraduate curriculum? And if learning, rather than training and political and ideological socialization, were to become the mission of American higher education, what would it look like?

WHAT IS TAUGHT, WHAT IS LEARNED?

CHAPTER 6

1

UNTIL THE 1980s, the focus of educational policy on questions of access overwhelmed curriculum issues. But the rapid growth of institutions of postsecondary education has posed once again the problem of what the missions of the universities and colleges are. Some have answered the question by framing the debate in terms of "mission differentiation," a phrase that tacitly acknowledges that liberal education is not for everybody and that some institutions should define themselves, frankly, as elevated trade schools. Even for those schools that lay claim to the liberal intellectual tradition, the insistent pressure from many quarters to define themselves as sites of job preparation has, as we shall see, clouded their mission and their curriculum.

Perhaps the most urgent questions today concern whether the academic system has a genuine role in providing the space for learning, whether or not its curricula are useful to the corporate order. Is a universal liberal education a legitimate goal in a pluralistic society? And, if so, who will provide it and in what does it consist? In different ways, both traditional liberal and radical educational perspectives are based on the critical appropriation of the main currents of human knowledge. By "critical appropriation," I mean the process by which students acquire the means to challenge—if not reverse—the technical divisions that fragment society as well as the higher learning, and perhaps most important, by which they are encouraged to become critical intellectuals prepared to swim against the current. When we inquire into the mission of higher education, two more questions emerge: Who can get into college, and what is taught when they arrive? These questions cut to the heart of what institutions of higher education purport to be doing and with how their mission statements square with what they are actually doing. In the past two decades, the weight of the debate has thus shifted to the issue of what is to be taught and, to a lesser extent, how?

Once the curriculum of colleges and universities reflected the assumption that the "liberal arts" were the appropriate foundation for all students, those in technology and the sciences, as well as those in the humanities. It was taken for granted that only in the upper division of undergraduate education should the student devote her energies to specialization. But for the last twenty years, the eclecticism manifested in such practices as "distribution requirements" has drawn criticism from all sides. Those who follow Allan Bloom contend that universities, at least those in the "elite" ranks, should abandon the effort to expose students to a smattering of diverse knowledges and, instead, return to the great texts of Western civilization. On the other end, the multiculturalists have excoriated the institutions for essentially ignoring subaltern (that is, subordinate and marginalized) cultures in core or distribution requirements and for failing to achieve what has now become known as "diversity" in the university.

When administrators and liberals and conservatives in the professoriate decided to remedy the "crisis" they perceived in the undergraduate curriculum, neither Bloom's call for a return to the sacred texts nor a more global understanding of processes of social and cultural transformation framed their intentions. Ironically, at most universities, these contentious intellectual debates have had little impact on the reversal of 1960s reforms that sometimes abolished distribution requirements, not to mention core curriculum, to a new "coherent" and "rigorous" regime and an "integrated" species of "general education." There is nothing in the elite institutions, any more than in third-tier schools, that points the way to a genuine revival of intellectual culture. Nor, indeed, do recent changes promote the formation of a sphere in which the middle class—still the basic constituency of these institutions—may develop the habit of critical thought so necessary for participation in public life as it has emerged in the last quarter century. And although curriculum reformers have failed to prepare students to face relatively new issues such as globalization, immigration, and cultural conflict, it cannot be said they are bent on reasserting the intellectual hegemony of traditional Western culture, as Bloom would have it. Only parts of the core curriculum are still derived from conventional academic disciplines. In fact, the core curriculum "movement" may be described as the elevation of incoherence to an educational principle, marked by the imposition of requirements that remain, in almost all cases, without intellectual justification.

2

Beginning with Harvard's adoption of a new core curriculum in 1979, curriculum reforms in major universities can be seen as a reaction to the changes ushered in by the student upsurge of the 1960s. Amid the tumult of antiwar protest, perhaps one of the most enduring changes on colleges campuses was that administration and faculty were forced to accommodate student demands for curricular liberty—the right to choose their own course of study. Institutions ran the gamut, from the "extreme" of Brown, which lacked a core curriculum, indeed, lacked any requirements at all, to the relatively rigorous program of Columbia University. But by the mid-1980s, most of the three hundred or so leading schools, and many in the third tier as well, had reinstituted required courses in the first two years of college. From the viewpoint of faculty and administration, the goal was to overcome "the fragmentation of knowledge, the loss of shared values and an increasing emphasis on professional specialization." According to a special group assigned at UCLA to revise the general educational requirements, "A general education curriculum should introduce the sources, assumptions and methods central to distinct fields of inquiry while encouraging courses and possible connections among those different fields. General education courses should also restrengthen basic intellectual skills, among them writing, quantitative reasoning, critical thinking, and information literacy." The overarching goal is to address "strains in our national culture" by enabling students to become "well-educated."[1]

By the consensus of educators and college administrators, the University of Chicago was the great exception among leading research universities in the gallop toward specialization and professionalization of the undergraduate curriculum. According to stubborn myth, its faculty and administration had resisted the relaxing of requirements, especially in the study of language and of classical, humanistic texts. But Allan Bloom, a Chicago professor on the Committee for Social Thought, disputed the idea that the Chicago tradition of focusing on the classical texts of Western civilization was in any way intact at the university. Bloom's *Closing of the American Mind* (1987) was published in the midst of what he considered a bowdlerization of the great core curriculum, built around the "great" books, that had been Chicago's claim to one of the few world-class undergraduate programs in the United States. Bloom's attempt may, in part, be understood as commentary on what he perceived to be Chicago's descent from the stern, rigorous course of study that Chancellor Robert Hutchins had initiated in the 1930s. Although at the time of its publication, Bloom's book was viewed chiefly against what came to be known as the "multicultural" curriculum—the rise of women's, Afro-American, and cultural studies programs, which Bloom viewed as so much populist drivel—this was not his main concern. The more pertinent target was the conception of liberal education as a Chinese menu of more or less disconnected courses masquerading as "breadth"—a student's brief sojourn with the arts and humanities before getting on to her "real" education, learning a marketable trade.

Bloom counted his own school, Chicago, among the philistines, for, among other reasons, its faculty and many of its students had displaced the privileged study of philosophy in order to pursue the social sciences. There is little question that, despite a remnant of the old commitment to sacred texts of the West, the university had slid quite far down toward rank mediocrity, at least by Bloom's classical lights. He ascribed Chicago's fall from intellectual grace to a long-term trend, rather than to the vicissitudes of the student and other social movements. As a Chicago undergraduate in the 1940s, Bloom tells us, he was exposed to the pernicious influence of Germans, some of whom were refugees from Hitler, and to Americans who had been prewar sojourners in Berlin and other cities in the worship of German thought. For Bloom, the main culprits in the pervasive dissolution of the faith in Western values were Marx, Freud, Nietzsche, and Heidegger. Also implicated was historicism, an intellectual movement that saw history not as the story of great, eternal ideas and values, or of the bold interventions of "great men," but situated events and knowledge and its meaning within the social environment. What united these otherwise diverse thinkers, and their followers, was their challenge to received wisdom. Bloom's professors "did not tend to be philosophic and did not dig back into the sources of the new language and categories they were using. . . . They were very much addicted to abstractions and generalizations." Bloom pined for a return to eternal "values" and to reason, a combination he asserted had ended, at least in German philosophy and social theory, with Hegel.[2] What remained was an appeal to the irrational, an intellectual tendency that, he implies, has left higher learning in disarray.

That Marx and Freud, to cite two of Bloom's main villains, saw themselves as continuing the Enlightenment questioning of all past knowledge in the search for new conceptions of life and mind did not impress Bloom, any more than the corps of conservative educators who have followed in his wake. In fact, neither Bloom nor his followers are friendly to critical theory or, for that matter, to science. Their conception of the proper ends of education remains deeply religious. They ascribe the decline and fall of civilization, not to the absence of a genuine, broadly engaged dialogue concerning society's present and future prospects, but to the dissolution of the academy's dedication to the monuments of Western culture. Bloom would rigorously exclude any ideas that point toward the disenchantment of the world—the "debunking" sciences of sociology and anthropology and, of course, of political economy, but also secular knowledges of all sorts that engage with the world rather than attempting to impose eternal forms on it.

If Bloom had not declared the last two centuries a moral disaster, and had confined himself to the statement that schools were engaged in promoting an educational concept that "impoverishes students' souls," his proposals would not have provoked intense controversy. But his cultural imagination was imbued with the profoundly undemocratic premises of the platonic "dialogue," whose premise is that we know only one truth, that of an unalterable human nature. For Bloom the task of education is to help the self discover its own nature by means of an intellectual encounter with the best that has been thought and said, in the first place, by Plato and Shakespeare, and to embark on the quest for our "essential being." That quest must eliminate, as much as possible, the "accidental" and contingent in our lives.[3]

The claims of those who take the intellectual standpoint of marginal and excluded groups and their critique of the mainstream curriculum—both the "core" and distribution versions—are in origin not at all trivial. In their most ambitious expression, critics of a curriculum that focuses, almost exclusively, on the mainstream texts of the Western cultural tradition not only argue against the exclusion of blacks, women, gays, workers, and other social categories from history, literature, and social and cultural theory, but challenge prevailing interpretations on the basis of these exclusions. In this view, history is not made by "great men" or by leading institutional actors alone. The actions of ordinary people are just as significant in structuring societies. The antebellum slave revolts, struggles for women's rights, working-class upsurge and resistance to corporate power in the nineteenth and twentieth centuries—in short, the culture and politics of the everyday lives of subordinate groups—are crucial to the configuration of social relations. Their movements and their cultures alter the strategies of dominant groups and, in the twentieth century, have radically altered the nature of economic, political, and cultural power. In sophisticated versions of this thesis, history is a mutually determining interaction between dominant and subordinate groups.

Concomitantly, cultural differences among subordinated groups and between their cultural formations and that of the dominant culture are significant sources of solidarity as well as of conflict. Solidarity manifests itself, for example, in the practice of making native languages the lingua franca of everyday life and treating English as a second, public language. And the novels, poems, music films, paintings, and other works of art springing from subordinated groups should not be viewed as "minor" or "genre" forms but as complex, indirect, and important aspects of world culture. It can be argued that black and Latino forms are the overwhelming influence in, indeed in many ways define, American popular music and that the films of black filmmakers are both part of the Hollywood system and independent of it. That minority cultural works must operate under conditions of integration as well as exhibiting difference is hardly open to question. What is in question is whether it is still possible to construct a canon or to narrate histories absent the struggles and representations of subaltern people.

To be sure, despite the massive attack on affirmative action in colleges and universities and the relative decline of minority enrollments in some elite institutions, "multiculturalism" and "diversity," the new euphemism for minority hiring, remain watchwords for faculties seeking to broaden the purview of their departments and disciplines. For example, traditional departments may hire black and women faculty to facilitate the development of programs that cannot hire on their own. The refurbished African American studies programs at Harvard, NYU, and Princeton, like the attempt of the Columbia administration to restore its sullied image in black and Latino communities by hiring some prominent black and Latino faculty, signify the institutionalization of one of the more significant gains of the freedom movement. Similarly, dozens of women have become academic stars in the push for diversity in faculty hiring. While their salaries do not, in general, match those of their male counterparts, some have made powerful inroads, even at the high and middle levels of academic administration.

Whatever its virtues on other grounds, we must revisit the intellectual merits of the so-called multicultural curriculum movements. Given the sordid history of academic exclusions, the development of women's, African American, Latino, Asian, and ethnic studies represents more than the fulfillment of political demands with places and jobs in academic precincts, for the impact of multiculturalism has been to produce entirely new space for subaltern approaches to knowledge. But its existence through the academic system and its substantial achievements as well as banalities do not adequately engage its critics. In particular, conservatives call attention to "dumbing down," to the "flattening of discourse," and, most notoriously, to what Allan Bloom calls a "closing of the American mind" as a direct legacy of the 1960s student revolt against all sorts of established authority.

Bloom's prescription to reverse the decline is to return to the quasi-theological study of sacred texts, ending with Hegel, a canon that drastically curtails, even eliminates, an examination of the most world-shaking ideas of the nineteenth and twentieth centuries. Moreover, he would de-canonize critical theory, which, in the last instance, presupposes scientific skepticism, and would restore the study of the "authentic values" abandoned by the "bad" universities of his own postwar youth. One might debate whether the last sixty years of mass higher education should be canceled, especially for the elite schools, whose task, under Bloom's directive, would be to form and preserve the ideal of a class of intellectual priests, and perhaps mandarins as well.

But paradoxically—as Lawrence Levine retorts—there can be no question of offering multiculturalism, diversity, and other democratic innovations as evidence that the American mind has, in fact, been opened. It may be argued to the contrary that, thirty years after multiculturalism's more radical emanations, many if not most, of its academic programs have been confined to two distinct corridors. One track has been assimilated into the disciplinary hegemony of the academic system, by constructing a canon, forming professional associations, and establishing departments, majors, and advanced degree programs. The other makes the multicultural curriculum into a "politics" with its own intellectual apparatus. Its leading ideas are appropriated from an understanding of Marxist theory that holds "standpoint" to be the basis of knowledge, at least in the human sciences, though some philosophers have argued for its application in the natural sciences as well.

A few works stand as models of subaltern studies in seeing black and women's history in the perspective of world history, plumbing the political economy and cultural depths of social oppression. I can cite as examples Paul Gilroy's *Black Atlantic,* Martin Bernal's *Black Athena,* Orlando Patterson's early work *Slavery and Social Death,* and W. E. B. Du Bois's great effort to rewrite the history of the most tragic, but significant event in nineteenth-century American history, *Black Reconstruction.* In the feminist literature one finds Charlotte Perkins Gilman's pioneering *Women and Economics,* Shulamith Firestone's bold *Dialectic of Sex,* and Nancy Hartsock's *Money, Sex, and Power,* which attempt to offer a feminist historical materialism. But these are notable exceptions, for in general multiculturalism as a both a slogan and an intellectual practice has signified integration and subordination into the prevailing disciplinary construction of American academic knowledge. On the whole, the movement no longer constitutes an alternative perspective on Western civilization and its history.

It may thus be argued that by mainstreaming themselves, women's, ethnic, and African American studies have become ordinary academic departments and programs. But an unintended consequence of "normalization" is that they have been placed directly in the line of fire. Since, in most institutions, "programs" do not hire their own faculty but must make their candidate acceptable to one of the disciplines, program directors find themselves defending their own academic integrity. What is worse, in the interest of getting their faculty on board, they must enter into the inevitable compromises common to all politics; frequently, they hire people to please their adversaries. But, in the main, their relatively weak academic position often makes them intellectually less daring. As a result, with the exception of programs with access to sufficient resources to hire high-profile academic stars, many of these programs have become less attractive to students. When students are not persuaded that they must choose pre-med, pre-law, and business majors, many prefer conventional disciplinary majors on the ground that they offer better opportunities for eventual academic jobs.

The second corridor comprises a reduced form of radical subaltern studies. Instead of placing oppression in the context of social structure and world history, the intellectual project is to link diverse cultural and political identities to intellectual paradigms perceived as oppositional to the disciplines. Because most philosophical, social, and cultural knowledges, as well as the natural sciences, are conceived as reflecting established ideas whose purpose is entirely ideological, students are advised to construe the past and social relations in images of exploitation, oppression, and domination. In the interest of overturning canonical texts, which perpetuate exclusions by obliterating popular protest and marginalized discourses, scholarly movements called "history from below," "subaltern studies," "postmodernism," and similar approaches have made considerable headway in the humanities. They have succeeded in rewriting history and in challenging psychology, literary theory, and philosophy to address their modernist presuppositions. In some fields, until the beginning of the 1990s backlash, it was no longer possible to maintain scholarly silence concerning what workers, blacks, and women contributed to history, politics, and culture.

But in the course of setting their collective shoulders against the wheel of academia, identity intellectual politics has succeeded only in creating a new set of mutually exclusive oppositions. Consequently, in some quarters "Western" civilization and culture are read as having little or nothing of value to offer present and future generations. The cost of such corrections has been considerable. Conservatives are right to insist that thoroughgoing skepticism and its twin, radical relativism and historicism, both of which vehemently deny both the possibility of objectivity in knowledge and transhistorical "truth," leave the intellect bereft, not only of certainty, but also of its bearings. As working-class, black, and women's history and cultural criticism have abandoned the point of view of the totality, that is, ceased to situate subaltern histories and cultures within a social structure, they have become genre histories and criticism. Often standpoint theorists and postmodern philosophers disdain dialogue; their dogmatism mirrors that of their adversaries. That the conservative project is to restore faith in what they describe as "common sense," "irrefutable" ideas, and tradition, I have no doubt. But to posit its mirror image is no solution. So the problem is whether one can imagine and, on the basis of these speculations, specify a radical intellectual project that comprehends historicity without falling into the pit of relativism; that welcomes the new without joining modern scientific thought's studied ignorance of its own history; that is prepared to concede that its perspective, however valid, is incomplete; and that supports student choice, but does not submit to the commodification of knowledge or require "usefulness" as a justification for study.

Whatever one may think of Bloom's prescription, or his critique of elite education, it is difficult to ignore his most important contribution to the debate: his analysis of the heart of the undergraduate education. In its 1997–98 catalog, the University of Chicago reaffirms its desire to shun "fragmentation" by resisting "the confinement of inquiry to any particular department yet offering "the finest scholarship that specialization can bring." In other words, even Chicago's famous core curriculum has devolved into incoherence. Proclaiming the pedagogical values of "breadth," "depth," and "independence," the university's core includes general education sequences in biological and physical sciences, humanities and social sciences. And, as a concession to students, it has a "New Collegiate Division" whose "role is to provide a place for diverse collegiate experiments unconstrained by those boundaries that separate the several departments and divisions of knowledge [by] cut[ting] across the familiar academic lines." Needless to say, only the humanities division promises to "open students' lives to significant human problems and pleasures while sharpening their perceptions and their capacities for analytical thinking." But, consistent with the skills orientation of a large number of core curricula, the university quickly assures prospective students that its courses are "designed to enhance careful reading, analysis, writing and argument" and to "train" in one of thirty languages.

Yet, as attractively eclectic as it has tried to portray itself, even the relatively comprehensive and rigorous core of the University of Chicago has proven incapable of resisting what a 1998 *New York Times* article termed "the winds of change." Facing sharp competition from other universities, whose dedication to rigor is mostly talk, by the late 1990s Chicago was having trouble recruiting students. According to the *New York Times* report, "Partly to make the university more attractive to high school seniors, and to make it seem less of a grind, it is reducing its core curriculum and expanding its recreation and service areas." "I don't know how many students we can attract if we go after those who only seek the life of the mind," said a new vice-president hired "to improve marketing and recruitment." Facing relatively high dropout and transfer rates, the university's president, Hugo F. Sonnenschein, declared that the university was trying to get in step with what he termed "commodification and marketing in higher education." He admitted these trends "are unmistakable today and we can't jolly dance along and not pay attention to them." After a series of "bruising sessions," during which it was suggested that the number of required courses be cut from twenty-one to nine in order to give students greater opportunities to choose electives, the faculty agreed to reduce requirements to fifteen or eighteen courses, "depending on how the foreign language requirement gets worked out." And the president told a reporter that, in order to comply with student and parent expectations, the university was improving its placement services, building a new swimming pool and sports center, and improving its volunteer program, among other reforms. Yet not all students were happy with the changes. One student ruefully observed "If you lose Chicago, I don't know what you have left."[4]

Judging from the catalogs, reports, and "mission statements" of a dozen of its competitors, not much. Chicago was the pinnacle of liberal education in U.S. research universities. Only some four-year elite schools like Hampshire, Bard, and a few other colleges even attempt to match its focus, at least with respect to the humanities. As to the others, from the University of California schools and those in the Big Ten to the Ivies such as Harvard and Pennsylvania, the core admittedly represents little more than a simulacrum of a liberal education. Perhaps only Columbia remains committed to offering a core curriculum grounded in the connection between canonical books and "Western civilization." But while Columbia's curriculum is relatively coherent and demanding, the problem is how the texts are treated, how civilization is construed. Few professors capture the irony of Gandhi's response to a reporter's question, "What do you think of Western civilization?" To which Gandhi is said to have replied, "It would be a good idea." In most classrooms, Plato and other sacred texts are mostly treated with reverence rather than critical scrutiny. Yet according to one student, the forty-credit core curriculum in literature, a philosophically oriented civilization sequence, music and art histories have small classes and, especially in literature, are discussion seminars based on close textual readings. In recent years, as the university has admitted more students to its college program, students complain that some instructors teach the core in the lecture format.

Since Harvard is often held up as the standard in undergraduate education and, as we have seen, initiated the new emphasis on the core in undergraduate curriculum, let us look more closely at its much-imitated version as spelled out in its 1979–80 catalog: "The philosophy of the Core Curriculum rests on the conviction that every Harvard graduate should be broadly educated." To this end, the core "does not define intellectual breadth as the mastery of a set of Great Books, or the digestion of a specific quantum of information, or the surveying of current knowledge in [a] certain field but, instead, [seeks] to introduce students to the major approaches to knowledge in areas that the faculty considers indispensable to undergraduate education." Harvard goes on to define the core as chiefly methodological: "It aims to show what kinds of knowledge and what forms of inquiry exist in these areas, how different means of analysis are acquired, and how they are used and what their value is."

It is not difficult to discern the debt of this educational philosophy to John Dewey's pragmatism, for one of the leading precepts of Dewey's "reconstruction of philosophy" was to emphasize method over substance. This outlook has informed, if not determined, much of what goes on in the teaching and practice of the social and natural sciences and has had its effect as well on literature, historiography, and philosophy.[5] Students are admonished to concentrate on the "how" of learning, to understand methods of "inquiry," to disdain speculation, and to put in question the idea of "substance" as such. Put another way, a good education tends to be construed within a framework of instrumental rationality and formalism. In this context, we are encouraged to digest, not knowledge, but techniques of research. Hence the invocation to the student to master "skills" such as quantitative reasoning and writing.

In 1989, ten years after its core philosophy was written, Harvard made further abridgments in the curriculum in favor of procedure, still evident in the 1998–99 version of its catalog:

> The Faculty of Arts and Sciences offers undergraduates a wide range of courses to satisfy individual objectives and interests. In defining the requirements for the Bachelor of Arts and the Bachelor of Science degrees the Faculty has sought to accommodate those objectives and interests and, at the same time, to establish a framework for study at the College that ensures involvement with important areas of general knowledge [the Core requirement]. In addition, students must demonstrate competence in certain skills reflective of the complex demands of modern society [the quantitative reasoning, writing, and foreign language requirements] and achieve a satisfactory level of performance in their work.

The satisfaction of requirements is designated in part, by a letter grade in eight of ten areas of the core curriculum, comprising two history, two science, and three literature courses, as well as one course each in social analysis, moral reasoning, and foreign cultures. Depending on the student's choice, two areas corresponding to their concentration are exempt.

The Harvard program purports to balance student interests with the faculty's conviction that such areas as "moral reasoning" correspond to a well-rounded liberal education and that one course in "social analysis" is sufficient to prepare non–social science students for the "complex demands of modern society." One can imagine the negotiations necessary to come up with these requirements at the faculty committees and faculty senate of the university. Such arguments are often bitter, and as with all cores, the outcome an unsatisfactory compromise among the contending disciplines. In none of the documents I have seen are the various components of the core and their corollary, the "skills" components, justified on intellectual grounds. Rather, they are presented as self-evident, equivalent elements of a well-rounded curriculum. Nor is the much-invoked criterion "coherence" explained. Needless to say, there is no attempt to justify, whether on the basis of learning theory or of educational philosophy, the choice of domains, except on the criterion of comprehensiveness or breadth. Taken for granted, and left unexamined, is the nineteenth-century German understanding of division of academic labor, in which knowledge is segmented into natural, social, literary, and arts domains and subdivided by convention into disciplines. And the idea that the student is best served by a sampling of the various disciplines, to which a skills menu has been added, is never questioned.

Why, for example, should the non-science student be required to take courses in "quantitative reasoning"? Granting that the sciences and the social sciences are largely quantitative, if not in their concepts then in their respective methods, are math and statistics fundamental for a "good" education for a prospective artist or literary critic, except as a means of socializing the student into the prevailing culture of our society? Even if so, do we really require math "skills" when computational instruments such as computers and calculators can easily provide whatever information the student might desire? For the sake of this discussion, I am not necessarily rejecting quantitative reasoning as a "core" knowledge, any more than one might challenge "information literacy" or literature. The question I am asking goes to coherence, the avowed goal of integrated learning, and to the underlying philosophy of the core.

The debate about what should be taught and what should be left out almost never asks whether the concept of "breadth" has pedagogical or intellectual validity. Is math taught as a series of algorithms, that is, procedurally, or is it taught conceptually? One might insist, for example, that a grasp of fundamental principles of number, of the aesthetics and philosophy of mathematics and the underlying logic of its wide application to human affairs, is vital for a good education and may be more apposite than learning a series of procedures for solving esoteric problems. In which case, what may be important is to understand how different cultures have addressed number and computation—for example, Greek, Egyptian, and Sumerian approaches. Why, for example, did the Sumerians use the number 60 rather than 0 as a base number, and what were the consequences of this choice? Does the math sequence include learning about the social imperative that things be quantifiable in order to predict their behavior and control their movements? Or is math treated as a reified object, independent of its own philosophical and theoretical premises, let alone its social uses and historical foundations? Almost no conversation about these issues takes place when quantitative reasoning is automatically incorporated into the core. The same might be asked of its other components.

The educational reform that reintroduced a fairly heavy sequence of requirements into the undergraduate curriculum was only peripherally motivated by concern for learning. Its real concerns lay in another direction. The Harvard core is a case in point. Compared to Chicago's fading commitment to a liberal education, which in principle still places "reading" close to, if not directly at the heart of, the core, Harvard's twenty-year-old educational reform is, at the bottom, profoundly ensconced in instrumental reason. Consistent with perceived student interests, it aims, perhaps, to help them address society's demands for a skilled, flexible labor force. The term "flexible" refers to preparation in the *approaches* to knowledge acquisition rather than a set of great books, which, because of their impracticality, might constitute an obstacle to fitting in to our rapidly changing and increasingly complex society. The educated student who chooses management, law, and other business-related fields such as accountancy or economics must be able to attend an opening of an exhibit, the opera, or a classical music concert with a visiting client and be able to have an intelligent conversation about these events. For there is little doubt that what one gets from an elite school that is generally not available for the rest is a portfolio of essential cultural skills that have practical value for those headed to the corporate, professional, and public bureaucracies.

Not unexpectedly, most schools that have submitted to the core curriculum have emulated Harvard, not Chicago or St. John's of Annapolis, which have traditionally pursued the "great books" approach. Needless to say, the recent core movement has completely overcome decisions many schools made in the 1960s and 1970s to reduce or completely eliminate the core. In fact, at Harvard and at the earliest of its emulators, Brooklyn, with eight to ten courses of core requirements in two years, in addition to ten to twelve courses of the thirty-six credit major, not to mention a minor, and miscellaneous requirements like physical and health education, students are fortunate if they manage to squeeze in a year's worth of electives. In some disciplines, notably the sciences, technologies, and the social sciences, the student is frequently encouraged, or coerced, to take "methods" courses beyond requirements or correlated courses in another discipline in order to enhance her skills, further reducing electives to just a few courses, or none.

One clue to the instrumental orientation of core curricula in major universities is their universal privileging of "skills" acquisition. As we saw in the case of UCLA, most include "information literacy" among the basic skills, alongside language learning, writing, and what is quaintly labeled "quantitative reasoning" rather than the scary term "math" or one of its subfields, "statistics." What are students supposed to learn under the rubric "information literacy"? Will an English major learn computer languages in order to become a programmer, how to configure operating systems, troubleshoot hardware and software problems? Does information literacy signify that the digital foundations of computing and alternative logics will be taught? Will students be exposed to the history of computers—Babbage's early model, Turing's philosophy of computation, and the debates surrounding new domains such as artificial intelligence, many of whose advocates accept Herbert Simon's conception of humans as information-processing machines—and other derivations in biology, physics, and social knowledge? Does "information literacy" include learning about the history and development of technology and its role in changing patterns of work and leisure? Or does "information literacy" consist in learning how to operate the word-processing programs, such as Windows 2000, work with spreadsheets and other statistical programs, and manipulating computer-stored data?

This brings us to the most uncontroversial of the requirements. Is "writing" a skill, an art, or a kind of critical literacy? Are its various forms—fiction, poetry, discourse, and argument, embodied in memos, papers, essays, and treatises—mastered by learning techniques and rules? If writing is a skill, then it can be compared to the instrumental activity of tying a shoelace, replacing a light bulb, operating a computer, a lathe, or a photocopying machine. We seldom think about what is involved in these activities because, after repetitive use, they become habitual. But learning a skill takes time, particularly for the neophyte. One must find out how to turn on the machine before discovering how to retrieve the work from a hard disk and use the various commands on the screen properly. The lathe operator must learn how to put the metal or the wood part into a chuck, the machine part that holds the work, before he gets started; the photocopier operator must know how place the paper correctly on the surface of the photocopier in order to get the job done.

Writing, too, would be a skill if its mastery were confined to habituating the student to such mechanical features. To be sure, writing incorporates skills: the practitioner must learn how to use pen or pencil or master the mechanics of typing. And in the case of computer-driven word processing, there are a fair number of technical features of some complexity to be assimilated, compared to the relatively simple operation of a typewriter. Further, the formulation of a simple sentence, which embodies spelling, grammar, and syntax, has certain skill components.

But since semantic issues always intrude in writing, making meaning is not a skill but both an art and a form of critical learning. If writing is an art—since it entails thought, the adroit use of language, and rules of expression, none of which is mechanical in nature—the process of learning involves imagination, genuine knowledge, and more or less self-conscious familiarity with logical sequences. Even the most mundane memorandum that goes beyond mere conveyance of information— "The office will be closed at 12:00 P.M. on Thursday, 31 December, for New Year's Eve"—and instead makes a proposal for a course of action, or contests a course of action proposed by another, entails complexity and narrative coherence. Learning the formal apparatus of a memo is a necessary step, but only a first step. Almost everything else must be artfully as well as skillfully wrought, both with respect to its order and its rhetoric, for the object of the exercise is to persuade others of the rightness of one's perspective. In this sense, rhetoric must not be understood pejoratively but in the sense used by the Greeks: like logic, it is inextricably intertwined with argument. It involves careful choices of words, a sense of dramatic presentation, an awareness of the questions that might arise from some of the author's statements, the mood of the audience, and many other considerations.

Every good writing teacher is aware of these and many other issues. She knows that, however much the visual has become a cultural force, words retain their power, and those who are able to use them effectively—to tell stories, invent slogans, construct arguments, and to paint word pictures that have visceral appeal—tend to acquire influence. In short, many writing teachers understand that the skills are subordinate to the art of writing. And they understand that writing is not only a form of communication and expression but signifies a content itself, modifying and infusing all other forms of knowledge. The notion of "writing across the curriculum" demonstrates at all levels of schooling that some teachers have become convinced that the idea that knowledge acquisition is independent of its expression is untenable. Yet few framers of the undergraduate core seem to have taken these insights into account; they persist in using the term "skill" to describe the nature of writing. This term reflects the persistence of the rest of the curriculum to transmit a fixed, specialized body of knowledge acquired by the instructor in graduate school and to which he has become habituated. That a sociologist or economist should consider himself a writing teacher and a guide to close textual reading would embarrass most professors in these fields, except some who understand that the reading and writing are properly learned at all levels of the academic system.

To be fair, the fault lies with society as much as with the faculty and administration, who, in the name of "accommodating" student interests, are prepared to submit to the zeitgeist. Student "interests," which with few exceptions have tended to the vocational, may be taken at face value or as a euphemism for their anxiety, even panic, regarding the future. While many parents are convinced that elite schooling will enhance their children's chances, few remain confident that the job market will continue to expand to make room for them. Parents and students are responding, not only to media hype, which heralds the value of job-preparedness, or to the unmistakable evidence of corporate concern that education be articulated with the needs of the employer, but to their own observations and, indeed, their own experiences of corporate downsizing. For sons and daughters who enter colleges and universities in the 1990s and beyond, the core curriculum cannot be forbidding. Nor are most prepared to follow Bloom's earnest plea to achieve genuine mastery of the cultural legacy upon which the claims of the West to moral and intellectual superiority were built. It is one thing to sample Great Ideas; it is another to pay careful attention to learning them and figuring out what they might mean today.

The "self-interested individual" is today the pervasive subject of postsecondary schooling. Whatever the specific content of the curriculum, successful outcomes are nearly always calculated in terms of letter grades and differential rankings as a prelude for differential access to the job market. During their school years, many students spend much of their time trying to decipher the professor's moral and intellectual code in order to give her what she wants to read or hear. Talk to any concerned professor. Chances are, she will complain about the difficulty, these days, of getting a discussion started in a class of eighteen to twenty-one-year-olds, let alone getting a paper that displays even a glimmer of originality or dissent from received wisdom. By many accounts, students sit in classrooms passively, waiting for the professor to tell them what to think and what to do. However horrific to the critical mind is the powerful academic practice of lipreading, many students know this is the way to get ahead. It is the key to getting the A's and B's that have become the norm of undergraduate as well as graduate school evaluation in elite private universities.

The self-interested student in elite institutions, where the stakes have never been higher, often regards his classmates as competitors rather than fellow learners. He usually directs his attention to the teacher alone, rather than seeking wisdom and counsel from peers, except on examination-eve occasion, when study groups might form. As at graduate schools, where the mood among students seems to have degenerated into an ugly competition for shrinking jobs, undergraduates are looking over their shoulders. For some, the pressure is so great and the consequences of failure sufficiently dire to prompt thoughts—occasionally deeds—of suicide. For the survivors, the option of transferring or dropping out seems preferable to completing their degree, at least in the prescribed four years.

There is thus not much evidence of real *learning* taking place at most postsecondary institutions, if by that we mean the process by which a student is motivated to participate in, even challenge, established intellectual authority. Although "critical thinking" is standard in the rhetoric of curriculum planners, it is a rare practice in most classrooms, occurring only by the efforts of individuals who labor under nearly insuperable obstacles. In third-tier schools, a valiant teacher may successfully make her classroom into a citadel of critical learning. Indeed, there are thousands of mostly isolated teachers who have tried to light a fire in the minds of eager students. The problem is not so much that these souls are absent from postsecondary schools. Over and over, students blessed with a semester of intellectual excitement in the classroom, complain that they can expect little or no continuity of perspective in their educational careers. We remember the singular teacher who "opens our eyes" to new possibilities—if we are lucky. In the elite as well as other schools, the classroom remains the boundary of critical learning. One cannot rely on colleagues or on student groups to carry critique or close textual reading and interpretation beyond its walls.

Most faculty have forgotten that the main function of the higher learning and of its faculty is not "teaching" but providing an intellectual environment that will encourage the learner to dispense with intellectual authorities and to become her own authority. In the main, the learner becomes autonomous when she can confront the letter and the meaning of a text directly, without the mediation of a teacher. This does not exclude the value of mentorship, but the object is to achieve separation rather than acolytism. As I have previously contended, most undergraduates are lucky if they have the mentorial services of a professor. But can there be any doubt that the best kind of schooling provides the student with the chance to become self-directed, and to rely as much, if not more, on her own peers as on the teacher? After all, possibilities for genuine social and cultural as much as scientific innovation depend, not on following others, but on the formation of an autonomous self capable of finding its own voice.

3

Until the late 1960s, graduate education in the United States saw little reason to undertake curriculum reform. The typical applicant for master's and Ph.D. programs was an undergraduate major in the discipline, and it could be safely assumed that most majors were familiar with its canonical texts and its methods. Graduate school was viewed by faculty and students as a training program in the methods of research and, in the case of medicine and other health science fields, of treatment practices. For these reasons course work, as opposed to fieldwork, was rather narrowly constructed. However, as the bachelor's degree became more common, higher education schools, professional associations, and licensing agencies began to ante up credentials. By the 1970s, master's and doctoral programs were expanding and, in these years, many schools and their departments had to consider curriculum revision. For one thing, many students entering advanced degree programs were not majors in their chosen discipline, and some hadn't taken even one course in their subject before entering graduate school. And a fair number of students entering graduate school expected to obtain the education they believed had been denied to them by an indifferent and less than rigorous undergraduate curriculum.

Most humanities and social science graduate students devote the first two or three years of course work to playing catch-up with the discipline. Regardless of a student's undergraduate major, graduate curricula these days customarily presuppose little or no prior knowledge of the central issues of the field. At best, a student may demonstrate superficial acquaintance with some canonical texts and, in the humanities, a minimum methodological competence. But since the social sciences yearn to emulate the ahistorical, quantitative orientation of the "hard" sciences, many undergraduate majors in fields such as economics and sociology have little historical perspective on the discipline. Except for a single semester "theory" requirement at the undergraduate level, most enter graduate school with little idea of how and by whom the field was developed, what the central problems it attempted to address were, let alone any awareness of its philosophical foundations. Most graduate physicists and biologists have never read, respectively, Newton's *Principia,* Darwin's *Origin of Species,* or Claude Bernard's *Essays in Experimental Medicine;* many social scientists ignore Adam Smith's *Wealth of Nations,* David Ricardo's *Principles of Political Economy and Taxation,* let alone *Capital* by Karl Marx. Ignorant of their forebears, students whose undergraduate major was in the natural sciences are nevertheless likely to have received much more "training" than students in other disciplines, at least in the well-endowed schools. Some social sciences have aspirations to methodological rigor and share the so-called hard science quest for precision in measurement and the predictive certainty long abandoned by many theoretical physicists. But in only a few instances does the undergraduate major prepare students to plunge directly into research and writing.

Graduate school is coded as the time when general education ends and boot camp followed by trade school begins. For students headed for academic careers, the path is an apprenticeship in appropriate institutional behavior and research methods. Most serve this apprenticeship on projects of their mentor or another faculty member who has money for research assistance. Student expectations often match those of the faculty. With the exception of a small number of required courses designed to acquaint them with some canonical works of "theory" and research methods, and under the strong urging of advisors and consistent with the culture of the program, most students quickly select courses directly related to their dissertation topic. In fact, in a considerable number of programs, the occasional learner who takes courses outside the discipline in order to explore unfamiliar intellectual territory risks being consigned to the margins. And if she chooses a dissertation study that might require advisors from departments outside the discipline, she may forfeit access to the networks usually necessary in the current academic labor market for finding a job in higher education.

As academic jobs have dried up in nearly all domains, since the late 1980s the pressure on faculty to forfeit or otherwise jettison experiments in transdisciplinary or interdisciplinary master's and Ph.D. programs has become intense. As a result the student hoping to use graduate school to achieve what has become difficult if not impossible at the undergraduate level—to explore intellectual options freely—finds departments becoming more protective of their turf and their disciplinary boundaries and hardening into academic fortresses. While there are a few pockets of learning offering students a strong transdisciplinary regime—programs that actively encourage students to explore their interests—they are more scarce than at any time since the early 1960s. Graduate education today is once again the site of the learner's socialization and acculturation to conventional professional roles, even as the nature of higher education rapidly veers away from these conventions, if not always for the better.

To take one of the most obvious examples, at a time when the teaching of literature has all but disappeared from the undergraduate curriculum in many four-year colleges, graduate English departments remain reluctant to offer a stream of courses that will prepare students to teach composition or to work as the language faculty in a vocational cluster. Many highly ranked Ph.D. English and comparative literature programs belittle "composition studies," but students know that there is where the jobs are. The distance between the conventional graduate school curriculum and the job market has led some, like Elaine Showalter of Princeton, and a former president of the Modern Language Association, to urge students to explore careers such as computer programming in corporations and public administration. Others on the senior faculty have come out forcefully for a two-tier credentials system. Instead of turning out more Ph.D.'s in, say, Milton or Blake studies, for whom there are simply no jobs, they have advanced the idea that a special credential be devised for composition teachers. Even if this degree is less demanding, it might prepare a considerable number of students otherwise destined for the part-time labor force or for law to take full-time jobs as directors and teachers in freshman composition. For Cary Nelson and Michael Berube, the authors of one of these proposals, the successful applicant might be required to teach more, and write less, to win a permanent job.[6]

These are the well-intentioned conclusions of an embarrassed senior professoriate that finds itself progressively helpless to assist its graduates in finding jobs, but has become resigned to the decline of full-time positions, the vocationalization of the curriculum, and the casualization of large sections of the academic labor force. These are solutions born of despair at a time when it has become difficult to envision an alternative future for the academic system. But, however unwittingly they reinforce the dominant trends in curriculum reform toward a two-tier educational regime, literature, philosophy, and science are increasingly reserved for a few elite institutions, albeit in a much degraded form. On the other side, the reduction of writing to a skill, applied ethics in place of metaphysics, and technical training in place of critical learning are paths that have begun to erode the resolve of many professors to hold out in defense of the intellect. As we have seen, the problem is that most who resist vocational training offer a curriculum that either preserves the truncated versions of knowledge production characteristic of the disciplines or extols the eternal truths and holy texts.

Most faculty in graduate programs actively discourage transdisciplinary learning or scholarship that exhibits much originality. According to the hallowed tradition, the dissertation is no time for dissenting scholarship; better the candidate follow the deeply furrowed pastures plowed by others, to fill in holes left by the pioneers for subsequent researchers. In no case ought the neophyte attempt to forge a new paradigm, or even suggest a novel interpretation that might offend the intellectual powers-that-be. The adventurous student is advised to save her new idea until after she wins tenure, when she will have shown her professionalism by producing books and articles evaluated by peers as competent and well within disciplinary boundaries. Of course, a minority of graduate advisors may urge the few intellectually ambitious students to "follow their hearts," to use the dissertation to experiment with forms of trans- or nondisciplinarity, and to choose unpopular topics and marginalized theoretical perspectives.

What is the alternative to these dismal scenarios? How can students and their teachers resist the seemingly inexorable trend toward the interlock between undergraduate and graduate tiering? Should students be advised to go with the flow? And if they choose to take their own road, how are they to survive? My answer is simple. I believe that advice that stifles the voice of the student who really has something to say, the intellectual means to say it, and the stamina to tolerate perpetual wagging heads is cockeyed and indefensible. The decision to conform to prevailing sensibility ultimately defeats the interest of maintaining some portion of the academy as a vital organism and can only destroy the spirit of the aspiring intellectual. Moreover, those who willfully trim their sails are causing the boat to founder.

The students who enter graduate school in their late thirties and forties have had the greatest difficulty finding full-time teaching jobs. Since many already have full-time jobs as administrators, community college and high school teachers, or as secretaries and researchers for nonprofit organizations such as schools and health care agencies, the term of their graduate study may be as much as twice that of younger peers. Many others are required to work at several part-time positions. For these reasons, they manage to finish only after eight to ten years rather than the typical five or six. When they are ready to look for a full-time teaching position, they may be pushing fifty. Older graduates face not-so-hidden age discrimination, even those who publish books, articles in peer-reviewed journals, and have sterling teaching evaluations. Since a newly earned Ph.D. usually qualifies the candidate for an entry-level assistant professorship, hiring committees know that salaries of older candidates may already be considerably higher than what the university is prepared to offer. Moreover, faculties prefer to try to shape the professional career of a relatively inexperienced young person, especially one with few obligations. The mature candidate may be more intellectually and politically independent and "disturb the delicate balance of the department," as one chair told me when I telephoned him in behalf of a candidate.

Discouraged, many who might have entered academic teaching, writing, and scientific research are deciding to seek occupationally oriented graduate degrees in areas such as computer science, business administration, and the law. Another group puts its collective head down and pursues an academic career, but on condition that they toe whatever line has been drawn by the discipline to distinguish the acceptable from the unacceptable. After years in the casual teaching force, many of these graduates also end up in computers, administration, and law. As we have seen, those who stick it out risk becoming part of the enormous casual workforce that now undergirds nearly all universities and many colleges. Or if they do creative and independent intellectual work and manage to land a full-time job, they are likely to find themselves in third-tier schools, where the routines of teaching resemble industrial labor and the opportunities for collegial intellectual work are few. Many teachers who end up in these schools become discouraged, but stay the course. They find people to talk to; they may still grapple with intellectual and political issues and write. Hope remains with those who take the risks.

4

It is no secret that education is one of the most labor-intensive industries in the economy. Like other public services—health care and social work come to mind—the delivery system has, conventionally, depended upon face-to-face interaction. At Oxford and Cambridge, the practice of one-to-one mentorship remains the substance of the pedagogical regime. Typically, the professor may offer three or four lectures a year. But his day-to-day work consists in a relatively small number of tutorials with students working, broadly, in the professor's area of special interest. The tutorial may be as intense as a weekly session devoted to certain texts or as loose as an occasional meeting to discuss the student's paper, or both. But only in cases where the instructor presides over or participates in a study group, usually consisting of five or six members, is there anything like a "class" or teaching in the common usage.

Long before the budget crunches of recent memory, the emergence of mass higher education in every advanced industrial society posed the problem of how to construct the learning regime. Clearly the tutorial method was too expensive unless the student's family could afford huge tuition fees, and even then costs would remain prohibitive for many schools to maintain the tutorial in anything like its pristine form. We have already seen that, even in elite universities, the German system of disciplines and specialization became the knowledge base, so that the concept of "general education" had to be brought back in to ensure some common ground, however fragmented and incoherent it might remain. At the level of instruction, in the overwhelming majority of American universities, the classroom replaced the tutorial as the pedagogical norm. However, as the professoriate became specialized and profession-alized, that is, as most schools required their faculty candidates to have a doctorate to qualify for a full-time and permanent position, it became increasingly difficult to distinguish the quality of education between elite and non-elite institutions. While the money needed to free faculty to pro-duce knowledge and to finance the material infrastructure of their activities, not to mention swimming pools and gymnasia, undergirds university prestige, it doesn't always work to enhance the academic program of the institution. Until very recently, many students who could not qualify for City College went to NYU and other New York area private colleges and universities where admission standards were considerably lower. NYU has upgraded its admission standards, but most area schools are scrounging for students.

The problem is complicated by the fact that most junior faculty get jobs where they can, and where they land is often a matter of luck. I know a few newly arrived Ph.D.'s who accept jobs in elite private schools because of location, or more frequently, because that was the only job they were offered. While I would not want to underestimate the importance of teaching loads in determining faculty "productivity," an easy distinction can no longer be made between colleges and universities and normal (education) schools. Reflecting, perhaps, their own career trajectories toward professorships in elite schools, and despite their own recollections of mediocre teaching, burdened as it was by heavy schedules, impoverished support, low pay, and no tenure, the City College of New York faculty managed to produce its share of knowledge. Even today, as working conditions in many public institutions deteriorate to the level of the 1920s and 1930s, many faculty members match, if not exceed, the achievements of their colleagues in private and public research universities.

But relentless cost cutting has failed to stem the tide of rationalization of the university. After sixty years, the already degraded pedagogies of mass education are themselves under siege. It is true that some state systems have managed to wring from legislatures enough money to keep up with the inflation rates, small salary increases for faculty and staff, and soaring costs of construction and maintenance of buildings and grounds. Among the factors that account for their success is a high number of alumni among state legislators and members of the executive branch. Especially in the Southeast and on the West Coast, these representatives and officials clearly expect that maintaining a solid scientific and technical establishment will attract and retain "high-tech" companies in their states. For example, a high percentage of public officials in the Midwest are Big Ten university graduates. Nevertheless, many states have suffered a twenty-year absolute or relative slide of education revenues: New York,

New Jersey, most New England states, California, even the research universities, and most of the Southwest states, except Arizona, are feeling the squeeze. In almost all states, including those of the Midwest and Southeast where public research universities remain relatively well funded, the community colleges and third-tier four-year schools are experiencing near-crisis conditions. In many community colleges, part-timers teach 75 percent of course sections. The teacher-student ratios in these schools have climbed over the past fifteen years from one full-time faculty member to twenty or twenty-five students to hover around one to forty. Even so, they are still too expensive for conservative state legislators aching to cut income and business taxes for their corporate sponsors, and for the ideologues, pushing more students out of public schools into private colleges.

Enter distance learning. At a mundane level distance learning is an extension to the Internet and to video of the old correspondence school principle. After World War One, at the historical moment when high-school dropouts exceeded graduates, a new economic niche was carved by educational entrepreneurs who offered working people the chance to return to school without having to attend classes. In the pre-electronic era, a student enrolled in a correspondence school would read several books and articles in a subject, receive study guides, take an exam and enjoy the rewards of preparation, even when the school was unaccredited by a recognized agency. But since the point of the curriculum was, and remains for some, to enable students to take the state or local community's GED examination, accreditation was not especially important. In other instances, the correspondence school was frankly directed to helping the student acquire specific occupational skills.

External bachelor's and master's degree programs mushroomed in the 1960s. Postsecondary distance learning began among the most far-sighted institutions, which sought to accommodate adult learners—those over thirty who simply could not attend night classes because of family and work obligations. A number of experimenting colleges—Antioch, Goddard, Franconia, and a dozen others that had conventionally relied on campus-based programs—began recruiting at bachelor's and master's levels for new external degree programs. At Vermont's Goddard College, for example, I was a member of a committee for a master's degree student in early childhood education. As a co-mentor I joined her at a two-week seminar on the college's campus. But she also had a "core" faculty member who resided in the college's community. The rest of her curriculum in both general and specialized subjects was fulfilled by correspondence, telephone calls with the core mentor, and by arrangements to take classes at local colleges.

By the 1970s, a number of new colleges, some which call themselves universities, had emulated the pioneers. Except these private, mostly entrepreneurial institutions needed accreditation, since no states provide examinations as sufficient criteria for awarding degrees. As with all other aspects of education, each regional accrediting association has slightly different standards for conferring degree status on applicants. Nevertheless, "external" degree programs on an expanded scale have been rapidly approved under pressure from business institutions such as AT & T, the corporate accounting firm Arthur Andersen, and other corporations that have used external approaches extensively and, in some cases, started their own universities and acted as lobbyists in behalf of the educational entrepreneurs. Some, like the University of Phoenix, Chapman University, and National University, which cast their respective nets over a geographically wide region, combine distance learning with on-campus instruction. Located in Orange County, California, Chapman has established small learning centers throughout this vast region and has an electronic instructional program as well.

By the mid-1990s, the trend toward distance learning had begun to pick up steam in postsecondary education. In 1998, under pressure to satisfy a surge of student applicants but also facing budget constraints that discouraged building new physical facilities, a group of western governors announced plans for a cross-state consortium to offer degree programs over the Internet and by video. Their proposal is patterned, at least organizationally, on the United Kingdom's Open University, with which the Western Governors' University will have a cooperative relationship.

Begun as a national university by the Labour governments of the 1970s, the Open University was, at its inception, viewed by conservative educators as a radical and ill-conceived experiment, inspired by 1960s countercultural and Marxist ideologies. The Open University differs from U.S. external degree programs in several important ways. First, fairly prominent professors recruited from established institutions are hired as a central faculty with two key functions: to write a set of texts and study guides integrating broad knowledge domains in the humanities, social sciences, and natural sciences; and to prepare videotaped lectures corresponding to chapters in the texts. The texts and the lectures might differ slightly, but they are meant to cover the same ground. Second, at the local level, a relatively low-paid tutor and discussion leader conducts classes around the text and the videotaped lectures, meeting in churches, community centers, and other nonacademic facilities, or in regional colleges. Evaluations are made at the local level, but the knowledge and curriculums are generated by the central faculty sitting in Milton Keynes, a suburb of London.

Some of the Open University texts are first-class treatises in their respective domains; others are generally fine summaries of prevailing knowledge, including the critical literature. In no way can these books be compared to the watered-down American textbooks geared to the lowest common denominator. International figures, including the cultural critic Stuart Hall, sociologist Veronica Beechey, and educational theorist James Donald, have produced some of the Open University works.

Distance learning in the United States is likely to emulate the American cultural ideal of possessive individualism. Sitting at a computer terminal or a VCR, or both, the student interacts with a packaged program, watching a lecture delivered by a prominent scholar on, say, African American literature, contemporary social problems, or problems in quantitative reasoning. Lessons are divided into units, which include the text of the lecture, questions, and problems for the student to answer. Once he has completed his unit test, the student can download his grades. In the better models, there might be online discussion groups, or an online tutor assigned. Although there are programs, for example, at Empire State College, that employ full-time faculty in small, but promising distance-learning programs, the discussion leader, tutor, or grader will almost certainly not be a credentialed full-time professor but is likely to be a member of the casual academic labor force. After all, the whole point is to reduce costs and, at the same time, maintain the promise of mass education.

The objective of the distance-learning planners is to be able to deliver an entire online and videotape or CD-ROM curriculum. If education conforms to the banking model—where the student opens her mind to a specified body of knowledge to be ingested and regurgitated—distance learning can work and will save the institution the expense of having to hire hundreds of high-priced professors. If writing and quantitative reasoning are taught as skills, distance-learning techniques may be almost as effective as classrooms. You can instruct a person to perform certain calculations or attain such "information literacy" as it takes to process words or operate the computer, including learning how to use program packages and find information on the Internet. Distance learning can be effective in technical subjects like mastering computer programs or languages. And since software for checking spelling is installed on most contemporary machines, and many even have dictionaries and a thesaurus, distance learning may be more effective than classrooms in helping students to learn the skills associated with writing. Parts of speech, writing a straightforward sentence, and learning models for letter and memo writing can be acquired through tutorial packages.

However, if what I have said earlier about writing and math is right, the semantic and conceptual contents of distance-learning techniques will be found wanting. The problem of learning how to make meaning is complex. As every writing teacher knows, the ability to convey ideas clearly, let alone develop a sense of style, sometimes takes years of practice, discussion, and rumination over the instructor's comments on dozens of papers. In order to gain confidence in their own authority, students should be able to exchange their papers with each other and be able discuss them for an hour or two over a cup of coffee. And if "subjects" are not defined as a fixed body of knowledge and the learner is defined as a knowledge producer as much as a receiver, the same conditions apply. Many learn by argument, even wrangling with fellow learners. These encounters are not subject to time and cost limitations, but require a luxury of space and time that may exceed the resources of an online conversation.

I do not demean the value of online discussion groups. I am a member of two very active groups from which I receive at least fifty messages a day. Imagine a small group of distance learners engaged in these conversations, or a tutorial between a single student and her tutor. Some have argued that one day the technology will be able to simulate face-to-face interaction, during which gestures, voice inflections, and other markers of meaning will operate. For the present, most of us are confined to words and are subject to delays of hours or even days before receiving messages. Chat rooms on some online service providers are better, but it is still difficult to be spontaneous in these venues. Ironically, if the tutorial model remains the preferred method, as one developer told me, distance learning will prove as labor-intensive and expensive as classroom instruction.

But the main problem in distance learning is that in its mass applications it tends to become an asocial activity. In some of its incarnations, the student never talks to a person but responds to packaged material, and is not encouraged to become a critical, autonomous learner. A curriculum consisting of packaged information and mostly mainstream lectures on videotape promotes the concept of the learner as consumer, not producer. It will be effective for training students to follow instructions, and to make the kinds of choices that our educational system has perfected: the student/consumer may choose from a menu of predigested knowledges.

In some elite schools, distance learning is employed as a supplement to classroom instruction. Equipped with their individual PCs, students engage in extensive evening discussions around themes posed during the class session by instructors. Indeed, if each student had her own computer, such conversations could enrich the learning regimes of any program of study. The problem is, most students in commuter schools, even some graduate students, do not have the money to purchase a personal computer; they rely on the institution's scarce resources, in which access for each individual is constrained.

It is not difficult, in these criticisms of the current curriculum to discern the outlines of an alternative approach. In the next chapter, I want to offer a philosophical and conceptual basis for a curriculum and pedagogy whose aim is to foster learning, even wisdom. This discussion is meant to be a prelude to a more detailed and concrete series of proposals. In the course of these ruminations, I will consider the question of whether the core itself has validity, as well as ways to resolve the conflict between "great books" and our urgent need to address problems of contemporary life in areas that are, for nearly all of us, profoundly perplexing: love and friendship and other forms of social life; work and family; the apocalyptic issues of nuclear destruction and ecological catastrophe; politics and culture. The premise of my proposals is that far from remaining blasts from the past with little or no contemporary pertinence, what are often called the "classics" remain so, not because they still sell, but because they still speak to our condition. If students are to become engaged in learning, their intellectual encounters must refer, in the first instance, to the formation of the self, which presupposes everything in the world. For we are our most interesting knowledge-objects, and it is on the basis of reflexive knowledge that we can reach out to the world in all of its richness and complexity.

CHAPTER 7

DISMANTLING THE CORPORATE UNIVERSITY

1

AMERICA'S COLLEGES AND UNIVERSITIES have assumed the task of preparing a substantial fraction of the adult population for professional and technical careers, but this cannot be the engine that drives higher education. In the era of globalization and rapid technological change, the advanced economies are likely to produce fewer jobs at decent pay relative to the qualified labor force. In many parts of the world, even in advanced industrial societies, economic stagnation has framed restructuring, technological displacement of labor, and consequent mass unemployment and underemployment. As I have previously argued, if we live in a global economy, the advantages the United States has experienced in the last half of the 1990s must be viewed, at best, as temporary.

Unless new institutional arrangements are enacted, the jobless future is no mere metaphor; it is a high probability for society in the twenty-first century. In the next century, technological displacement will probably force many to work at paid labor for a shorter portion of their active lives, without disturbing overall productivity.[1] Even against their own ideological objections, legislatures may be obliged to enact such measures as guaranteed income—a major demand of most European labor movements—in order to stave off serious social upheaval resulting from inequities and unemployment. In response to these changes, the long-held, but suppressed, belief in lifelong education may return with a vengeance as workers with time to spare decide to return to school, whether for vocational or general education objectives.

As the number of secure, well-paid full-time jobs continues to shrink in relation to an expanding workforce and as many of those employed work fewer hours at full-time jobs, education as a form of life becomes a practical alternative. This situation suggests the need for noncredit programs for older adults. Courses for nontraditional students would employ both full- and part-time faculty and would be granted credit-bearing status if the candidate decided to pursue a degree. If universities are to be public spheres, they may become sites for a wide array of cultural activities: art, music, theater, and writing schools for citizens and professional students alike, concert series in jazz, popular, and "classical" music, as well as museums, current affairs programs, and other activities.

The current academic system has fudged the distinctions between training, education, and learning. Administrations of most colleges and universities have responded to the economic and cultural uncertainties provoked by budget constraints and a volatile job market by constructing their institutions on the model of the modern corporation. Consequently, many have thrust training to the fore and called it education. Lacking a unified national culture into which to socialize students and in any case lacking an educational philosophy capable of steering an independent course, the academic system as a whole is caught in a market logic that demands students be job-ready upon graduation. Under these imperatives colleges and universities are unable to implement an educational program that prepares students for a world of great complexity. Instead, academic leaders chant the mantra of "excellence," the new horizon of university administration, as corporate slogans corresponding to bottom-line corporate practices drive higher education's goals. Excellence means that all of the parts of the university "perform" and are judged according to how well they deliver knowledge and qualified labor to the corporate economy and how well the administration fulfills the recruitment and funding goals needed to maintain the institution.

Although thousands of full- and part-time faculty work, often under onerous conditions, to advance education and learning, America's colleges and universities have, in the main, abandoned these missions as their defining goals. The university administration has devolved into the means by which the machine runs smoothly, which translates into fundraising and crisis management. The research faculty "produces" useful knowledge, which can be measured by the amount of grant money, commercial applications, or critical recognition they receive in appropriate circles and which may enhance the institution's prestige. And the valued student is the one who earns good grades, which in many cases means only that she tests well and gets good job offers. The doctrine of excellence requires the student to perform according to rules over which she has no control and which proscribes thinking. For real thinking entails marching to your own drummer, ignoring rules the thinker regards as arbitrary. In the service of reflection, the thinker may even choose to be less "excellent." Thinking means questioning the nature and the content of approved knowledge.

It may be that undermined by transnational movements of capital and labor, the nation-state no longer provides the basis for education-as-socialization. The current drift may result, in part, from economic globalization and from the profound changes taking place in the makeup of the population of the United States. In the past two decades, as many immigrants have crossed U.S. borders as entered between 1880 and 1920, the apex of the second great migration. But unlike earlier periods, schooling as a primary mechanism of assimilation is in serious disrepair. Skeptical of the image of America as a land of unlimited opportunity, many immigrants have arrived acutely aware that they have been pushed here by poverty, by diminished expectations, or by one of the innumerable little wars that dot the globe, rather than being pulled by glittering prospects. The melting pot is frozen; assimilation is at best partial and is often more successful at the economic than at the cultural level, since America seems to have unlimited room for low-wage and marginal entrepreneurial labor.

Next to severe budget cuts in public schools, the most important factor in the intellectual decline of higher education is the disappearance of opportunities to explore knowledge domains whose only attraction is that the student's curiosity has been piqued, and of occasions for reflection on self and on society. In order to remain in school, even many who are coded as "full-time" students are obliged to obtain paid work, typically more than twenty hours a week. Under these circumstances, they simply don't have the time to consider learning as anything more than the rituals necessary for obtaining credentials. Whether or not they manage to learn a series of marketable skills, this has become the sufficient justification for spending years attending school.

As higher education gropes for a new mission and tries to come to terms with these conditions, most public universities and many private schools find themselves caught in a permanent fiscal crisis born of the disparity between burgeoning demand for postsecondary schooling and restricted resources. Even as some private universities receive large donations from grateful alums, in most smaller, non-elite private schools, donations barely keep up with rising costs and competition prevents them from closing budget gaps by raising tuition. Congress and many state legislatures have ruthlessly trimmed one of the great engines of the postwar expansion, student aid. To keep enrollments up, many administrations have been forced to transform their faculties into a casual labor force; to postpone needed maintenance and repairs indefinitely; and to cut back or eliminate "nonessential" academic programs such as languages, geography, and linguistics and, in some schools, to close nursing and other occupational programs.

Now more than ever, the imperatives of fundraising drive higher education. We have seen how officials scurry to forge alliances with large donors, offering to dedicate buildings and compromising chunks of the curriculum in return for financial support. Corporate sponsors and panicked parents and students alike demand programs oriented to "job readiness." As a result, many schools have succumbed to pressure to spruce up their placement, or in contemporary parlance, "career" services, introducing vocational courses into the curriculum, and encouraging internships—often coded as "experiential" learning—aimed at inducing employers to hire their graduates.

This mad race toward occupational education, and to the intellectual bottom, comes at a time when good jobs are disappearing and competition is sharper than at any time since the Great Depression. For the truth is that, despite glowing reports of economic boom, there are fewer jobs, if by a "job" we designate work that provides health and pension benefits, offers long-term continuity with a single employer, and income commensurate with qualifications. Even many corporations in the most dynamic sectors of the economy—communications, entertainment, and information services—prefer to hire temporary and contingent labor and retain only a small corps of permanent employees at all levels of the occupational structure. In response colleges have, under the rubric of providing "skills" in "logic and rhetoric" (composition) and "computer literacy," added vocational and remedial elements to the core curriculum.

Despite apparent short-term gains for some universities and colleges, vocationalization is the wrong way to go. Notwithstanding their anxiety about the future, students are ill-served by educational regimes that tailor their learning to a rapidly changing workplace whose technological shifts belie the assumptions driving many specialist curricula. Ironically, the best preparation for the work of the future might be to cultivate knowledge of the broadest possible kind, to make learning a way of life that in the first place is pleasurable and then rigorously critical. For it is only when the learner loves literature, enjoys puzzling out the meaning of art works and those of philosophy, is intrigued by social and cultural theory, or becomes an indefatigable researcher that she acquires intellectual habits that are the precondition for further learning. The learner who really understands the economy knows how fragile is the concept of career.

But students cannot expect to get much help from economics departments. Economics today is taught either as a branch of mathematics or, at the introductory level, as a branch of social psychology. According to many textbooks, economics boils down to individual choice. The individual makes rational choices between competing products on the basis of her conception of (usually short-term) comparative advantages. In the long run, the buyer of an automobile, for example, might be better served by considering a durable, but more expensive brand. But this choice might require a steep down payment and higher monthly payments. So, the budget-conscious buyer often chooses the cheaper, more brittle model, which, over time may prove equally or even more expensive. Yet this decision is considered entirely rational, within the limits imposed by the buyer's income.

Given this orientation, it is no wonder that the typical student who takes an economics course leaves college with absolutely no idea of the dynamics of the labor market and its relation to broad economic arrangements. But most students do not take such courses. They are required only to fulfill a breadth requirement by selecting from a diverse social science menu. Only by accident are they likely to learn about the impact of corporate decision making on work, or the role of technology in the labor process, the knowledge of which is crucial for their future. The tiny corps of economists who teach from a critical perspective are rarely to be found in the leading schools. Since the small blip of critical thinking in the 1960s and 1970s, economics education has reverted to cheerleading for capitalism, and many professors earn considerable sums moonlighting as consultants for large and medium-sized corporations.

2

Since I hold that the emergence of the new corporate university is in the interest of neither faculty nor students, nor, indeed, of our country, what follows is not consonant with most proposals for educational reform. I doubt that higher education institutions will adopt an alternative vision and program for those who wish to preserve or advance John Dewey's celebrated but largely ignored concept of education for democracy and democracy in education. Democratic reform, let alone fundamental change, seems beyond possibility, at least for the time being. For reform to succeed in the current conservative cultural environment, its protagonists must accept the underlying framework of current educational practice and the prevailing philosophy of governance. Otherwise they are likely to be dismissed as cranks or "pie-in-the-sky utopians." The main line of the current reform program in higher education—appropriately referred to by some as "tinkering"—is to maintain its expansion of access of the last twenty-five years for those traditionally excluded, and to provide them with the means to fare better in the changing labor market.

In the name of "relevance," many reformers accept the trend toward a more vocational curriculum. They argue that working-class students need credentials and some practical tools to enter the labor market on more favorable terms than would otherwise be available to them. Among their amendments to current practice are proposals to make the curriculum more responsive to racial minorities, to women, and to the handicapped. And instead of demanding a more rigorous core curriculum, significant currents of progressive opinion have excoriated the canon and its acolytes as "elitist." While some trumpet multiculturalism as the key to revitalization of a tired faculty and an outmoded curriculum, few multiculturalists challenge the main drift of higher education toward intellectual downsizing. After scarcely two decades of effort, many of these programs have been successfully integrated by the mainstream, but most have lost the critical edge that once gave them some purchase. They are content with providing an add-on to an essentially unchanged core and a series of discipline-based curricula directed toward training professionals.

Bluntly said, in the light of pervasive intellectual inertia we can expect further stratification of the American academic system. Some universities are accumulating huge endowments from wealthy alumni desperate for tax shelters, while those that are chiefly tuition driven are condemned to scrape along. And even when public universities hasten to privatize by selling research capability and some of the curriculum to corporations, seeking thereby to build their own endowments, many lack a pool of rich donors. So where are the incentives for learning? Certainly not in the top-tier universities, whose commitment to "research"—a "mission" acquired during World War Two—now seems set in stone. As for the public schools and private four-year colleges, unless prospects for income from reluctant legislatures and smaller donors improve, at the peril of sinking further, they are likely to continue the trend to privatization.

Today, those who, in the name of the higher learning, seek to establish a community of critical scholars while extending learning opportunities to wider sections of the population are faced with the arduous task of producing their own space within and without the academic system. And it is almost inevitable that, for the foreseeable future, this space will be relatively small. Yet without efforts to produce new forms of governance and of learning, the drift toward the corporate university will turn into a tide. In several short years, battered graduate programs in the arts, humanities, and the sciences are likely to restrict admissions to those for whom fellowship money is available. In fact, many humanities programs have already imposed these restrictions in the hopes of tightening the labor market for their graduates. Some less prestigious programs are bound to close. Once inspired to seek careers in college teaching and humanistic scholarship, but driven by the perception that jobs exist elsewhere, young people in greater numbers than ever will turn to business administration, law, and low- and middle-level technological applications. If the critical intellect is today on the defensive, without "pie-in-the-sky" thinking, tomorrow it will survive only underground.

On what basis should this effort proceed? To specify a "wish" list of curricular suggestions without addressing the burning issue of governance condemns any effort to mere abstraction. In the current academic system, the flight of many faculties from responsibility for curriculum, hiring and firing, and other issues has left the administration in control. Having themselves been transformed from a community of scholars to a collection of individual entrepreneurs in the research universities and to employees of a fairly enclosed bureaucracy in the others, the faculty has conceded much of its prerogatives to the permanent academic government.

3

The formation of a permanent administrative bureaucracy in education was the crucial internal precondition for the gulf that now separates faculty and students from educational leaders, leading to the development of the corporate university. The decline of academic life represents, in part, the degree to which the faculty has surrendered autonomy, that is, a governance and curriculum system that is largely self-generating and self-reproducing. Instead, as we have seen, the learning enterprise has become subject to the growing power of administration, which more and more responds not to faculty and students, except at the margins, but to political and corporate forces that claim sovereignty over higher education.

Over the past thirty years, administration has become a separate career in academic life. Although most deans, provosts, and presidents of academic institutions begin as scholars and teachers, for many the life of the mind offers paltry rewards in comparison to administration. Having been invited to become department chair, some are happy to seek higher office in the university. While there are still deans and even college presidents who, after serving in these posts, return to the classroom, to research, and to writing, many discover that the comparative advantages of administration are greater. For some administrators, the choice is dictated by the will to power or, what amounts to the same thing, the conviction that they can serve the institution better. For others, the move to administration is a tacit acknowledgment that they have exhausted their academic or intellectual contribution and that administration is a choice that saves them from plunging back into routines that no longer excite their passions. Still others are motivated by the large incomes they may earn in comparison to the relatively small recompense of ordinary professors.

What are the consequences of administration as a career? First and perhaps foremost, career administrators tend to lose touch with the educational enterprise. Their allegiances and self-conception become increasingly corporate as they gradually surrender any pretense of doing consistent writing and teaching. They take the standpoint of the institution against those who would resist the "necessary" and "rational" decisions that any administrator must make in the face of relative scarcity—a perspective emblematic of even the most profitable corporations. As the department chair rises to dean, instead of regarding administration as a temporary tour of duty and welcoming resumption of his academic work, he tends to look forward to the next niche in the administrative hierarchy, vice-president for academic affairs or provost. It doesn't take long before he views himself as a member of a separate social layer within the academic system and sees the faculty and students as adversaries or, at least, as a different stratum. Indeed, in recognition that administrators constitute a separate social layer, many institutions have different personnel and benefits policies for their official cadres than those offered to the professoriate and to the staff.

In the 1960s and 1970s, student protest led to a new, incipient partnership of students, faculty, and sometimes administrators in university governance. Since the late 1970s, student participation in the various committees of faculty and institutional decision making has become token at best. These relationships should be renewed; without a voice in the life of the university or the college, students become akin to alienated labor. This deprivation may account for the current conflict between graduate employees on the one side and faculty and administration on the other. For, with some exceptions, most boards of trustees and collegewide committees have no student representatives. While inclusion would not solve the problem of social and political distance between the constituents of universities, it might enhance dialogue and avoid some unnecessary misunderstandings.

The AAUP, America's pioneering faculty organization, has issued many statements calling for "shared governance," the term a tacit acknowledgment that the intrusion of administration into vital academic functions has gone so far that a return to the principle of autonomous faculty governance is virtually unthinkable. Needless to say, even this moderate concept of shared decision making has suffered considerable erosion in the past quarter century. While faculty through departmental and divisional professional and budget committees still have, in most instances, primary responsibility for recruiting, interviewing, and making selections of new faculty and have similar functions in the tenure process, in the overwhelming majority of schools these decisions are never final. They remain in essence recommendations, because administration retains its right to exercise veto power. Until the 1970s, few administrations actually did more than rubber stamp faculty choices. Now this regime is under scrutiny in the light of the growing authority in every aspect of governance of deans and provosts, the frontline representatives of the administration. For example, in some schools, faculty search committees are required to submit more than one candidate for any given position in order to give the dean the final say among the alternatives.

The systematic centralization of decision making in administrative hands has disempowered faculty at all levels of the academic system, not only in the lower tiers. A recent tenure decision at Harvard illustrates the generality of the problem. The candidate was overwhelmingly approved for tenure by a major department in the social sciences. The administration rejected their recommendation, despite the fact that the candidate had support from some of leading scholars in his field. The message? Even the support of academic "stars" and other established faculty cannot assure the job security of a young scholar. What was remarkable about the case is that the candidate sued, but not on affirmative action grounds, because he was white. Although by no means a radical scholar, he challenged the rule of secrecy in tenure and promotion decisions, which denies the candidate access to records of the proceedings and especially to the final vote. In effect, he made an issue of what has been one of the crucial prerogatives of faculty and administration: the right to make decisions in absolute secrecy in order to avoid outside scrutiny and the prospect of legal sanction. The growing corporatization of leading universities means that, even in the most hallowed academic precincts, the CEO and administrative minions control many aspects of the academic program, not only hiring and firing, but which departments and programs will survive, what criteria will determine their survival.

Major decisions over the academic program, including hiring, firing, tenure, and curriculum, should be returned to the faculty, and students should play a larger role in school governance. Today in many universities chairs are appointed by the college president, with only the advice and not necessarily the consent of faculty. Chairs should be elected by their peers unconditionally, rather than being subject to administrative veto, as is the practice in many institutions. Administrations should revert to their traditional role: to facilitate, coordinate, and raise the money needed to sustain the institution. Administrators as policymakers demean the sovereignty of those most qualified to control the academic program: the learning community. Academic senates are only one form of participation. Faculty unions might be another. In connection with this proposal, academics might consider reverting to the practice of rotating administrative responsibilities and jobs. According to this tradition, department chairs, deans, provosts, and college and university presidents serve for limited terms, after which they are expected to return to the classroom and to writing and research. Traditionally these practices were oriented to retaining power in the hands of the faculty, preventing the emergence of a permanent educational bureaucracy that owes allegiance to itself rather to the community.

What are the curricular criteria that correspond to making learning the heart of the university or college? My proposals for faculty-student dominance in governance may be perceived as a partial return to tradition, but they are in the service of democracy. Much of what I propose should have been part of the high school curriculum. Teenagers possess the energy and can muster the enthusiasm to learn new things, tackle difficult texts, and solve complex problems. Some may need help learning how to "read" in both senses of the term: breaking the elementary codes of literacy and learning how to decipher concepts. But given sufficient space and time—mostly freedom from the obligation to work after school and the psychological freedom whose presupposition is some kind of economic security—most can master any knowledge placed before them and acquire the structures needed to be knowledge producers themselves.

When conditions fail to free the student's imagination, by the time he enters college at almost any level, he has become persuaded that the main point of education is to earn the credentials needed to enter the work world with some kind of comparative advantage. Education becomes almost entirely instrumental to professional and career goals. The student may perform well in her courses, and occasionally she may encounter an instructor who is able to ignite some kind of spark. Yet for most students and many faculty, secondary schooling is a ritual performance. With the exception of secondary school English, where the tradition of reading literature is still alive in some places, the typical practice is to lard teaching and learning with the watered-down material presented in textbooks. Only in exceptional high schools are students afforded the chance to read original works of history, social analysis, and scientific discovery. In many places, and not only in the southeastern states and cities, vigilant right-wing and socially conservative professional and citizen watchdog groups make sure that the creative teacher, the enterprising school librarian, or the innovative school administrator is kept in line. Today, there is more censorship in K–12 schools than at any time since the McCarthy period, only the rhetoric has changed from fighting political subversion to safeguarding religious conceptions of sexual morality and science.

"Common denominator" thinking is pervasive in secondary education because, even if much of the curriculum bores the teacher and students to distraction, it is safer. For this reason, to propose something that is strikingly different entails the recognition that only a minority will acquire real learning, however much most students could, given proper circumstances, gain from it. At the same time, I maintain that anyone who has the will to learn in the fullest sense of the term already has the potential and often the capacity to succeed in enlarging her intellectual horizon.

The current model of postsecondary schooling presupposes that the student has already received a good general education in high school and, for this reason, that college is a time of specialization and preparation for a professional identity. The appearance of the core curriculum movement in many colleges and universities is a tacit admission by faculties and administrations that this supposition no longer holds, if it ever did. But for most universities and colleges, caught in the vise of the school-to-work ethos, the core is best described by the invocation to "breadth." College becomes an interlude before specialization in a discipline or, more precisely, a boot camp for the student to demonstrate her capacity to endure the rigors of cultural capital accumulation. Clearly, few core curricula provide the student with a systematic, critical introduction to the intellectual traditions that inform or challenge the precepts of contemporary life.

My views converge with those of some in the conservative camp who would restore many of the so-called classical components to the college and university curricula. Like them, I reject the idea that in our postmodern culture it is too late for intellectual rigor, least of all for a learning regime that offers the students the opportunity to grapple with writings that have shaped Western thinking. Where I depart (in two respects) from the conservative prescription is first on the scope of the canon and then on its intended constituency. My approach does not assume the superiority of the conventional over the alternative or oppositional canon, only its power. We must substitute critique for reverence. I am convinced that virtually all postsecondary students should encounter the crucial elements of the canon of Western thought, not only because it contains much of value, but because the knowledge provides the basis for any critique and transvaluation of that canon.

Herein lies my most vehement disagreement with the conservatives. As is plain to see, few educational philosophers or academic planners favor extending the encounter between canonical works and works of subordinate cultures to working-class students in third-tier schools. Indeed, their policy is one of benign neglect of both domains for students in these institutions. For anyone interested in the democratic purposes of the higher learning, this is an unacceptable position. To confine access to the jewels of Western culture to students attending elite institutions is to devalue these works. For how is it possible to claim their universal stature when access to them is restricted? And how can we renew their stature unless students are offered alternatives for comparison? Proponents of the canon who would make only the elite school curriculum more rigorous admit, tacitly, that the works of Plato and his successors are not identical with what we mean by the Western intellectual tradition. Instead, through the concept of "mission differentiation"—which implies that although all students have access to higher education, some have more opportunities than others—they cynically refashion the canon as cultural capital. Its value consists precisely in the clear delineation of who is admitted to the realm of intellectual property and who is excluded from it.

But addressing alternative canons can enable a student to deal with the fundamental issue of self-formation, to recognize the place she and her peers have in the social world, both in everyday life and in "history," as well as to understand the system of social and political power. The basic question is not whether to read the ruminations of a series of "dead white men," but what the point of the sojourn might be. Of course, there is no way to avoid cultural capital accumulation. The task of pedagogy is to encourage the surplus—the elements of the canons that transcend the sacred texts by putting them in their historical context and into the debates that formed them.

One of the chief differences between American and European higher education is that Europe's system is more relentlessly meritocratic but, like all other levels of schooling, is funded from general revenues. In most European countries, although enrollments in technical and professional schools have increased over the last half century, the higher academic learning remains a privilege for the relative few, and emphatically not a right. The American meritocracy is no less exclusionary if access to knowledge rather than admission to some institution is taken as the criterion. Rather than restricting admission to high achievers, American higher education, in the sense of access to the Western intellectual tradition, operates more openly, albeit often in truncated form, at the level of the elite schools—the Ivies, prestigious private colleges, and leading state universities.

While in the United States a much larger proportion of the population is afforded the chance to attend some postsecondary institution, most students are denied the time and the opportunity to study literature, history, science, and philosophy, the key domains by which the tradition was forged. And sooner or later, many graduates from elite schools discover that the curriculum has left huge gaps in their education. Most are not required to study philosophy, social theory, and the metatheoretical or philosophical foundations of the sciences. Often they find that their undergraduate degree signifies status, but not learning, even in their major field. The same can be said for many European, Asian, and Latin American students, whose schooling has become increasingly specialized as their own societies have sought to emulate the American model.

With more than 60 percent of U.S. high school graduates entering postsecondary institutions, tuition has become just another user tax, like highway tolls or fees for the use of recreation areas or for motor vehicle registration. In the United States, after a generation during which the state afforded nearly every high school graduate the opportunity to attend college, the higher learning is once more treated as a privilege. At the same time, educators and public officials remind us that it is no longer merely a stepping stone to the middle class but has become a necessity in our knowledge-based economy. If this is so, a fundamental political question remains: How can we generalize tuition-free higher education and make it a major priority of public expenditures?

The key to the creation of spaces that are, even in a small measure, sites of learning is to radically separate all or part of teaching and learning from specialization. By specialization, I do not refer to a learning regime that focuses on a profound exploration of a few domains of knowledge. Indeed, I subscribe to Alfred North Whitehead's dictum: "Do not teach too many subjects—What you teach, teach thoroughly."[2] By specialization, I mean a pedagogy that requires students to, as quickly as possible, narrow their focus to a single discipline, which in most instances means putting on intellectual blinders against the distraction of other knowledges.

There is, of course, a place for in-depth focus on technical education in the undergraduate curriculum. But it should not be exclusively oriented to the practices and technologies of existing jobs. Its aim should be consistent with the general purposes of learning: to enhance the student's grasp of conceptual thinking, as well as to provide a practical path to attaining control over a body of knowledge that might or might not become useful for specific occupational purposes. For example, it would be refreshing if "computer literacy" included, in addition to programming, knowledge of the science behind these programs. The student could benefit from learning the history of computers, including Babbage's idea of the differencing machine, the socioeconomic functions of current and future computer applications, their relation to the configuration of the labor process, changing occupations and their applications in play. Needless to say, a program like this would transform the meaning of technical education; it would make it critical, since its focus would be on the social relations of technology while, at the same time, helping the student to gain mastery over technics.

Nor do I oppose postsecondary science programs designed to prepare students for medicine or nursing, medical technology, computer programming, and many similar trades. The point is, today even some of the most prestigious technical institutes, including Rensselaer Polytechnic, Carnegie Mellon, and Case Western Reserve Universities, permit students from the inception of their academic careers to fill their curriculum with technical and technoscientific subjects, relegating the arts, humanities, and social sciences to the periphery. The student arrives at the end of four years a techno-idiot. In the Greek meaning of the term, "idiot" signifies a person with only specialized knowledge, someone who, in all other respects, is ignorant. I suppose for those sufficiently talented in and entirely dedicated to their narrow interests this appears to be a reasonable option. The question is whether this kind of learning is consistent with the objective of providing a learning regime that prepares the student for life?

If learning as a form of life could be even partially severed from the credentialing system, the university would welcome the broad participation of working adults as much as it now does traditional full-time students, encouraging the formation of intellectuals as well as bestowing credentials. Even though higher education would still serve the practical needs of society, it would not define society primarily as "business." In short, the whole spirit and purpose of higher education would change, returning to the time when, at least rhetorically, universities and colleges saw themselves as sites of critical thinking. It might be possible to show that the virtual abandonment, by today's educational leaders, of the goal of providing for society a layer of critical intellectuals is a response to the upsurges of student activism in the 1960s. In this light, the turn toward vocationalization and toward a reduced conception of learning may be part of an effort, openly urged by many on the right, to make sure the 1960s never happen again.

4

The fundamental mission of higher education should be to play a leading role, perhaps the leading role, in the development of general culture. This mission falls on colleges and universities because, for historical reasons, they have been endowed with the intellectual and physical resources to occupy this space. To the academic system falls the task of providing access to a substantial portion of the population to the rich intellectual and cultural traditions that make up American society, of which the Western is, of course, the most important but not the only strain. As I have already suggested, this implies that colleges and universities must become public spheres, available to the larger community as well as to the community of scholars. They must be centers of learning, but also sites of discovery, not only in the natural sciences but also in the social sciences and the humanities. And universities, especially public institutions, should be places where debates on public issues occur, where public life, which has been eclipsed in all but the most local ways, can be restored.

Universities are still the centers of the development of most socially useful science and an increasing proportion of technoscience, that is, science oriented to practical ends. But government funds for all types of scientific research are shifting from military-related physics and chemistry to commercially oriented molecular biology applications, chiefly for agricultural and drug corporations. In many leading universities, a new pharmaceutical-corporate complex is slowly displacing the older military-industrial complex, which nevertheless retains considerable power over scientific work. And government funding, especially for pure science or basic research is, relatively speaking, declining, because these activities formerly had military cover. It seems that in the wake of post–Cold War science policy, the scientific enterprise must justify itself on commercial grounds until a new military danger appears.

Scientists themselves are seeking private corporate sector support for their work. In the bargain of receiving corporate funds, scientists have shifted their priorities to activities whose goal—direct as well as indirect—is to provide commercially useful knowledge, but the price of funding is to surrender intellectual property. For example, the corporations often own the patents for new life forms outright, or at least share the title with the scientist. In recent years, patent law has been interpreted by the Supreme Court to mean that corporations can own all of our collective genes; consequently, if anyone wishes to use her own genes for any purpose, she must obtain permission from the patent holder. As a result, where government has pulled back, philanthropy has been called upon to assume a larger responsibility for funding medical research, especially in areas such as cervical, ovarian, and breast cancer, where there is not yet a "magic bullet" cure. But areas such as ecological science, research on diseases that have a smaller base of public support, and knowledge that is in practical terms "useless" but in cultural terms significant are being shortchanged.

National science policy needs to recognize these problems; only new infusions of public funds can preserve entire areas of science, like cosmology, that have hitherto received public support largely in relation to military and commercial priorities in conjunction with space exploration. In addition, just as under pressure brought by social movements, substantial infusions of public funds have been directed to AIDS research, the role of the public sector in cancer research must grow. At a time when one of three people can expect to suffer from the disease, private donations cannot hope to meet the heavy costs of research and development of treatment regimes. None of these arguments nullifies the value of private giving. But however necessary, private philanthropy is neither quantitatively or qualitatively sufficient.

We need a new national policy for educating and employing scientists and mathematicians. Since the end of the Cold War resulted in relative declines in education and research funds to the sciences, many of the best students are choosing careers in law, medicine, and business. There are simply no jobs for even the most qualified students in the "hard sciences," especially in universities. One of the reasons for the current situation is that, lacking the domestic resources for training and education, U.S. businesses and university education and research programs are draining other countries of their talent, especially where universities educate scientists, engineers, and physicians but the economy cannot employ them. Many U.S.-based corporations and academic physics and chemistry Ph.D. programs rely on the migration of Indian, Korean, Russian, Philippino, and Taiwanese students and researchers for their sustenance. Under these circumstances, there is little or no incentive to pay attention to the large-scale drift away from the sciences among native-born young people. As, however, the economies of developing countries start to emerge, they will begin to offer their own scientists and engineers more opportunities. The United States is thus ill advised to rely on outside talent and the market to solve their knowledge-based labor needs. Given the length of preparation required to be a competent research scientist, only serious planning can improve and expand science education at every level of schooling and once more build the cadre this country needs in these fields.

The renewal of science education as part of a general education program is important beyond its uses in refurbishing scientific cadres. For there is little question that ours is a scientific/technological era. Science and technology have shaped every aspect of our lives, especially our thinking and the use of what was once termed "free time," the hours away from paid labor. From the invention of nuclear weapons, which has transformed global politics and international relations, to the emergence of communications and information technologies as tools of business, forms of conviviality, and no less important, sources of pleasure, the human "soul" has been hardwired and partially programmed. That we have become cyborgs—half human and half machine—seems clichéd to some, but remains one of the presuppositions of social life.[3]

Where are the learning programs to address this radically novel phenomenon? How can we teach and learn ethics, science, social science, and contemporary literature and other arts without a thorough knowledge of the historical rupture that has occurred since World War Two? How we can avoid taking science and technology as the significant "other" of the self? Having declared these commonplaces, any honest look at the curriculum would soon reveal that our most established disciplines have taken great pains to ignore the scientific and technological imperative, abdicating their responsibility to expose generations of students to the most salient forces in contemporary life. This is not the place to elaborate the historical and ideological roots of this neglect. In the present context, it may be sufficient to note the lack of conceptually based science education as an indication of how utterly blind our leading academic disciplines are.

Certainly, in every field there are exceptional individuals among the faculty who have made these issues their major work: philosophers of an earlier generation—Martin Heidegger, Herbert Marcuse, and Hans Jonas—and more recently philosophers Don Ihde, Sandra Harding, Andrew Feenberg, Evelyn Fox Keller, and Steve Fuller. Among natural scientists, the work of Richard Lewontin, Richard Levins, Jonathan King, and Stephen Jay Gould in biology stands out. And the social and philosophical ruminations of physicists Albert Einstein, Niels Bohr, and Werner Heisenberg have provided a necessary counterweight by drawing attention to the social consequences of their scientific discoveries to the otherwise unmitigated celebration of their achievements. Joseph Weitzenbaum and Seymour Papert have, from different perspectives, discussed the educational and social implications of computer science; social investigators such as Donna Haraway, Shoshanna Zuboff, Sherry Turkel, Bruno Latour, Andrew Pickering, Steve Shapin, and David Bloor have, in different ways, invented a whole new knowledge domain, the social studies of science and technology. Historians Lewis Mumford,

Thomas Kuhn, David Noble, William Leach, and Stuart Ewen have subjected scientific and technological change to close scrutiny, as have literary historians and critics such as Leo Marx, Richard Deinst, and Cary Wolfe.

These are among the handful of intellectuals who have distinguished themselves precisely by their attempts to understand the meaning of science, technology, and the rise of information and mass communications as characteristic human activities. All of them have called attention to the profound alteration of what Heidegger has called the transformation of the "world picture" initiated by discoveries such as relativity, quantum mechanics and its indeterminacy principle, complexity and systems theory. Social investigation has shown that just as fundamental physical and biological relations are valid only within a specific frame of reference, scientific discoveries are not free of social and cultural embeddedness. On the contrary, their truths are historically situated and always linked to human purposes.[4]

Scholars in all disciplines may readily acknowledge the world-transforming effects of the scientific revolutions of our own time, but they often resist the connection to social life. They prefer to erect a "Chinese Wall" around the achievements of science and technology, declaring their autonomy from culture and social relations. In many universities, a sometimes acrimonious debate rages around these conflictual claims. This is not the place to rehearse the issues separating the combatants, only to indicate that the terms of entry into the debate requires students to have some familiarity with the history, politics, and culture of science and technology above and beyond the algorithms of (past) scientific practices. I shall return to this and related questions of curriculum below.[5]

5

The evolution of the curriculum in the last century has paralleled the growth of knowledge specializations, which in turn correspond to the emergence of scientific, technical, and organizational knowledge as key actors in the industrial and service workplaces. The narrowing of the definition of these knowledge domains has also been linked to the transformation of philosophy into science, the human sciences as well as the so-called natural sciences. Increasingly, the unity of the sciences is provided by method rather than by a substance they all share. But experimental and quantitative methods in fact constitute the substance of science; in social as well as natural sciences, to be is to be measured. Thus the humanities have been defined by their historical and interpretative approaches to knowledge and, consequently, relegated more and more to serving as ornaments in the academic system or, worse, to places where students obtain "skills."

Since the disciplines have been constituted historically rather than being a force of nature, they can be changed. Ironically, the natural sciences have been most open to these reforms: biochemistry, molecular biology, biophysics, and several other hybrids resulted from the actual interdisciplinary practices of the sciences themselves. Many have discovered that the separation of physics, chemistry, and biology no longer addresses the knowledge-object, which, it turns out, can only be grasped adequately by combining and transfiguring the traditional disciplines. In contrast, facing fewer student enrollments and less money, the humanities and social science disciplines have jealously guarded their turf, except English and its stepsister, American studies, which have experienced something of a revival over the past decade as a result of their embrace of cultural studies. However, I do not wish to promote indiscriminate interdisciplinarity in undergraduate learning. I want to argue for an approach that concentrates on the study of four key knowledge domains, at least in the first two years: history, literature, science, and philosophy.

My fundamental strategy employs all of these domains to explore specific historical periods, with the goal of showing their interaction rather than a logical and traditional separation. Every domain within a specific place and period participates in, and is influenced by, the prevailing spirit of the time, but each has its own internal history as well. One need not adopt a particular theory of knowledge determination—by the economic infrastructure, by Power, taken here as a migrating Will, by Great Ideas, or any other category. In fact, issues of determination might be treated dialogically, that is, as a subject for discussion. The point of the core is to find articulations between economic, political, and social currents, social and cultural movements, and knowledge orientations and, perhaps, to discover unexpected relationships with other cultures and contexts.

There are two possible approaches to historical knowledge. First, one can study the forces and events that have shaped human societies and, second, one can pursue philosophical and theoretical considerations as a way of understanding nature and the practices of human groups, both in the anthropological sense and in their representations, especially art, science, and philosophy. For example, instead of the pervasive practice among teachers of treating Plato's *Republic* as the starting point, the key texts for a study of ancient Greek civilization might include contemporary accounts by Thucydides and Herodotus, as well as works such as Josiah Ober's *Mass and Elite in Democratic Athens* and M. I. Finley's *Ancient Economy*. In addition one might turn to writers like Pierre Vidal-Naquet to establish a social and political context for the study of the pre-Socratics, who were both the philosophers and the scientists of their era. Thales, Anaximander, Anaximenes, and Heraclitus would be treated as pioneers of cosmology, physics, and chemistry, as well as shapers of philosophical discourse. Students might read the best collection and one of the better commentaries on these works, G. S. Kirk, J. E. Raven, and M. Schofied's *The Presocratic Philosophers* and John Burnet's *Early Greek Philosophy*. They would also do well to pick up the collection of critical essays edited by Alexander Mourelatos, especially Mourelatos's essay on Parmenides, Gregory Vlastos's essay on Anaxagoras, and the section on Heraclitus, which, among other discussions, contains Kirk's commentary. These works could be supplemented by Bruno Snell's *The Discovery of the Mind* and Werner Jaeger's *Paideia*. Snell's work would give students a solid background to the pre-Socratic era, and Jaeger would provide an overarching perspective on philosophical, pedagogic culture. F. M. Cornford's *From Religion to Philosophy* is indispensable for showing the transition from myth and religion to philosophy and science and provides a pivot for understanding feudal society. The epic works of Homer, Aristophanes, and Euripides, the development of mathematics, and the study of Greek architecture and sculpture would be interweaved with history, science, and philosophy.

In other words, Plato's dialogues would no longer be viewed as the record of genius at work without regard to the historical context within which Socrates and Athenian democracy worked. The science, philosophy, and (social, economic, and political) history of ancient Greece would form the context for readings in Plato's dialogues—the *Symposium*, the *Phaedrus*, and *Parmenides*, as well as the *Republic*—Aristotle's *Metaphysics*, *Poetics*, and *Politics;* and the Romans, for example, Lucretius, Virgil, and Cato. The student would thus come to see, for example, that

Plato was not just engaged in a discussion with his immediate interlocutors, but also with the entire early scientific and philosophic tradition. And she would see the relation between Aristotle and his teacher, Plato, and his relation to the earlier Milesian philosophers, the Eleatics, and the Pythagoreans, for the Socratic and Platonic view that truth lies in the permanence of forms was disputed by their predecessors as well as by Aristotle. Plato's metaphysics was, in part, a reading of Parmenides and Zeno's philosophy, but not the only possible reading. Plainly, a deep study of the so-called ancient world should take up at least one full-year course.

Early Greek thought was deeply influenced by the science and philosophy of the East. Thus, the exclusion of the pre-Socratics from the canon is every bit as ideological as the neglect of the philosophy of North Africa, India, and China, for it is among the pre-Socratics that "non-Western" influences are most pronounced, especially in their belief in flux, and in change as a consequence of natural strife. It might seem logical to assume that the call for explorations in Eastern philosophies—whose history is coincident with and, in some respects, predates ancient Greek science and philosophy—is the unique contribution of the multiculturalist movement. Indeed, it may surprise some multiculturalists to learn that G. W. F. Hegel's *Philosophy of History* begins with an extensive treatment of the "Oriental world" and that his *Lectures in the History of Philosophy* starts with Eastern philosophy, not the Greeks. Two of Max Weber's earlier writings, *The Agrarian Sociology of Ancient Civilizations* and *The Religion of India*, remain of contemporary interest, especially the latter work's sensitive study of Hinduism and its relation to the caste system. Louis Dumont's *Homo Hierarchicus* and the fine essay by Barrington Moore at the beginning of *Injustice: The Social Bases of Obedience and Revolt*, on discontent among India's untouchable caste, provide a counterpoint to Weber's treatment. A century after its publication, *The Agrarian Sociology* remains one of the great treatments in the literature, containing discussions of Mesopotamia, Egypt, and Israel and providing a historically situated political economy of the ancient world, of the Roman republic in particular. The "Near Eastern" forerunners of Greek science and philosophy are explored in J. B. Pritchard's edited volume *Ancient Near Eastern Texts and Their Relation to the Old Testament*. And one can still profit from the idiosyncratic but towering work of Karl A. Wittfogel, *Oriental Despotism*, which if used carefully still offers one of the best interpretative histories of China. Of course, the magisterial multivolume *Science and Civilization in China* by the English Marxist scientist and historian Joseph Needham awaits a shorter version suitable for classroom work. Yet the discerning teacher might be able to extract key sections from the five volumes.

An interesting question is why, for more than a century, Western education "forgot" the Chinese, African, and Indian roots of what has been considered unique in the European and North American tradition. Scholars have long insisted on the syncretic relation between Western and non-Western thought, but since the nineteenth century, the educational system steadily narrowed its horizon. It would be worthwhile to address this question in a core program, to trace the process and the influences that made the "forgetting" probable. It might be discovered that the loss of a global perspective was inversely linked to the turn-of-the-century colonial and imperial reach of Western societies, which was accompanied by the academic movement to confine traditional study to "Western" civilization. One could cite England's dominion in the Americas and in Asia, the French incursions into Asia and North Africa, the American expansion in the Southwest, the Caribbean, and Latin America, and its displacement of the older Spanish colonialism. In the context of aggressive economic and political penetration by technologically and industrially advanced Western societies, it was simply not convenient to acknowledge the "Oriental" influences, the African, or in general, those of the subaltern or subordinate cultures. Nor, until recently, did mavens of "high culture" come to terms with folk music, blues, jazz, and "primitive" visual forms as some of the major influences on contemporary art. In the context of the lost history of academic commitments to global culture, is it too much to suggest that multiculturalism is the return of the repressed, even if in different forms?

In a two-year period, neither a full survey of the millions of years of archaeological and anthropological records of human development nor of the five thousand years of "written" history can be adequately covered. Indeed, "coverage" is quite beside the point. But students do need a vision of the sweep of the development of the natural and human sciences as well as exposure to differing and conflictual theories of historical periodicity. The canon might include a range of historiographic works. It might begin, for example, with selections from Hegel's *Philosophy of History* and from the first part of Marx and Engels's *German Ideol-*

ogy, both of which suggest definite stages of historical development. Moving on, twentieth-century reflections such as Lucien Febvre's *A New Kind of History* and R. G. Collingwood's *The Idea of History* stress ideas more than social forces but retain a clear sense of structure. More contemporary works, such as Siegfried Kracauer's *History*, Jacques Le Goff's *History and Memory*, and Michel de Certeau's *The Writing of History*, may be viewed within the framework of modern science's discoveries of indeterminism, even chaos and complexity, as the context of events and social life. In addition, relevant anthropological and archaeological studies of early peoples would be a central concern of this course.

A third course of study would explore the feudal epoch, the period between the fall of the Roman Empire and the early Renaissance. Here too philosophy would be the starting point: Augustine, Thomas Aquinas, and Duns Scotus from the Christian canon, Maimonides from the Jewish tradition, Muslim writings, particularly selections from the Koran, and Confucian works from this period. Students would study the science of Aristotle, whose *Physics*, essays on meteorology, colors, and biology, embodied in his five essays on animals and his *Plants* essay dominated Western science for a thousand years. And his followers would also be included in our curriculum, particularly Ptolemy, Archimedes, the later Epicureans, and, of course, the Roman Lucretius, whose *On the Nature of Things* points a way forward from the Master. For the historical context, Marc Bloch's two-volume *Feudal Order*, Eileen Powers's *Medieval People*, and Carlo Ginzburg's more recent *The Cheese and the Worms*, as well as Mikhail Bakhtin's *Rabelais and His World*, provide a solid grounding in the economic and social history of feudalism and segue to the early modern period and its conflicts. Finally, the student would read some of Dante's *Divine Comedy*, Cervantes's *Don Quixote*, and of course, Rabelais's *Gargantua*.

A fourth year-long course on Enlightenment philosophy and science in the context of the development of capitalism and the Industrial Revolution—again combining history, philosophy, science, and literature—might begin with one or more of many excellent shorter treatments of the Industrial Revolution in England, France, and the United States, such as Deane's *Industrial Revolution* or Hobsbawm's *Industrial Man*. For science, Thomas Kuhn's *The Copernican Revolution*, Gaston Bachelard's *The New Scientific Spirit*, and I. Bernard Cohen's *Revolution in Science* might provide a framework for understanding the nature of the scientific enlightenment. Selections from Hans Blumenberg's vast *The Genesis of the Copernican World* would be useful as well. These should be supplemented by readings from Galileo and other innovators, and by contemporary essays such as A. Rahman's "Sixteenth and Seventeenth Century Science in India and Some Problems of Comparative Studies," Roy Porter's "Rise of the Science of Geology," Stephen Jay Gould's collection *Time's Arrow, Time's Cycle*, and Robert Young's great monograph "The Historiographic and Ideological Contexts of the Nineteenth Century Debate on Man's Place in Nature." The intersection of technology and economics is addressed by David Landes's *Unbounded Prometheus* and E. P. Thompson's "Time, Work-Discipline, and Industrial Capitalism," and by Anson Rabinbach's *Human Machine*, which takes the story into the early twentieth century.

This is the place to deal with the great migrations endemic to industrialization, especially the slave trade addressed in Orlando Patterson's *Slavery and Social Death*. For a global perspective and a sample of the many important works of the Americas, we have Eugene Genovese's *Roll, Jordan, Roll* and Gilberto Freyre's classic study of slavery in the development of Brazil. To these must be added the work of Oscar Handlin and other historians who have contributed to the myth of the success of the second-wave immigrant experience, but also that of Brinley Thomas and Paul Gilroy, who have challenged the thesis of assimilation. In *The Atlantic Migration*, for example, Thomas argues that southern and eastern Europeans were never fully assimilated into the United States and other Atlantic societies. And following W. E. B. Du Bois's concept of double consciousness, Gilroy claims in *The Black Atlantic* that there is a black identity (his "black Atlantic") that for cultural as well as economic reasons remains in, but not of, the dominant societies, and, instead, is linked across national borders.

A fifth course, on modernity, might be distinguished from that on the Enlightenment only by its emphasis on philosophical and political as opposed to economic and social history, and by the study of literature. Clearly, Descartes, Spinoza, Hobbes, Locke, Berkeley, and Hume are crucial figures for grasping the new industrial and scientific mentality. Students would read Descartes's *Discourse on Method*; Spinoza's *Ethics*, which is a counterpoint to prevailing epistemological approaches to knowledge; parts of Locke's *Essay Concerning Human Understanding*, especially his analysis of "the self," which constitutes one of the founding essays on social psychology; and Hume's A *Treatise of Human Nature*, particularly part 1, "Of the Understanding." Perhaps the apogee of the philosophical celebration of the scientific enterprise is the work of Immanuel Kant, whose *Prolegomena to Any Future Metaphysics*, "What Is Enlightenment," and *The Critique of Judgement* comprise his most accessible short statements. But this is also a period of democratic revolutions, especially the epochal French Revolution, treated with degrees and variations of enthusiasm by R. R. Palmer, Georges Lefebvre, Albert Saboul, and George Rude, whose classic *The Crowd in the French Revolution* emphasizes the role of the crowd in social change. For counterviews, one can turn to Tocqueville and, more recently, François Furet. Modernity comes into its own in this period and, in this regard, no better source than pertinent selections from Hans Blumemberg's spirited defense *The Legitimacy of the Modern Age* can be recommended. There are many excellent treatments of the Industrial Revolution in England, France, and the United States.

The literature of modernity may be said to begin with Dante, not overlooking Marlowe and Shakespeare's plays and sonnets, the poetry of Dryden, Spenser, and especially Milton. But its representative form is the novel. Thus, the eighteenth-century books of Fielding, Defoe, and Richardson initiate the literature of the urban and industrial periods of capitalist development. To which must follow the great works of Dickens, Austen, the Brontës, Thackeray, Trollope, and Collins, to mention only the most prominent. Of course, the Americans Cooper, Whitman, and Hawthorne, Russians Tolstoy, Gogol, Turgenev, and Chernyshevsky, and the great French novelists Balzac, Victor Hugo, and Emile Zola provide a feast from which to make selections. The eighteenth and nineteenth centuries are also moments of vast changes in Japan, which, during this period debates and struggles with the issues of modernity. A good collection on modern Japan is R. P. Dore, *Aspects of Social Change in Modern Japan*. Donald Keane's excellent *Anthology of Japanese Literature from the Earliest Era to the Mid-Nineteenth Century* would be helpful for all of the courses, but the last section "The Tukugawa Period, 1600–1868," is particularly useful for the transition to modernity.

My sixth and final course would cover the twentieth century and thus presents the most serious difficulties. The twentieth century has been framed by the crucial events of two world wars, by the advent of the nuclear and the computer ages, and by a second wave of political revolutions, notably the Russian, Chinese, and Cuban upheavals. It has witnessed the nationalist revivals, especially in the conquered nations of Central and Eastern Europe, Asia, Africa, and the Caribbean, some of which identified themselves with socialism and communism. In the advanced industrial societies, the turn of the century saw the rise of the labor movement, which embraced millions. In most of the countries of Western Europe these movements formed class-based political parties that became challengers to political and economic power.

Just as important, our century has been a time of scientific and technological transformation. The world as we knew it just a few years ago looked and felt very different, whether we are talking about Einstein's discovery of relativity and the development of quantum mechanics, which together overturned the Newtonian worldview; the emergence of electricity and chemistry as characteristic industrial processes; or the profound applications of solid state physics to communications and information technology, the most ubiquitous of which has been the widespread application of cybernetics and its characteristic technology, the computer.

And this century has given birth to a host of new social movements: the fight for racial freedom in North America and South Africa, but also in Europe; two waves of feminism, beginning with the prolonged struggle for voting rights in England and the United States and ending with the struggle for sexual freedom and economic equality; the extension of the struggle for sexual freedom to lesbians and gays; and the emergence of a worldwide movement for constructing economic life, consumption as well as production, on ecological bases. The literatures of these movements make up a vast collection, as do the works written in reaction to them. Some, like W. E. B. Du Bois's *Souls of Black Folk* and Simone de Beauvoir's *The Second Sex,* are not only fine social analyses of the nature of the "problem" but compelling works of literature in their own right. Du Bois's book could be read in the context of post-Reconstruction reaction to the Civil War and the Emancipation Proclamation, but also in relation to the social psychology of William James and of George Herbert Mead, and of Dilthey's philosophy of history, which influenced Du Bois's concept of double consciousness. And Beauvoir's work may be seen in the light of feminism as a social movement but also through the prism of phenomenology, of which she was a major postwar proponent.

The difficulty of limiting the number of textual sources must be apparent to anyone conversant with the complexity of this century. Eric Hobsbawm's history, *The Age of Extremes,* possesses the virtues of being well written, comprehensive, and partisan. The partisanship saves this compendium from soporiferousness, a characteristic that condemns many similar texts. E. H. Carr has written a massive account of the Soviet experience, the first three volumes of which cover the Bolshevik revolution, and there are many other accounts recommended in his bibliography. Isaac Deutscher's biography of Stalin has been criticized for being a backdoor justification of his brutal dictatorship, but, together with Robert Tucker's more unswerving condemnation, it is among the best we have. Work on the Chinese revolution is less accessible, but the histories by Stuart Schramm and Edward Friedman might be profitably read. And, of course, the age of revolution quickly prompted a vigorous counterrevolution. The rise of fascism has been well described by many writers; my favorite for Nazism is Franz Neumann's great *Behemoth.* It is not the most up-to-date account but remains powerful and pertinent. For more recent evaluations, the collection of articles by German scholars edited by David Crew, *Nazism and German Society, 1933–1945,* provides a number of valuable recent perspectives. There are now several quite good biographies of Hitler—the most comprehensive is by Alan Bullock—as well as two recent biographies of Mussolini, to which should be added Victoria De Grazia's *Culture of Consent,* one of the better social histories of Italian fascism.

Einstein's essays and his student Abraham Pais's superb biography, which is an account of both his life and his work, might provide a starting point for understanding the twentieth-century scientific revolution. In another biography, Pais has also done well by Niels Bohr, who carried the revolution to places where the master was not prepared to go. In addition, there are many accounts of these changes directed to the general reader that stress the key concepts and avoid technical language. Fine biographies of Werner Heisenberg, the discoverer of the indeterminacy principle and the leading scientist in the German effort to build an atomic bomb; Leo Szilard, one of the crucial figures in the development of nuclear weapons and an important opponent of their postwar uses; and of others, such as J. Robert Oppenheimer and David Bohm, might give the student insight into postwar relations between science and political power.

Undoubtedly the most important scientific event of the last half of the twentieth century, James Watson and Francis Crick's discovery of the double helix structure of the DNA molecule led to the emergence of molecular biology at the center of the life sciences. With the development of genetic engineering, we have witnessed the virtual merger of science and technology. Watson and Crick have written highly readable accounts of their work. At the same time, critics such as evolutionary biologists Geerat J. Vermeli, Richard Lewontin and Richard Levins, Stephen Jay Gould, and Francisco Ayala have called attention to the reductionism and linear thinking pervasive in the new biological paradigm. They and other writers have also shown the close link between scientific practices and the ecological crisis. Rachel Carson, Barry Commoner, and many others have argued that the fruits of technoscience and its collaboration with large drug and agricultural corporations have produced some of the deleterious environmental effects of the last four decades. Lewis Mumford, Murray Bookchin, and Hans Jonas are among the philosophers who have called for an imperative ethic of responsibility. While most scientists remain unfazed by the consequences of some of their discoveries, the voices of critics have become increasingly insistent and have contributed to the emergence of a worldwide ecology movement that has challenged the industrial-scientific-university complex.

Twentieth-century philosophy has been preoccupied with the dominance of science and technology over everyday life. Whatever their concerns with other issues, nearly all of the leading philosophers of the pre–World War Two era and many of more recent vintage have felt constrained to address contemporary scientific knowledge and its consequences for our understanding of the modern world. For example, Henri Bergson, perhaps the most widely read philosopher of the first decades of the twentieth century, especially his *Creative Evolution*, wrote a major commentary on the theory of relativity, as did John Dewey, whose *Quest for Certainty* was a commentary on the so-called Copenhagen school of quantum interpretation. Alfred North Whitehead's *Science and the Modern World* stands among the leading early-twentieth-century treatments of the relation of science to culture and society. Karl Popper wrote *The Logic of Scientific Discovery* as a contribution to the movement to install science and its methods as the final arbiter of truth. This defining work in the philosophy of science could be contrasted with readings from critical admirers, notably Thomas Kuhn's influential essay *The Structure of Scien-*

tific Revolutions and especially Paul Feyerabend's *Against Method,* which has elicited considerable controversy.

Modernist literature actually predates the twentieth century. French writers from Mallarmé, Baudelaire, and Rimbaud to novelists such as Flaubert and Proust, the Russian Dostoyevsky and the American Edgar Allan Poe foreshadowed and influenced Joyce, Kafka, Döblin, Aragon, Céline, Eliot, Pound, and Faulkner, the great modernists of the first half of the century, as well as many others in virtually every country. But modernism, among whose characteristic movements were surrealism, dadaism, and futurism, also spurred the development of a new "realism." Hemingway was perhaps the most influential writer of this movement. His "surreal" style consisted in a parody of the staccato verbal performances of ordinary speech, which in turn became huge factors in the transmutation of the detective genre and in American and Caribbean black literature. In this connection, Dashiell Hammett, Raymond Chandler, and Cornell Woolrich deserve an important place in the modernist canon, as do Richard Wright, the great Caribbean writer George Lamming, Langston Hughes, Zora Neale Hurston, and Chester Himes. Indeed, Himes's detective fiction ranks among the best of this genre, even as many critics have discovered the importance of his early novels *If He Hollers Let Him Go* and *Lonely Crusade* and his great two-volume autobiography, *The Quality of Hurt.* Ralph Ellison's *Invisible Man,* whose debt to Dostoevsky and to Wright is as profound as it is obvious, also has an honored place in this company.

The writers of the so-called Latin American boom of the postwar era stand out in world literature as among its most powerful and original invocations of the modernist struggle. Writers such as Juan Rolfo, Jorge Luis Borges, Gabriel García Márquez, Mario Vargas Llosa, Julio Cortázar, and Manuel Puig should be read in connection with their contributions to literary modernism, particularly magic realism and the integration of indigenous myth and popular culture. Again, these works would not be read for their aesthetic value alone but as *situated* knowledges linked to the history and politics of the region and its relation to Europe and the United States. This link is especially apposite in the light of García Márquez's leftist and Vargas Llosa's center-right candidacies for president of their respective countries, Colombia and Peru, but also for the unique role many Latin America intellectuals have played in public life in this century. The neoliberal Brazilian president Ferdinand Cardozo is a Marxist academic economist by training; the Chilean Nobel Prize–winning poet Pablo Neruda was his country's ambassador to France and a leading member of the left unity administration of socialist Salvador Allende; and Mexican writers Octavio Paz and Carlos Fuentes played prominent roles in their country's politics and culture for decades.

I want to offer an illustration of a transdisciplinary approach to the conflicts and confluences in North Africa. It may help clarify how one might address the need to place writers from different domains in juxtaposition. Frantz Fanon's *Wretched of the Earth* towers in the growing field of African/diasporic studies, together with Albert Memmi's *The Colonizer and the Colonized*, the more contemporary essay by Gayatri Spivak, "Can the Subaltern Speak?"—one of the most anthologized in the postcolonial critical literature—and Edward Said's *Orientalism*. These are arguably four "classic" works in the countercanon, but any core curriculum would be hard pressed to omit a serious examination of some of these texts. In contrast to the way these works have been opposed to the "Western" canon, my inclusion treats them as having been deeply influenced by aspects of the Western philosophical and social theoretical canon as well as constituting counterpoints to them. A unit on colonialism and postcolonial thought might, for example, focus on Fanon's dialogue with psychoanalysis, phenomenology, and Marxism. It would obviously incorporate the fiction of the African independence movement, notably the work of Achebe, whose classic *Things Fall Apart* is, in addition to being an affecting story, a crucial account of the emergence of modernity in black Africa. Other voices include Julius Nyerere and two novelists whose reflections on Africa are as significant as any history, Nadine Gordimer and Doris Lessing, and films such as *The Battle of Algiers*, a docudrama of the struggle for national independence in North Africa. In addition to selections from Fanon, Memmi, Spivak, and Said, the readings would include the works of those who have had the greatest influence on Fanon and Memmi—Freud, Sartre and Camus, and Marx—as well as accounts of the economic and political history of French colonialism. The study of colonialism might be capped by some discussion of the influence of contemporary philosophers, such as Jacques Derrida and other intellectuals of the colonized era, on critics such as Said and Spivak.

6

In the best pedagogical scenario for this curriculum, the students would take no other courses in the first two years. Indeed, the "course" and "credit" model would be jettisoned, since it still participates in the rationalization of knowledge. Students and faculty would work together in one rolling seminar. The learning community would organize its time according to its own convenience rather than accommodating to university rules. My strategy for the core is to see science, philosophy, and literature within a historical framework. Those who object to this approach are invited to adopt their own framework. One might proceed from literature, science, or philosophy, subsuming history and the remaining domains. These decisions would be left entirely to the curriculum planners, as long as these domains are addressed conceptually and critically. For example, in previous chapters I have argued for a conceptual approach to the three-thousand-year history of science and technology, and I would not want to insist on a particular perspective, only that it not be either primarily procedural or reverential. After all, the point is to assist students to think again what is usually taken for granted.

What is objectionable, in my view, is the current practice of treating canonical texts as independent of their contexts, and the tendency to exclude economic, political, and social history. The canon is also meaningless without a critical understanding of science and technology, and a grasp of contemporary thought, especially the philosophy and literatures of the margin and their histories within many cores. Among other reasons, it is arguable, for example, that the Latin American boom and genres such as detective and science fiction are not only the popular reading of our time but among its best literature. And I insist on these specific domains because they embody the most salient areas of what is the Western intellectual tradition.

If the goal is to help students become autodidacts, education must emphasize *pedagogy*. This is the main innovation of my model, for pedagogy has largely been ignored by most academics. Of course, the real object is to help students acquire the habit of reflexivity, but this aim cannot be realized unless students are genuinely empowered in the learning process. This means that the object of the curriculum is to engender the critical self-learner. Drawing from literary studies, I advocate "close" reading in the classroom, so that everyone is on the same page and the authority of the teacher may be put into question by the ambiguity of interpretation. In contrast to the Socratic method, with the instructor posing a question for which there is always a correct answer—as represented in the film and television series *The Paper Chase*, where the law professor was always in control, drawing responses from his students—the discussion would always be open. The instructor's questions would presume no "correct" interpretation and would invite students to teach each other as well as the professor. For my method assumes that the student enters the classroom, not as a blank sheet of paper, but with some knowledge and perspective to contribute.

Working study groups would also become key pedagogic tools, so that students could teach each other. The instructor would be on hand to provide information not easily available to students and perhaps interpretations that entail concrete knowledge of the intellectual and historical context within which the texts were produced. The instructor's role would be to encourage students to perform the research needed to adduce these contexts because this is a way to help them acquire the "skills" of inquiry.

These modes are appropriate, not only for the already literate, but for all students. By mastering the key texts of legitimate academic knowledge, the collective student body may be empowered to deal with many intellectual problems. "Mastery" cannot be achieved by ways of learning that are largely passive, such as being fed information through lectures or, what amounts to the same thing, through textbooks. There is no substitute for the encounter with complex arguments made through the use of rhetorical strategies that can themselves be studied. This encounter involves individual study, but also collective reading and inquiry.

There are three remaining issues, which are by no means easily solved: Who will teach the core? Who will learn its contents? And is this ambitious program suitable for two-year colleges and third-tier four-year institutions? I must confess that at first glance this curriculum proposal seems daunting, especially for a professoriate trained during the past five decades of relentless specialization. I do not mean to romanticize the academic system of the pre–World War Two period. Long before the war, most colleges and universities had abandoned a global approach to literature and philosophy; and outside anthropology, some subfields of sociology, such as religion and comparative politics and economics, few educated Americans knew anything about non-European and North American societies and their cultures. Moreover, this was a period when knowledge of the other was largely disdained by most faculty and students; after all, it was an appropriate attitude in the American Century. But it remains true that many schools required one or more courses in philosophy and literature. Some even required courses in Greek and Roman classics, and the typical graduate of a four-year program had a working knowledge of at least one other language besides English.

Most professors in the human and natural sciences would require considerable reeducation to be able to teach my model curriculum. For unlike other core programs, the trans- or cross-disciplinary approach to knowledge, situating it in a historical context, would not subdivide the subject matters into disciplinary units but would seek linkages among domains. It would probably work best if two or more instructors worked together with a large group and took responsibility for small study groups and tutorials or directed readings with individuals. And this curriculum would require holding faculty development institutes, which might focus on both the pedagogy and the knowledges. Surely the core I propose would be impractical without this preparation.

Can and will students embrace this rigorous program? I must confess that it will be an uphill battle. We know from the recent past that some societies have been able, in a relatively brief period, to achieve astounding literacy rates and to develop a considerable stratum of scientific and humanistic intellectuals, where once only a small group of these people existed. One model is suggested by military necessity. During World War Two, the United States military educated and trained almost a million servicemen and -women to read and write and operate complex technology, sending thousands on to colleges and universities for further education and training. Since the armed forces provided the time and money for this enterprise, and the alternatives were worse, enlisted men responded affirmatively.

The second model was born of ideological and political conviction as well as military need. The Soviet Union, China, Cuba, Israel, and revolutionary movements in Central America and Africa made education a centerpiece of their revolutionary and national programs and succeeded in creating within decades a scientific, technical, and cultural class where, in most cases, it had not existed. In these cases, the state appealed to its citizens to defend the gains of the revolution and to benefit individually by acquiring knowledge. Mass education in revolutionary societies inspired education, and even some learning, for considerable periods.

Even when revolutionary fervor cooled, developing industrial countries were able to maintain a high level of enthusiasm for education because they were in the process of economic expansion. Industrialization extended to the countryside as well as cities and literally made trade and academic schools the major after-work activity for millions.

What will inspire skeptical, not to say cynical, students who, having been encouraged to turn away from knowledge for its own sake in favor of the most practical conception of the role of education, may believe that general education is "useless"? In elite institutions, it may be that students are sufficiently motivated by status and the promise of job success to undertake such a program, especially if it is mandatory—better to expound the value of critical thinking and the knowledge that can grease its wheels. The problem is most severe in third-tier schools, where neither status nor money drives the educational regime. In these schools, the faculty is likely to find it necessary to articulate motivating arguments. In my experience as a community college instructor in the 1970s in a predominantly white working-class community, and in the 1980s at a workers' education center that awarded a baccalaureate to adult, mostly minority municipal employees working in low-level jobs, I found that students responded to two appeals. The first was to the idea that critical thinking and substantive knowledge of history and social theory, and not only in the procedural sense, might lead to group and self-advancement—a point made with considerable ideological content, with references to issues of class and labor politics, and to the largest interests of blacks and Latinos. The second could only be convincing in process: learning this stuff was intellectually challenging—and fun.

My students were often well prepared to read some of the canonical works I assigned, but not all of them. I found—and with my current graduate students, I still find—that reading the text paragraph by paragraph in class, stopping to answer questions of definition as well as interpretation, and meeting privately with those who have specific reading and writing difficulties are often effective in overcoming problems students encounter with unfamiliar material. Needless to say, I have had to adduce examples, illustrations, and demonstrations of many of the arguments and concepts. Having said this, I find that students are excited to be learning the real thing. But in order to pull it off, I have had to reinvent my own teaching style, think through the conceptual issues in situating knowledge in its own traditions, as well as in its social milieu. I have had to relate the most difficult concepts to people's concerns while not simplifying or distorting them, work very hard to learn things I once scorned or ignored, and to be open to new ideas without pandering to fashion.

Sometimes I fail to reach a group of students in a class, and it's usually because I have been unable to find the match that might light a fire in their bellies. Mostly when I don't make connections, it's because I haven't tried hard enough. Occasionally, the problem resides in students' inability to focus because of personal problems such as work and family, which demoralizes them when it does not prompt them to drop out. But I have a lot of evidence from my own teaching, and from that of others, that most students at every level of the academic system will rise to the challenge to *learn*. But they will strive only if they are convinced the professor is there beside them and has equal dedication, something far more valuable than charisma.

Are there those who are prepared to undertake this improbable adventure? If I didn't believe there were, I would not have written this book.

Notes

Chapter One

1. National Bureau of Higher Education Statistics, *College and University Enroll- ments, 1997* (Washington, D.C.: National Bureau of Higher Education Sta- tistics, 1998).
2. David Nasaw, *Schooled to Order* (New York: Oxford University Press, 1976).
3. Bill Readings, *The University in Ruins* (Cambridge: Harvard University Press, 1996).
4. Matthew Arnold, *Culture and Anarchy*, edited by Ian Gregor (Indianapolis: Bobbs-Merrill, 1971).
5. Readings, *University in Ruins*.
6. Paul Willis, *Learning to Labor: How Working-Class Lads Get Working-Class Jobs*, with an introduction by Stanley Aronowitz (New York: Columbia Univer- sity Press, 1981); Pierre Bourdieu and Jean Passeron, *Reproduction in Educa- tion, Society, and Culture*, 2d ed., translated by Richard Nice (London: Sage Publications, 1990).
7. Basil Bernstein, *Class, Codes, and Control: Theoretical Studies toward a Sociology of Language* (New York: Schocken Books, 1975).
8. National Bureau of Higher Education Statistics, *College and University Enroll- ments, 1997*.
9. Alain Touraine, *The Academic System in American Society* (1971; reprint, with a new introduction by Clark Kerr, New Brunswick, N.J.: Transaction Books, 1997).
10. "What Professors Earn," *Chronicle of Higher Education*, 23 April 1999.

Chapter Two

1. Christopher Lucas, *American Higher Education: A History* (New York: St. Mar- tin's Press, 1994), 86.
2. Ibid., 192.
3. Thorstein Veblen, *The Higher Learning in America* (1918; reprint, with a new in- troduction by Ivar Berg, New Brunswick, N.J.: Transaction Books, 1993).
4. Irving Howe, *A Margin of Hope: An Intellectual Biography* (New York: Harcourt, Brace and Jovanovich, 1982), 63.
5. National Bureau of Higher Education Statistics, *Colleges and Universities in the U.S., 1997* (Washington, D.C.: National Bureau of Higher Education Sta- tistics, 1998).

6. Clark Kerr, *The Uses of the University* (Cambridge: Harvard University Press, 1963), xiv.

7. David Lance Goines, *The Free Speech Movement* (Berkeley: Ten Speed Press, 1993), 103.

Chapter Three

1. Martin Kenney, *The University Industrial Complex* (New Haven: Yale University Press, 1986).

2. Fritz Machlup, *The Production and Distribution of Knowledge in the United States* (New York: Columbia University Press, 1969).

3. Jonathan R. Cole, introduction to *The Research University in a Time of Discontent,* edited by Jonathan R. Cole, Elinor G. Barber, and Stephen R. Graubard (Baltimore: Johns Hopkins University Press, 1994), 10.

4. Ibid., 31.

5. Ibid., 32.

6. Walter E. Massey, "Can the Research University Adapt to a Changing Future?" in Cole, Barber, and Graubard, *The Research University,* 191–92.

7. Donald Kennedy, "Making Choices in the Research University," in Cole, Barber, and Graubard, *The Research University,* 91.

8. Frank H. T. Rhodes, "The Place of Teaching in the Research University," in Cole, Barber, and Graubard, *The Research University,* 180–81.

9. Ibid.

10. Steven Brint and Jerome Karabel, *The Diverted Dream: Community Colleges and the Promise of Educational Opportunity in America, 1900–1985* (New York: Oxford University Press, 1989).

11. Lewis Feuer, *The Conflict of Generations: The Character and Significance of Student Movements* (New York: Basic Books, 1969).

12. Roger Kimball, *Tenured Radicals* (New York: Free Press, 1989).

13. Joseph Berger, "Remediation at CUNY Shifts to Community Colleges," *New York Times,* 27 June 1997.

14. Lucas, *American Higher Education,* 197–200.

15. Alan Trachtenberg, *The Incorporation of America* (New York: Hill and Wang, 1982).

Chapter Four

1. Courtney Letherman, "Teaching Assistants Plan Slowdown over Unionization," *Chronicle of Higher Education,* 13 November 1998.

2. Allen L. Sessoms, interview with Stanley Aronowitz and Jessie Klein, 16 June 1998.

3. Janny Scott, "Discord Turns Academe's Hot Team Cold," *New York Times,* 21 November 1998.

4. As reported on the FairTest Web site, April 1999 (http://www.FairTest.org).

5. Ibid.

Chapter Five

1. National Bureau of Higher Education Statistics, *College and University Enrollments, 1997.*

2. Brint and Karabel, *The Diverted Dream.*

3. David Lavin and David Hyllegard, *Changing the Odds: Open Admissions and the Life Chances of the Disadvantaged* (New Haven: Yale University Press, 1996).

Chapter Six

1. Faculty Committee on General Education, *General Education at UCLA: A Proposal for Change* (Los Angeles: University of California, 1998).

2. Allan Bloom, *The Closing of the American Mind: How Higher Education Has Failed Democracy and Impoverished the Souls of Today's Students* (New York: Simon and Schuster, 1987), 150.

3. Ibid., 20.

4. Ethan Bronner, "Winds of Academic Change Rustle University of Chicago," *New York Times,* 28 December 1998.

5. John Dewey, *Reconstruction in Philosophy* (1920), in *John Dewey: The Middle Works,* vol. 12, edited by Jo Ann Boydston (Carbondale: University of Southern Illinois Press, 1982).

6. Cary Nelson and Michael Berube, "Introduction and Report from the Front," in *Higher Education under Fire,* edited by Michael Berube and Cary Nelson (New York: Routledge, 1995).

Chapter Seven

1. For a fuller treatment of these themes, see Stanley Aronowitz and William DiFazio, *The Jobless Future: Sci-Tech and the Future of Work* (Minneapolis: University of Minnesota Press, 1994), and Jeremy Rifkin, *The End of Work* (New York: Holt, 1995).

2. Alfred North Whitehead, *The Aims of Education and Other Essays* (1929; reprint, New York: Free Press, 1967), 2.

3. Donna Haraway, "The Cyborg Manifesto," in *Simians, Cyborgs, and Women: The Reinvention of Nature* (New York: Routledge, 1991).

4. Martin Heidegger, "The Age of the World Picture" and "The Question Concerning Technology," both in *The Question Concerning Technology and Other Essays,* translated by William Lovitt (New York: Harper Colophon Books, 1997).

5. For opposing perspectives on the science wars, see the critique of scientificity in Stanley Aronowitz, *Science as Power: Discourse and Ideology in Modern Society* (Minneapolis: University of Minnesota Press, 1988), and the passionate and unequivocal defense of contemporary science in Paul R. Gross and Norman Levitt, *Higher Superstition: The Academic Left and Its Quarrels with Science* (Baltimore: Johns Hopkins University Press, 1994). Andrew Ross, ed., *Science Wars* (Durham: Duke University Press, 1996), also assembles some of the more important critiques of the social relations of science.

Acknowledgments

Many people have contributed to making this book better than it might have been. I am grateful to my friends and colleagues Patricia Clough, Joan Greenbaum, Jay Lemke, Donaldo Macedo, Michael Peleas, and Nancy Romer for their comments on several chapters. Henry Giroux gave rigorous reading to the entire manuscript and made salient suggestions, which I have incorporated into the final version. As is her wont, Ellen Willis sent me back on more than one occasion to the drawing boards and was especially helpful in suggesting structural changes in some of the chapters. My editor, Micah Kleit, paid close attention to every paragraph and shared some of his ideas and his own educational biography with me. Without his attention, completing the book would have been a much more difficult task. Finally, I want to thank my agent, Neeti Madan, and Beacon's editorial director, Deborah Chasman, for their confidence in this project.

Index

keeping technical programs current, 111; minimization of liberal arts programs at, 110; numbers enrolled in, 102; and remedial programs, 63, 106, 109–10

composition studies, 146. *See also* writing

Conant, James Bryant, 31, 38, 39

Consortium for Worker Education, 95

Cooper, James Fenimore, 183

Copernican Revolution, The, 181, 182

Cornford, F. M., 178

corporate partnerships, 43–44, 82–83, 160

corporate university, 6, 11, 49–50, 158–59, 163; and business ethic, 16–17; and downsizing and restructuring, 62–67; and ending of the Cold War, 83; and faculty restructuring, 73–74, 80–81, 84; and privatization, 82; as training ground for industry, 17; and use of business of practices in, 83–84, 85

corporations: and research universities, 6, 36, 43–44, 49–50; and science, 18, 173; and support of postsecondary education, 81

correspondence courses, 151

Cortázar, Julio, 187

cost: of postsecondary education, 122. *See also* funding for postsecondary education

Creative Evolution, 186

Crew, David, 185

Crick, Francis, 186

crisis of higher education: and Bill Readings, 37; solutions for, 108

critical appropriation, 126–27

Critique of Judgement, The, 183

Crowd in the French Revolution, The, 183

cultural capital, 7–8

culture, general, and development of by postsecondary education, 172–76

Culture of Consent, 185

curriculum: debate relative to, 126–56; and development for business, 81–82, 112–13

curriculum, graduate, 144–49; distance from job market, 146–47; revision of, 144; and two-tiered educational regime, 146–47

curriculum, undergraduate: and Bloom's quest for essential being, 129–30; and general education, 127, 149; and identity intellectual politics, 133–34; and "inquiry" rather than substance, 136; and lack of general education, 170; liberalization of in 1960s, 127; and multiculturalists and diversity, 126, 128, 130–33; proposed new model of, 178–88; and course on ancient world, 177–79; and course on Enlightenment philosophy and science, 181–82; and course on feudal epoch, 181; and course on modernity with literature, philosophy, and politics, 182–83; and course on non-Western perspectives, 179–81; and course on twentieth century, :83–88; implementation of, 191–93; and pedagogy, 189–90; and question of breadth, 137–38; and radical intellectual project, 134; reform and

Kissinger, Henry, 40

knowledge: cultural, 45–46; monopoliza-
tion of natural and scientific by universities since World War Two, 41; production of new by universities, 30–31,
41; sharing of, and privatization, 48

knowledge factory, 35; Kerr's delineation
of, 31–34; and Mario Savio, 33; as purpose of university, 38

Koran, 181

Kracauer, Siegfried, 181

Kristol, Irving, 23

Kuhn, Thomas, 176, 181, 186

Labor Action, 24

labor and employers interest in excess of
qualified employees, 26

labor force, lack of education about, 161–
62

Lamming, George, 187

Landes, David, 182

land-grant colleges, 16, 18, 39, 44

Lash, Joseph, 24

Latinos: and antipoverty programs in
1960s, 114–15; occupation of CUNY
chancellor's office, 116. *See also*
minorities

Latour, Bruno, 175

Lavin, David, 117

Leach, William, 176

learning, 143–44; as a way of life, 161,
172; and curiosity, 159–60; definition
of, 1, 158; education as rather than
vocational, 167; lifelong, 158; and proposed new curriculum, 189–93

Lectures in the History of Philosophy, 179

Lederman, Leon, 49

Lefebvre, Georges, 183

Legitimacy of the Modern Age, The, 183

Le Goff, Jacques, 181

Lentricchia, Frank, 87

Lessing, Doris, 188

Levine, Lawrence, 131–32

Levins, Richard, 54, 186

Lewontin, Richard, 54, 175, 186

liberal arts program: change in required
education in, 126; and Columbia's
core curriculum, 135–36; and cutting
of New York programs for, 97; and
declining numbers of native-born science majors, 37, 56; declining of
majors in, 29, 55; and Harvard's curriculum, 136; and invasion of political
correctness, 37; and University of Chicago curriculum, 128, 134–35

liberals and refusal to enter into educational dialogue, 98

lifelong education, 158

Lincoln, Abraham, 16

linguistic codes and socialization, 7

Lipset, Seymour Martin, 59

literature: and national identity, 5; and
proposed new curriculum, 178, 181,
183, 187–88; and social and cultural
values, 4

Llosa, Mario Vargas, 187

Locke, John, 182

Logic of Scientific Discovery, The, 186

Lonely Crusade, 187

Lucretius, 178, 181

specialization and its separation from
learning, 171
Spenser, Edmund, 183
Spinoza, Baruch, 182
Spivak, Gayatri, 45, 52, 188
sports programs violations, 88–91
Stalin, Joseph, 185
standardized tests, 104; and high school
preparation, 105–6
Standard Oil, 18
Stanford, Leland, 17
Stanford University, 15, 28, 40; and cor-
porate partnerships, 43–44
Starr, Paul, 52, 53
State County and Municipal Employees,
69, 92
Staten Island Community College, 110
State University of New York (SUNY):
and end of mass public education,
63; and United University Profes-
sions, 95
Steinmetz, Charles, 19
Stern, Leonard, 86
Steven Technical Institute, 110
Strauss, Leo, 37
Structure of Scientific Revolutions, The,
186–87
Student aid, reductions in, 160
student protest movement and partner-
ship of postsecondary school governance, 59–60, 165
student response to educational dismantling, 96–101
Sykes, Charles, 61

Symposium, 178
Szilard, Leo, 185

teaching assistants, 70–71, 72
Teaching Assistants Association (TAA),
68, 69, 70, 71–72, 73, 78–79, 92; and
University of California system, 79.
See also Graduate Assistants
Association
tenure, 51–54, 55, 61, 65, 66, 84; and
early retirement packages to mini-
mize, 80, 85; proposal and desire to
abolish, 65, 76, 84; replacement of
with temporary and contingent posi-
tions, 73–74
Thackeray, William, 5, 183
Thales, 178
Things Fall Apart, 188
Thomas, Brinley, 182
Thompson, E. P., 182
Thucydides, 178
"Time, Work-Discipline, and Industrial
Capitalism," 182
Time's Arrow, Time's Cycle, 182
Tisch, Lawrence, 86
Tocqueville, Alexis de, 183
Tolstoy, Leo, 183
Trachtenberg, Alan, 66
training, definition of, 1, 158
Treatise on Human Nature, A, 183
Trollope, Anthony, 5, 183
Tucker, Robert, 185
Tugwell, Rexford Guy, 40
Turgenev, Ivan, 183

Printed in the United States
by Baker & Taylor Publisher Services